Donald C. M...

P190 ① complacency } led to defeat
② waywardness

He Gave Some
PROPHETS

The Old Testament Prophets and Their Message

BY

SANFORD CALVIN YODER, A.B., S.T.D., D.D.

President Emeritus, and Professor
Emeritus of Bible

Goshen College, Goshen, Indiana

HERALD PRESS,

SCOTTDALE, PENNSYLVANIA

Dedicated

To My Former Students

and

Those Who Follow in Their Train

PREFACE

It may seem unnecessary or even presumptuous, in view of the literature available on the life, ministry, and messages of the prophets of the Old Testament, that another venture should be made in that field. Hence it was not without hesitation, and some misgivings, that the task of preparing the material for this treatise was begun. However, during the long years of my ministry and my experience as instructor in the classroom I became deeply impressed with the lack of knowledge and interest in this area of Biblical study. All too frequently, and I say this advisedly, the only use that is made of the messages of the prophets is to take portions, often out of their setting, and use them as proof texts to establish some theory or doctrine of the New Testament, or to confirm some dogma that has grown up through the years. Then, too, some of my students were kind enough to suggest that what was taught in the classroom should be reduced to written form in order to make it available to a larger group. These suggestions are perhaps by now forgotten, but the lack of material in this field still persists, and it is the hope of the author that this attempt to help supply this need will be acceptable and will fulfill its purpose.

It is, then, the aim of the author to set forth the gist of the content, and the purposes of the ministry and labors of the prophets in the historical, geographic, political, and religious setting out of which these writings came. The prophets deal with people and nations which no longer exist and of whose history the ordinary layman too often knows but little. It is not an easy task to fit the people, their leaders, their countries, and the dates of their existence together. All of this material hangs unattached and unrelated and has little meaning for many people, unless it is located on a map, dated and arranged in proper order. Nor can the motive or the meaning of the messages of these great spokesmen for God be fully realized unless one understands something of the social, religious, and political situations out of which they came.

This, then, is not a critical study of the literary or the

theological aspects of the subject. It is rather intended for the minister, the teacher, the student, and lay people who have neither the time, the training, nor the urge to approach the field from a critical, scholarly standpoint. Those who wish to do so will find that there is already much material on hand on those phases of the subject. Some recent books that deal with Old Testament history contain sections that are helpful. Among them we find Bright's *A History of Israel;* Schultz's *The Old Testament Speaks;* and Gottwald's *A Light to the Nations.* Other volumes that are helpful are Young's *My Servants the Prophets* and his commentaries on *The Prophecy of Daniel and Isaiah 53;* George L. Robinson's *The Twelve Minor Prophets* and *The Book of Isaiah;* also the five-volume commentary on the *Minor Prophets and the Book of Isaiah,* by George Adam Smith. There is available, also, the recent reprint of Pusey's scholarly two-volume set on the *Minor Prophets.* Among the more lucid, though no less valuable, works are Leslie's *The Prophets Tell Their Own Story;* Harrel's *The Prophets of Israel;* Ellison's *Men Spoke from God* and *Ezekiel, the Man and His Message;* and Herring's *Studies in the Prophets.*

This humble effort is sent forth with a prayer that it may stimulate an interest in this portion of the greatest of all literature which the church has inherited from the past. May it also lead to a deeper realization and fuller appreciation of the task, the faith, and the courage of the men through whom God chose to make known His purposes, His resources, and His power to generations that have long since passed, but who speak to the needs, the hopes, the aspirations, the desires, and the problems of our day. May these voices be helpful to the saints at this time when formalism, ritualism, dogmatism, and criticism threaten Christendom as they did in the days when God bypassed the chosen priesthood that had become chiefly concerned with the ritualism of the altar, and raised up fearless and devoted men who, though classed as alarmists in their day, spoke again to the masses the things of God that had to do with faith and morals and the spiritual resources and power that made people strong to resist the corrosions of earthliness and earthborn weaknesses and desires.   The Author.

INTRODUCTION

Tremendously important in God's revelation to men was the ministry of the Old Testament prophets. Through them came some of the sharpest moral and spiritual insights. Through them God affirmed again and again His own character and the nature of His covenant with His people. The prophets thundered the judgments of God against wickedness and breathed the tenderness of His mercy for those who repented of their sins. The prophets showed the meaning of contemporary events and pointed the directions of history to the end of time. Detail by detail they built up the Coming One who should redeem the world and bring the affairs of the world to consummation. One after another the Old Testament prophets rang the changes of warning and promise, of the terror and the blessedness of the Day of the Lord.

It is a tragedy that so many people, even Bible readers, have so little acquaintance with the writings of the prophets. Except for a few of the greatest passages, this is the Dark Continent of the Scriptures, unexplored and unknown. One of the reasons for this, one must quickly admit, is that these books are often difficult to understand. In no part of the Bible are the services of a competent guide so much needed and appreciated.

Therefore it is a joy to see another book added to those which aid in the understanding and appreciation of the work of the Old Testament prophets. For here is lucid comment and interpretation that any layman can understand. Here a veteran Bible teacher presents the gleanings of a lifetime of reading and study. He sets each prophet into his place in history, for only so can the prophets be understood. He summarizes their spiritual teachings and distills their contribution to Christian thought of today. The author's own dignified eloquence shows that he has long drawn from the springs of prophetic orators and poets.

This book, published on Sanford Calvin Yoder's eighty-fifth birthday, is a fitting crown to the list of books which he has authored. Those who sat in Dr. Yoder's classes will be glad to have his inspiring teaching in this permanent form. And those who never had that privilege will be happy to get at least this much of the inspiration and help of a great man of God as he presents the Word of God which he believed.

—Paul Erb

CONTENTS

1 | The Prophets

The institution of prophetism is an old one. The writer of the epistle to the Hebrews says that "God, who at sundry times and in divers manners spake in time past unto the fathers by the prophets, hath in these last days spoken unto us by his Son" (Hebrews 1:1, 2). These men are also spoken of as preachers of righteousness, the spokesmen for God. They are designated by the writers of the Scriptures as servants of Jehovah (Deuteronomy 34:5); man of God (I Samuel 9:7, 8); the man of the spirit (Hosea 9:7); the watchers (Habakkuk 2:1, 2); the messengers of Jehovah (Malachi 3:1).

The call to the prophetic ministry was as varied as the conditions under which these men lived and the nature and disposition of the one that was called. For example, Moses received his call at "the burning bush" in the desert of Midian. Samuel heard "THE VOICE" in his childhood during his sojourn in the home of Eli, the high priest. Isaiah "saw . . . the Lord . . . high and lifted up" in the temple in the year that King Uzziah died. The word came to Jeremiah during the crisis in Josiah's reign. Ezekiel was with the exiled Jews by the River Chebar in Babylon when an incomprehensible image arose out of the whirlwind and gave him his commission to go and preach to a "rebellious nation . . . impudent . . . and stiffhearted." Others say merely that the "word of Jehovah came" and from then on they "spake as they were moved by the Holy Ghost."

Religion and worship during the patriarchal period were largely in the hands of the clan, the head of which was the family priest. During the centuries of their residence along the Nile and the adjacent plains they retained in a remarkable way their racial solidarity, but there is evidence that they were greatly influenced in their worship by the religion of the Egyptians among whom they lived. They were no longer a mere clan. They had become a host that had practically attained the stature of a nation. Joseph, one of their number, served as prime minister of Egypt and was empowered with authority to transact the business of the nation. Another one, a foundling by the water of the Nile, was adopted by a princess of the royal household, was reared in the palace, and given all the advantages, social and educational, that belonged to one of that position. Exodus 2:2-10. It is said that he was learned in all the wisdom of the Egyptians. This was the man Moses, who volunteered to assist his people who were then oppressed, and as a result became involved in an episode that made it necessary to flee from the country and spend forty years in the desert. Exodus 2:11-15. From thence he returned at the call of God to deliver his people—a race with a destiny—from the bondage into which they had fallen. Under his leadership they were led to the foot of Sinai on the Arabian peninsula, where they were given a code of laws that set forth the fundamental principles by which they were to live, and a mode of worship that was adapted to their need as well as to their mental and spiritual conditions.

God did not only provide a mode of worship that was suited to their condition, but He provided also modes of administration and instruction that were adapted to their needs. One whole tribe, the descendants of Levi, was set apart as the group from which their priests were to be drawn to administer and make meaningful the sacrifices, ritual, and ceremonials of their worship. Those who were not included in the priesthood were to be scattered throughout the land, among the eleven tribes, as teachers and to assist by turns in the temple service. Forty-eight cities, with suburbs for their cattle, were allocated to them.

The spiritual condition of these people rose and fell throughout the centuries as the faith and loyalty of their godly leaders ebbed and flowed. In times of depression God raised up prophets, great preachers of righteousness, like Samuel, Nathan, Elijah, and Elisha, to call the people back from their waywardness to higher levels of faith and life. The priests had, by the eighth century B.C., become so formalized as a body and so concerned with their own well-being that their value and influence as leaders were largely gone. The host of prophets, some no doubt self-appointed, no longer spoke to the needs of the people, but used their office to promote their own welfare. So evident had this become that Jeremiah, one of Judah's greatest spokesmen, said, "The prophets prophesy falsely, and the priests bear rule by their means; and my people love to have it so" (Jeremiah 5:31).

We read of prophets in the early history of the race, but the era of prophetism reached its height during the late ninth and eighth centuries B.C., when the voices of Amos, Isaiah, Hosea, Micah, and others shook the nations with their fiery eloquence. Ezekiel ministered to the displaced survivors of the Southern Kingdom during the years of their exile in Babylon, and Jeremiah disappeared in Egypt whither he was carried by the fugitive remnant that sought refuge in the lands along the Nile when Jerusalem fell in 586 B.C.

During the years of captivity a new set of leaders known as the scribes arose. After the exile they largely supplanted the influence of the prophets and took over the spiritual leadership of the people, and continued until the voice of John, the Messianic herald, rang out of the wilderness to announce the presence of the greatest of all the prophets of all time, Jesus Christ, Lord of lords, who came to establish a new priesthood, the universal priesthood of believers, the redeemed saints, who have direct access to the throne of God through the mediation of Him who came to save the people from their sins. It is through them, prophets, spokesmen for God, priests of the Most High, that move in the Spirit of Him by whom they have been redeemed, that the Lord is now calling the lost of humanity unto Himself.

They constitute a priesthood after the order of Melchizedek, an order that is not based on ancestry nor upon tribal or family connections but upon personal worthiness.

2 | The Prophets: Their Mission, Call And Message

Their Mission

The prophets of the Old Testament were *forth-tellers,* preachers of righteousness, who spoke in behalf of God to declare His will for mankind. They were also *fore-tellers,* that is, they foretold events that were made known to them in divers manners by divine revelation. Their messages had to do with a range of subjects that were as wide as the needs of humanity and as lofty and deep as the grace and love and wisdom of Him from whom they came. They dealt with people's responsibility to God, to themselves, to their families, to their neighbors, and to the nations. They were not only concerned with persons and their ways of life, but also with the world in which they lived and the things with which they had to do.

The purpose of their ministry may be gleaned from their divinely inspired and orientated messages which were delivered, from time to time, over a period of many centuries.

1. To make known to man the nature and will of God, and to set up standards of righteousness.

2. To rebuke sin and bring the wayward and erring to
   repentance.
3. To initiate religious, social, moral, and political reforms.
4. To warn the erring, the unruly and undisciplined, of the
   judgments of God.
5. To encourage the faithful with messages of hope and
   consolation and comfort.
6. To make known the greatness and goodness and mercy of
   Him who is greater than all the needs of mankind and
   is able to deliver people and nations regardless of what
   their problems and limitations may be.

Their Message

As to the manner by which the prophets received their
messages, one can only say that there seems to have been no uni-
form pattern. The Scripture says that "prophecy came not in
old time by the will of man: but holy men of God spake as they
were moved by the Holy Ghost" (II Peter 1:21).

This statement made centuries later by one of the apostles is
in full accord with what the writers of the Old Testament say:
"The Lord spake unto Moses face to face, as a man speaketh unto
his friend" (Exodus 33:11; cf. Numbers 17:6-10). The Spirit
rested upon the society. Numbers 11:24-26. Samuel heard a voice
in the night at the time when there seemed to have been no
frequent visions. I Samuel 3:4-14. There were visions and
dreams and special messengers. Sometimes angels bore messages
from heaven by which they made known to prophets the mind
and will of God.

The manner in which these spokesmen for God delivered
their messages was as varied as was the nature, language, and
natural abilities of those who wrote or spoke. Rarely was there
bestowed upon the prophet a new gift. When Moses was called
upon to plead the case of Israel before Pharaoh, he pleaded his
inability to speak. Instead of imparting unto him the fluency
which he lacked, God promised that Aaron, his brother, should
speak for him in the presence of the Egyptian monarch. Exodus
4:10-16. There were, however, no doubt instances where the
natural gift of the speaker was exalted or heightened in order

to make it possible for him to do what he was enjoined to do, and things that could not be ascertained by the natural faculties were made known through visions and dreams or by such other means as God bestowed.

Some of the prophets reduced their messages to writing. Others delivered them orally and what we know of their content is what the historians of their time recorded. The practice of writing their messages became more prevalent among the later prophets. Isaiah was the literary artist who possessed the rare gift of creating mental pictures by putting words together in a beautiful and effective way. He set forth impressively by this means the great divine truths that came by inspiration and made them available, not only to the people of his day, but also to those of all time. Ezekiel dealt with imagery, symbolical acts, parables, illustrations, and figures of speech. Amos, the shepherd of Tekoa, shook the population of the Northern Kingdom with the rugged language of the desert herdsman. The earlier prophets, Nathan, Elijah, Elisha, and others, though among the most courageous and ablest, left no writings except what historians of that time recorded. The writings of Moses, who is ranked highly among Israel's prophets, have to do largely with the legal and worship aspects of the new nation that was to be established in Palestine. However, the few addresses of his that remain, such as Deuteronomy 31, 32, 33, are of a high literary quality.

False Prophets

There were, in the days of the prophets, also false prophets whose testimony ran counter to that of the true prophets. The call of these impostors was earthborn and their messages were attuned to the ears and desires of the rabble. They seem always to have been the bane of Israel as they were and are of all nations and people of all time. The Scriptures speak of them as having false visions and of speaking lying and flattering divinations and of seducing people by crying "peace when there is no peace." Ezekiel 12:24; 13:6.

The mark that distinguished the false from the true prophet was always whether his messages were in harmony with the mind and will of God and whether he had the faith, courage, and boldness to face the situations as they were. His fortitude and fearlessness in confronting kings and priests, as well as the multitudes, with their wicked and nefarious devices, stand ever in contrast with these "time-servers" who courted the favors of the godless with pleasing messages that enabled them to continue their evil practices and enjoy their sinful ways.

The Schools of the Prophets

There are a number of references in the Scriptures to the *sons of the prophets,* who it appears were quartered in groups. They are, by some commentators, considered as schools or institutions of learning that were established to educate and train men for the prophetic ministry. They bear some of the marks of such establishments. Their patrons lived together in common quarters and ate at a common table. (See II Kings 6:1-4 and 4:38-44.) Some of them were skilled in the art of music and the use of instruments. I Samuel 10:1-5. The purpose of these fellowships or institutions may not be categorically defined, but the writers of that time spoke of them as men who prophesied. I Samuel 19:20-24. There is, however, nothing definite to indicate that they were novitiates who were being trained for the prophetic ministry. Such institutions existed at Ramah (I Samuel 19:20), Bethel (II Kings 2:3), Jericho (II Kings 2:5), and Gilgal (II Kings 4:38). "It should be noted that these were associations or brotherhoods established for the purpose of mutual edification rather than education. . . . Nevertheless," says the commentator, "we cannot conceive of the element of religious training as being entirely absent."[1] It is not known whether any of the recognized prophets of the Old Testament belonged to these associations. Amos says definitely that he did not. Amos 7:14. Elisha, it appears, had rather close relationships with them. II Kings 4:38-41; 6:1-7.

The Writings of the Prophets

Not all prophecy is predictive. The larger part of it is hortatory. By that we mean that it was given for admonition, exhortation, correction, and instruction in righteousness. Nor is

1. See *International Standard Bible Encyclopedia,* Vol. 2, p. 901.

all of it to be taken literally. Prophets like Isaiah, Ezekiel, Amos, and others make wide use of figures of speech, parables, illustrations, and symbolism to exalt or clarify their messages or to make them impressive. People of all times, seemingly, enjoyed hearing great truth expressed in that way. The Apostle Paul, centuries later, says, "But he that prophesieth speaketh unto men to edification, exhortation, and comfort" (I Corinthians 14:3).

There is, however, an important element of prediction found in the messages of the prophets. Some of it is based on conditions. Other parts of it are unconditioned. Isaiah 53 is an impressive example of the latter. Jeremiah's prediction concerning the destruction of Jerusalem and the exile of Judah is in part based on conditions. There was a time during his ministry when repentance and a sincere return to God could have forestalled the catastrophe that took place in 586 B.C.

The earliest trace of predictive prophecy appears in Genesis 3:15, when after the tragedy that had taken place in Eden, a promise was made to Adam and Eve that spans the ages and covers the duration of the race. "And I will put enmity between thee and the woman," God said, "and between thy seed and her seed; it shall bruise thy head, and thou shalt bruise his heel." From thence the prophetic stream began to flow with varying, though increasing, measure until the close of the Old Testament period. We hear it again in New Testament times when the voice cried out of the wilderness and announced the arrival of the greatest of all the prophets, Jesus Christ, the Son of God, the one of whom his predecessors had spoken. Following John the Baptist the apostles continued to sprinkle their messages with futuristic predictions that gave hope and courage to the saints of their day and of all time.

During the period of the eighth-century prophets the literature became greatly enriched with Messianic and kingdom ideas. The descendants of Israel were then no longer living in alien territory. They had become a great and important nation. At one time their territory reached from the great river, the Euphrates, to the ends of the earth, the Mediterranean Sea, and was on the verge of becoming an empire. In fact, Pfeiffer in his Bible Atlas calls it "The Empire of David and Solomon."

They had become deeply rooted in the soil of the land which Jehovah, their God, had promised them. During their stay in Egypt their faith had become greatly influenced by the religion of the people among whom they lived. They were not anxious to leave their homes on the fertile delta of the Nile. They rather wanted the government to ease its persecutions and allow them to live in peace. The task of Moses was, for this reason, constantly made more difficult by their desire to return to "the leeks and the onions" and "the flesh pots" of the well-watered lands that for so long had been their home. Hence, when their deliverer tarried long on the mountain at Sinai, where Israel was encamped, until the multitude despaired of his return, they reverted to the type of worship which they had known in Egypt and in which they had likely participated.

Now all this was changed as a result of the tremendous experience at Sinai on the day when the *mountain burned* because the Lord had descended upon it and spoken to them face to face. They were in the process of becoming a nation with a homeland and an established religion and form of worship that was suited to their needs. Maclear, the historian, says:

> But while idolatrous forms of worship were rigorously forbidden, the Almighty condescended to make known to His people a way in which He was willing to receive their adoration. Stooping to the infirmities of a nation just delivered from degrading bondage, He took them by the hand and provided for the wants of their religious nature, in a way marvelously adapted to their native genius and character as well as to their previous habits and modes of thought.[2]

Prior to their descent into Egypt during Joseph's premiership, the mode of government and control was that of the patriarchal type. The father was the head of the clan, the family priest, and on occasions he performed the role of a prophet. Genesis 20:7. Under the Sinaitic covenant this was changed. The priests and Levites became the religious leaders and teachers. There were, however, times during the period of the judges and the monarchy when even these God-ordained men could

---

2. *A Classbook of Old Testament History*, p. 118. Reprint by Wm. Eerdmans Publishing Company, 1955.

not hold the people to their faith, and they themselves apostatized. It was then that these chosen leaders were reinforced with prophets who rose to preach the judgments of God as well as His love and His mercy in order to restore the waning faith of the people through whom He had chosen to make Himself known to mankind. These prophets had not only an erring people to deal with. The priests, too often, became absorbed with the externals of the ritual and forms of worship and the emoluments of their office and catered to the wishes of the people rather than their needs. It was then that these heaven-ordained messengers came forward and proclaimed in strenuous tones the will of God and His righteousness, in order to turn them back from their erring ways to their divinely appointed mission and way of life.

Inspiration

One cannot write or speak about the prophets without having to face, somewhere along the way, the question of inspiration. It is well to remember, when dealing with this subject, that the question of inspiration persists, whether or not it can be explained or defined fully or satisfactorily. Dr. Fouts of Northern Baptist Theological Seminary, one of my ablest teachers, one time said that "Apart from the study of the Scriptures and a living Christian experience, there is little hope of understanding the doctrine even partially. For the Scriptures," he said, "have a testimony concerning their own origin, design, and authority which is informing, and especially so, to one whose life is under the control of the Holy Spirit."

The inspired Scripture, then, has in it a divine as well as a human element. The Bible says, "The Spirit of the Lord came upon [clothed] Gideon" (Judges 6:34), as He gave him the messages he was to proclaim to the people. Elihu, when speaking during Job's controversy with his friends, recognizes the value of experience and the wisdom one accumulates throughout the years, when he says, "I said, Days should speak, and multitude of years should teach wisdom." But Elihu says also, "there is a spirit in man: and the inspiration of the Almighty giveth them understanding" (Job 32:7, 8). Moffatt, a modern translator, renders this passage as follows: "Yet God inspires a man, 'tis the Almighty

who breathes knowledge into him." In other words, there is a
source of knowledge above and beyond that which age, maturity,
learning, or experience brings. This was so whether the com-
munication came orally, or by and through dreams or visions,
or otherwise.

This then raises the question as to what effect the inspiration
of which Elihu speaks had upon the speaker. Was the recipient
entirely passive and were his natural faculties active or had they
ceased to function? Or did they deliver the content of their
messages in their own formulations which may or may not have
been amplified by the Spirit? No all-inclusive answer can be
given to questions such as these. Certainly the style of Isaiah is
not that of Ezekiel or Jeremiah. Nor is the style of Amos that of
Micah. Whatever the effect of inspiration on the state which it
induced in the speakers may have been, it did not obliterate the
personality of the prophet or reduce him to a mere automaton
or machine to be operated by the Almighty. The form of com-
munication, the imagery with which the messages of inspiration
were clothed, the symbols and illustrations that were employed
to make it clear or emphatic may be considered as its garb or
dress. This was determined by the mental and intellectual
character of the speaker as well as the training, associations, and
feelings of the spokesman. Hence we may say that regardless of
whether the prophet, during moments or times of inspiration,
wrote or spoke of things not previously known to him, that which
was revealed amounted to guidance, suggestion, revelation, or
dictation. Therefore, whatever their differences of style or
modes of expression may have been, we can still believe that the
Scriptures were the product of men who "spake as they were
moved by the Holy Ghost," and that "all scripture is given by
inspiration of God, and is profitable for *doctrine*, for *reproof*,
for *correction*, for *instruction in righteousness*."

Regarding the character of the prophetic messages we may
say with assurance that in the highest sense they were ethical,
spiritual, and practical. The speakers were not so much concerned with forms, ceremonials, and external and outward
religious observances or practices—the priests took care of that—
as they were with personal and national righteousness. What the

prophets tried to bring about was repentance, justice, honesty, and truth, without which all sacrifices, offerings, and ceremonies are vain.

The question of how one may know whether a prophet is an authentic one or whether he is an impostor has always persisted. This was a problem in ancient times as it is in our day. The writer of the Book of Deuteronomy gives us the answer. "When a prophet speaketh in the name of the Lord," he says, "if the thing follow not, nor come to pass, that is the thing which the Lord hath not spoken" (Deuteronomy 18:21, 22). The Apostle John, who wrote centuries later, admonishes the people to whom he wrote to try the spirits. "Beloved," he says, "believe not every spirit, but try the spirits whether they are of God: because many false prophets are gone out into the world" (I John 4:1).

The character of the prophet is also to be considered. Balaam is an example of one who was persistent in his endeavor to please his patron by destroying the people of Israel who were invading his country en route to their homeland. His name and his sin are recorded in the most widely read book in existence— the Bible. His teaching, "the doctrine of Balaam," has become a proverb that carries a blight which centuries of time have not extinguished. (See Numbers 22:2 and Revelation 2:12-14.) The final and supreme test was and is whether the thing that was prophesied was righteous and just and whether it came to pass.

Sometimes prophetic predictions were based on conditions. For example: "If my people, which are called by my name, shall humble themselves, and pray, and seek my face, and turn from their wicked ways; then will I hear from heaven, and will forgive their sin, and will heal their land" (II Chronicles 7:14). A large part of the prophetic messages were based on conditions. Others again were positive statements of facts or occurrences that were to come to pass. The great Messianic declaration of Isaiah 53 is not limited by or based on any conditions. All of its implications, however, were not realized until their fulfillment at Golgotha and on the day of Christ's resurrection.

The Interpretation of Prophecy

Some of the messages of the prophets lend themselves to different interpretations. Some have reference to events that were and have been fulfilled in the past. Others have reference to events that still lie in the future. In fact, when they are separated from the time and situation in and for which they were given, the meaning they had may not be clear. Some guidance, then, is necessary in order that the student or reader may not arrive at confused or erroneous conclusions.

1. *The subject should be approached prayerfully and with a mind open to the illumination of the Spirit.* Aid should be sought from the best minds that have studied the problem, not to substantiate some theory, but to arrive at the true meaning which the prophet had in mind when the words were spoken. Sometimes the spokesmen themselves did not comprehend fully what the Spirit led them to say.

2. *The historical setting* out of which the message came must be taken into account. Israel and the surrounding nations, their rivalries, aspirations, ideals—political, commercial, and religious—are often involved in the situations to which the prophets spoke.

3. *The style of writing and the subject matter are important.* Orators, preachers, and writers of that day, as in ours, made use of figures of speech, illustrations, parables, comparisons, and symbolical language in which the great truths of prophecy were clothed. Hence, it is important to determine whether the language is figurative or literal, poetry or prose, history or allegory, and whether the promises or forecasts are conditional or unconditional.

4. *Prophetic passages should be compared with other Scriptures* that bear on the same subject. It is often best to ascertain the meaning and purpose at the time the message was spoken, and also the application and meaning for our time.

5. *The prophets spoke to people and conditions that existed in their time.* Hence, one should seek to understand the situation that existed at the time when the words were spoken and to

ascertain its meaning and purpose at that time, as well as the lesson it has for our day.

6. *A knowledge of the chronological order of events is helpful.* Dates and place names, as well as names of persons, are important. Though they are often difficult and bothersome, they are, nevertheless, very necessary.

7. *One should keep in mind the perspective of the prophet.* For example, events yet far distant, in his time or ours, may be spoken of as being close at hand. (See Isaiah 10:1; Jeremiah, chapters 50, 51; Matthew, chapters 24, 25.)

8. *One must take into account how the writers of the New Testament Gospels and epistles handled the prophecies and predictions* of the Old Testament, especially the Messianic prophecies.

9. It is well to remember that prophecies that deal with the future *are best fully interpreted after they have been fulfilled.* Note what the Apostle Peter says about this. He describes prophecy as "a light that shineth in a dark place"—squalid surroundings—with feeble rays as compared with the light that comes with the dawn. II Peter 1:19.

10. *Messianic prophecies.* "The testimony of Jesus," one of my teachers emphasized, "is the spirit of prophecy" (Revelation 19:10). It is the organizing principle in which all revelation centers. Jesus during His ministry found proofs in the Old Testament for His claims to Sonship, Messiahship, and teachings. "And beginning at Moses and all the prophets, he expounded unto them in all the scriptures the things concerning himself" (Luke 24:27).

Conclusion

All through the millenniums of human history God has had His spokesmen who came and went with the years. The line begins in Genesis and runs through the historical books, the Psalms, and other poetical writings. Its richest flowering, however, is found in the works of the four major and twelve minor prophets. These great men, who moved under the impulse of the divine Spirit, gave to the world, by inspiration of God, a body of literature in which people and nations have found hope and consolation, correction and reproof for their day and ours.

3 | The World in Which The Prophets Lived

We live today in a world that is far removed in time from the one in which the prophets lived and worked. We see those people beclouded in the haze which the centuries have accumulated. They, together with the culture of their time, have disappeared. Their cities have fallen and become heaps of rubble and in many instances lie buried under the dust of the centuries. Their kings and great men lie moldering in the earth or in the vast mausoleums or tombs, or in the pyramids of the deserts. They are today to most of us only names on the pages of history. Except for such knowledge as archaeologists gather from the ruins which they uncovered, we know only what the Biblical records briefly give. They were, however, at one time great men who ruled vast empires, built great cities, occupied spacious palaces, led large armies, and enacted laws by which the life of their day was governed. All of the discoveries which modern students, scholars, and excavators have made enable us to realize, at least in part, what sort of folk these people of Biblical times were and what wonders they achieved.

One who wishes to see what these ancient craftsmen wrought needs only to follow the River Nile, in the land of the Pharaohs, where remain the ruins of Thebes and Memphis and the Great Pyramids. Or he may go eastward to ancient Babylonia, whose barrenness was made fertile by the waters of the Tigris and Euphrates rivers, which flowed through a vast network of canals and made the wastes of Mesopotamia, the land between the rivers, productive and furnish sustenance for the millions that thrived there. Or he may go yet further eastward across the mountains into what were at one time the strongholds of the Medes and Persians and there view the remnants of their culture and architecture which still remain. Nations of today might even profit by the example of the spirit of benevolence that occasionally marked the treatment of their exiles and subjugated nations and people, two and one-half millenniums ago.

North of Palestine, in Asia Minor as well as in northern Palestine and Syria, the Hittites have left their footprints on the "sands of time." They were once—not so long ago—a fabled race which were thought to have existed only in people's imagination. Today, thanks to the labors of patient scholars, their cities have been uncovered, their language has been deciphered, and the story of the people of this lost empire and their achievements is laid open to the world of our time. The northern Mesopotamian kingdoms, 1700-1550 B.C., and the Assyrian Empire, 1100-612 B.C., were one time great nations and world powers. History tells the story of their ruthless conquests. Nineveh and Damascus were beautiful cities, the marts of trade and the home of kings. Only remnants of the heyday of their glory still remain. Specimens of the architectural accomplishments and other tokens of their culture have found their way into the museums of Rome and London and other places where such ancient treasures are hoarded. The massive figures of lions carved in stone, which once guarded the palace gates at Nineveh in the day when Isaiah rocked the kingdom of Judah with his eloquence and warned the king and the populace of the Assyrian menace, are now in the British Museum in London, and the "hypocritical nation" of which he spoke no longer exists.

Such was the world in which Israel lived, but the small, rugged, little land of Palestine, the "Promised Land"—*Das Gelobte Land*—was their homeland. It was surrounded on three sides by great and powerful nations and on the west by the Great Sea—the Mediterranean. It was promised to Abraham while he still lived in his Babylonian home, centuries before his posterity had become a nation.

Palestine proper resembled in shape and area our own state of Vermont. Its size is entirely disproportionate to the place it fills in history. When one considers the achievements of its people, its place in past world events, and its influence upon mankind throughout the centuries, he becomes impressed with the fact that the greatness of a nation is not to be measured by the number of square miles in its area, nor by the size of its armies, but by the character and accomplishments of the people who occupy it.

Palestine is a small country. It lies between the River Jordan and the Dead Sea on the east and the Mediterranean Sea on the west. It is approximately one hundred and forty-four miles in length from north to south, and varies in breadth from ninety miles in the south to twenty-five miles at its northern border. East Palestine, with the consent of Moses, was occupied by the tribes of Reuben and Gad and one half of the tribe of Manasseh at the time of the invasion and conquest by Joshua. Joshua 1:16. In extent it was practically one hundred and fifty miles long and varied in breadth from eighty miles in the north to thirty miles in the south.

The Lebanon Mountains to the north, though not a part of Palestine, nevertheless determine to a large degree the character of the country. It is here that the Jordan River gathers its waters from the melting snows of the mountains and the rains of the higher altitudes, during the spring and summer months. When the snows that crown its peaks melt, the Scripture says, the "Jordan overfloweth all his banks all the time of harvest" (Joshua 3:15).

The Arabian poet sings of the influence of these lofty mountains and hills and says: "The winter is upon its head, the spring upon its shoulders, the autumn in its bosom, and at its feet slumbers the summer." This together with the breezes of the Mediterranean Sea gives it a wide variety of climate, products, and native life, such as is seldom found in a land of so small an area. Long ago, the youthful philosopher of Job's day said, "Fair weather cometh out of the north," and centuries later Jesus said, "When ye see a cloud rise out of the west, straightway ye say, There cometh a shower; and so it is. And when ye see the south wind blow, ye say, There will be heat; and it cometh to pass" (Luke 12:54, 55).

Few lands so small have such diversified topography, such impressive scenery, and such a wide range of climate and products. No better description can be found than that which Moses gave after their flight from Egypt. He says:

The land, whither thou goest in to possess it, is not as the land of Egypt, from whence ye came out, where thou sowedst thy seed, and wateredst it with thy foot, as a garden of herbs (Deuteronomy 11:10). For the Lord thy God bringeth thee into a good land, a land of brooks of water, of fountains and depths that spring out of valleys and hills; a land of wheat, and barley, and vines, and fig trees, and pomegranates, a land of oil olive, and honey; a land wherein thou shalt eat bread without scarceness, thou shalt not lack any thing in it; a land whose stones are iron, and out of whose hills thou mayest dig brass (Deuteronomy 8:7-9).

Such was the homeland of Israel, the chosen people of God. They were located at the crossroads of the world, where the traders, the merchants, the adventurers, and people of other nations passed by. The markets of Samaria, like those of Damascus and Tyre and Sidon, were destined to become filled with the clatter of wares and the din and noise and confusion of those that buy and sell.

After seven and one-half years of warfare, under the leadership of Joshua, the Israelites finally won possession of the land and subdued its inhabitants. But the struggles were not over. Surrounding nations looked with envy upon the new conquerors and within the borders of the country were pockets of subdued but unhappy and dissatisfied remnants of people who had formerly occupied the land. Tyre and Sidon, the Philistines of the maritime plain, Damascus, Moab, Ammon, and Edom were not pleased with the accomplishments of these people from the Nile Valley, who had come up through the desert and dispossessed them of their holdings. They were to pose a threat to the security of these invaders for many generations. Again and again throughout the centuries these newcomers—Israel—had to muster armies, to repel invasions and subdue insurrections that were instigated by the dissatisfied populace that remained in the country.

But more serious even than the political aspects of the situation throughout the years were the moral, religious, and spiritual influences of their pagan neighbors among whom they lived or by whom they were surrounded. In spite of all the provisions that had been made for the establishment and perpetuation of their faith, there were times again and again when apostate religions were given a large place, not only among the common people but in high places as well. During Ahab's reign in the Northern Kingdom, 875-853, this influx of outside influences reached its climax. Jezebel, a princess of Sidon, became the wife of Ahab and queen of Samaria, and her religion, Baalism, was made the state religion. Like an evil contagion this apostasy spread to the Southern Kingdom when her daughter, Athaliah, became the wife of Jehoram, king of Judah. The historians of that time tell the story of the tragic consequences that followed.

It was then when the leadership faltered or became corrupted that the stern voice of the prophets rose above the confusion and corruption of the palace, the home, and the sanctuary, or the din of the market place, to institute reforms and save the day for Jehovah's cause.

4 | The Early Prophets

The prophets with whom we are most familiar are those whose messages are handed down to us in written form. These men were, however, preceded by earlier ones whose line reaches far back into the history of the race. We know nothing of them and their work except what the historians of the Bible record. Noah predicted the coming of the flood, and admonished the people to desist from participating in the evils of their day. Abraham was designated as a prophet at the time when God spoke to Abimelech in a dream and ordered him to restore to the patriarch his wife, whom the offending king of Gerar had taken to be his own. "Now therefore restore the man his wife; for he is a prophet, and he shall pray for thee, and thou shalt live" (Genesis 20:7). When Moses was asked to plead the cause of Israel before Pharaoh, he insisted upon his inability to speak. He was then given assurance that his brother Aaron would be his spokesman. "See," He said, "I have made thee a god to Pharaoh: and Aaron thy brother shall be thy prophet" (Exodus 7:1). At the close of his career Moses himself is spoken of as a prophet. The writer of the Book of Deuteronomy says, "And there arose not a prophet since in Israel like unto Moses, whom the Lord knew face to face" (Deuteronomy 34:10). Hosea, when referring to him centuries later, says: "By a prophet the Lord brought Israel out of Egypt, and by a prophet was he preserved" (Hosea 12:13).

This great emancipator of Israel, who played such a large role in the history of his people, figures prominently also in the writing of all of the five books of the Pentateuch which in addition to other names bear also his name—the First, Second, Third, Fourth, and Fifth Books of Moses. He stands out in history not only as a prophet, but also as a great statesman and the formulator of a legal code by which the newly founded nation was to be governed. His sanitary and health regulations indicate a knowledge and understanding that is not generally credited to his time. He set up also a system of worship in accordance with the design given him at Sinai, that fittingly served the spiritual needs of the people. He was an organizer and writer of a high order. His accomplishments fully justify the statement of Stephen, who centuries later said: "Moses was learned in all the wisdom of the Egyptians, and was mighty in words and in deeds" (Acts 7:22). His faith, his humble spirit, his accomplishments in the religious, secular, and political affairs of the newly founded nation have borne fruit that lasted through the millenniums until now. *The Song of Moses* (Deuteronomy 32) and *The Blessings of the Twelve Tribes* are crowning literary achievements that fittingly mark the close of a life filled with the care and concern for the people whom God had designated him to lead.

Moses and Aaron were, however, not the only recognized prophets that came out of this period. Miriam, their sister, is spoken of as a prophetess. The writer who narrates their flight from the "house of bondage" says that when they saw the pursuing Egyptians engulfed in the Red Sea, Miriam the prophetess with timbrel in her hand and all the women went out with timbrels and dances. Exodus 15:20. When a food crisis arose during their journey from Sinai to Kadesh-barnea and Moses became overwhelmed with the cares and complaints of the multitude, he was divinely authorized to call together seventy elders to whom the Lord imparted His spirit and they prophesied. When complaints arose that two of the group, Eldad and Medad, had remained in the camp and had not gone with the others into the tabernacle, but prophesied in the camp, even Joshua protested and asked Moses to silence them. But Moses replied, "Would God that all the Lord's people were prophets, and that the Lord would put his spirit upon them" (Numbers 11:29)!

Balaam

Balaam, the son of Beor, came from Pethor of Mesopotamia. He is known in history as the man who badly misused the prophetic ministry to satisfy the wishes and expectations of those who solicited his services. However, in spite of his base intentions he made some lofty predictions that found their way into the inspired record.

Israel was on the move from the desert to the Promised Land. The people who occupied the territory through which this vast multitude with its herds and flocks was to travel were loath to grant them permission to do so. Armed resistance seemed to be unavailing; hence, they called for the prophet from the east to block the way and thwart the design of the invaders by calling upon them the curse of divine disapproval. The writer of the Book of Numbers records the failure of this effort and reports that instead the prophet was constrained to pronounce upon them the blessing of the Almighty. He said:

How shall I curse, whom God hath not cursed?
Or how shall I defy, whom the Lord hath not defied?
    For from the top of the rocks I see him,
    And from the hills I behold him:
    Lo, the people shall dwell alone,
    And shall not be reckoned among the nations.
                    —Numbers 23:8, 9.

The Lord his God is with him, and
The shout of a king is among them.
    God brought them out of Egypt;
    He hath as it were the strength of an unicorn.
                    —Numbers 23:21, 22.

How goodly are thy tents, O Jacob,
And thy tabernacles, O Israel!

Blessed is he that blesseth thee,
And cursed is he that curseth thee.

—Numbers 24:5, 9.

I shall see him, but not now:
I shall behold him, but not nigh:
There shall come a Star out of Jacob,
And a sceptre shall rise out of Israel,
    And shall smite the corners of Moab,
    And destroy all the children of Sheth.

—Numbers 24:17.

The writer of the Book of Numbers says later that Balaam,
the man so gifted in the use of words, caused "Israel to sin" by
the perverse counsel he gave to those who had solicited his services. (See Numbers 25:2 and 31:16.)

Prophecy During the Period of the Judges

When the Israelites entered Canaan, they had a well-or-
ganized system of worship and a code of laws that was based
on the divine principles of righteousness and justice. It set forth
the relationships between persons and persons, as well as between
persons and property, and between the people and God. It
provided for legal remedies as well as such procedures in equity
as were suited to their needs and to their time. The provisions
of their sanitary code were remarkable for their day. The leadership that was provided to carry forward their worship was largely
responsible to govern also their secular and social relationships.
There was to be no king. All the ostentation, extravagance, and
expense that usually attaches to the court was to be avoided, and
every aspect of their life and activity was to originate and operate
in a religious setting and be carried through in a religious spirit.
Hence, the leadership that was provided to direct their worship
was largely responsible to govern also their secular affairs and
human relationships.

They had subdued, after seven and one-half years of warfare under the leadership of Joshua, a large part of the inhabitants
of Canaan. Their army was largely disbanded after the conquest
and the troops had gone home. Their great leaders, Moses,

Aaron, and Joshua, were dead, and new men came on the scene to reckon with the problems that time was sure to bring with it. They were surrounded by neighbors whom they had dispossessed of their lands and dangers of uprisings were always imminent. Many of these people traced their ancestry to the same source that Israel came from. The Edomites were descendants of Esau, Jacob's twin brother. Between them there was an agelong feud that had never been healed. It had its origin in a hasty transaction between the two brothers which eventually resulted in the loss of Esau's birthright. Genesis 25:27-34 and chapter 27. The Midianites were descendants of Midian, the son of Abraham by Keturah, whom he espoused following the death of his wife Sarah. The Ishmaelites were descendants of Ishmael, the son of Abraham by Hagar, Sarah's maid. Moab and Ammon descended from Lot, Abraham's nephew. The Amalekites are said to trace their ancestry to Eliphaz, the son of Esau.

It is altogether possible, along with other things which caused the tensions between clans and tribes, that these people shared and carried with them something of the bitterness that grew out of the episode that had taken place between Jacob and Esau centuries earlier. Memories are long and feuds die hard! Any lingering feeling which traced its origin to the event that had taken place in Isaac's home before the time of his death could now find full play in the "Law of the Desert" which Moses tried to forestall among the Israelites by setting up cities of refuge throughout Palestine. Here the accused could find protection from the avenger until his case was properly adjudicated. If found guilty, he would be punished according to the provisions of their criminal code. If innocent, he would be assured of security.

These neighboring tribes of common ancestry, together with others who occupied the territory adjacent to Palestine, as well as the former occupants of the country that was taken over by the Israelites, looked with resentment and hostility upon the invading host that came up from the Nile country and dispossessed them of their lands. Throughout the centuries that followed they contested, again and again, Israel's right to the territory that lay between the Jordan River and the Mediterranean Sea, and also that which lay on the east side of the Jordan which was occupied by the Israelite tribes of Reuben, Gad, and one half of the tribe of Manasseh.

Deborah the Prophetess

It was during, or following, the twenty-year period of oppression by Jabin, king of Hazor, that the prophetess Deborah and her army under the command of Barak met the forces of the Canaanites at the River Kishon. The story of this conflict is told by the prophetess herself in the fifth chapter of the Book of the Judges. She describes, in highly picturesque and graphic language, the noise of the warriors, the clash of arms, and the roar of the storm which raged during the battle and swept away part of the army. She depicts also in a striking manner the defeat of the enemy and the murder of Sisera, the commanding officer of the invading army, in the tent of Jael, where he sought security and refreshment after his defeat. She gives, in the conclusion of the tragic story, a glimpse of the inevitable heartbreaks of war—an anxious mother sitting by the window of her home and looking through the lattice for a son who would never return. Even then he lay in the tent of a foreigner with his head severed from his body! Her song, recorded in the fifth chapter of the Book of the Judges, is one of few literary remnants that has come down to us from that ancient period.

> I, even I, will sing unto the Lord;
> I will sing praise to the Lord God of Israel.
>
>   ❋   ❋   ❋
>
> The stars in their courses fought against Sisera.
> The river of Kishon swept them away.
>
>   ❋   ❋   ❋
>
> Then were the horsehoofs broken by the means of the
>   pransings,
> The pransings of their mighty ones.
>
>   ❋   ❋   ❋
>
> The mother of Sisera looked out at a window,
> And cried through the lattice,
>   Why is his chariot so long in coming?
>   Why tarry the wheels of his chariots?
>   —See Judges, chapter 5, for the entire narrative.

The Unnamed Prophet of the Judges

In addition to Deborah, the chronicler of the Book of the Judges mentions only one other person, an unnamed prophet who came on the scene during the invasion by the Amalekites and Midianites. He says:

> They encamped against them, and destroyed the increase of the earth, till thou come unto Gaza, and left no sustenance for Israel, neither sheep, nor ox, nor ass. For they came up with their cattle and their tents, and they came as grass-hoppers for multitude; for both they and their camels were without number: and they entered into the land to destroy it (Judges 6:4, 5).

It was then, when the children of Israel cried in penitence, that the Lord sent a prophet among them to show them the way out of their trouble. He took Gideon from the threshing floor to lead the army of deliverance and free them from the bonds of their oppressors. Judges, chapters 6, 7.

Samuel: Prophet, Priest, and Judge

Samuel stood at the dividing line between the period of the judges and the establishment of the monarchy. He saw the rule of the judges come to its end and helped to inaugurate the kingdom. It seems that during the period of the conquest and settlement of Canaan there was no organized central government. The affairs of state were largely in the hands of the priests and prophets. Judges arose during times of crisis and led armies who delivered them from invaders and oppressors. After the uprising had been subdued these men continued to direct the affairs of the country until their deaths.

The greatest and most outstanding figure among the judges was Samuel. His home was at Ramah and "there he built an altar unto the Lord" (I Samuel 7:17). It appears that at times he performed, also, the functions of a priest. I Samuel 2:11; 7:12. The writer says that "Samuel judged Israel all the days of his life." His judicial circuit embraced Bethel, Gilgal, and Mizpeh, where he held court and adjudicated the causes of those who brought their problems to him. Important though his work as priest and judge was, the greatest contribution he made to the nation was without question his ministry as a prophet. It was his divinely directed spirit that, no doubt, seasoned his judgment in all the official functions he performed. The records indicate that he was closely associated with the sons of the prophets and that they depended upon him for help in times of need or of trouble. II Kings 4:38-44 and 6:1-4. He had no armies or officials to enforce his policies or execute and carry into effect his decisions or verdicts. He ruled, it seems, by the sheer force of his character and personality. He denounced vigorously the alien influences that imperiled the faith and life of his people. He emphasized also in positive terms the principle that the primary requisite of true religion and godliness does not consist in the performance of rites and ceremonies or in the observance of external formalities, though he gave them their proper place, but in righteous and godly living.

The Beginning of the Monarchy

However, the time was ripe for a change. The judgeship of Eli was drawing to its close. It appeared evident that his sons, whom the writer of the Book of Samuel designates as the "sons of Belial . . . [who] knew not the Lord," were planning to take over the judicial affairs of the nation at their father's death. They had, in fact, already done so and behaved so badly in the administration of the sacrifices that "men abhorred the offering of the Lord" (I Samuel 2:12-17). During the invasion of the Philistines, both these sons were slain in battle and the ark of the covenant, which they had taken with them into the conflict, fell into heathen hands. When news of the overwhelming disaster was brought to Eli, he died.

The house of Samuel, the faithful servant of Jehovah, fared no better. His sons, who held judicial positions in Beer-sheba, walked not in the ways of their father, but took advantage of their offices to exact bribes from their clients and perverted judgment in the administration of their official affairs. I Samuel 8:1-3. It was then that the elders of Israel called upon Samuel and petitioned for a king. Moses had foreseen this possibility centuries earlier and had given specific and definite instructions as to what the people, in such an event, should look for in the way of qualifications. He said:

Keep the heart from turning away

Thou shalt in any wise set him king over thee, whom the
Lord thy God shall choose: one from among thy brethren
shalt thou set king over thee: thou mayest not set a stranger
over thee, which is not thy brother. But he shall not multiply
horses to himself, nor cause the people to return to Egypt,
to the end that he should multiply horses: forasmuch as the
Lord hath said unto you, Ye shall henceforth return no more
that way. Neither shall he multiply wives to himself, that
his heart turn not away: neither shall he greatly multiply to
himself silver and gold. And it shall be, when he sitteth upon
the throne of his kingdom, that he shall write him a copy of
this law in a book out of that which is before the priests
the Levites: and it shall be with him, and he shall read
therein all the days of his life: that he may learn to fear the
Lord his God, to keep all the words of this law and these
statutes, to do them: that his heart be not lifted up above
his brethren, and that he turn not aside from the command-
ment, to the right hand, or to the left: to the end that he may
prolong his days in his kingdom, he, and his children, in the
midst of Israel (Deuteronomy 17:15-20).

After having reviewed these instructions of Moses, Samuel
yielded reluctantly to their demands. I Samuel 8:7-18. Knowing
the people as he did, he no doubt had forebodings of what would
take place if a king should be placed at the head of the nation.

Then began the quest for a suitable person to assume the
new office. The prophet, following the leading of God, met Saul,
the son of Kish, a young man from the tribe of Benjamin, and
privately anointed him to become Israel's first king. This anointing was later confirmed at a convocation of all the tribes of Israel
when they met at Mizpeh. I Samuel 10. The selection of Saul
from the plebeian class was not satisfactory to everybody. The
children of Belial said, "How shall this man save us? And they
despised him, and brought him no presents" (I Samuel 10:27).

Samuel followed with deep interest the affairs of Saul from
the day of his anointing until he died. He saw this timid youth
rise out of obscurity to a place of high honor and renown and of
grave responsibility. His early attitude and achievement gave
promise of a successful reign. His victory over the Ammonites

established him in the hearts of his people, but his willfulness soon became evident. After the defeat of the Philistines he took it upon himself, in the absence of Samuel, to perform the functions of a priest. I Samuel 13:8-10. When later he returned from the battle with the Amalekites and brought with him the spoils of war which he had been admonished not to take, he was met by the prophet, who sternly rebuked him for his disobedience. I Samuel 15:1-24. Samuel left him that day and saw him no more until the tragic night at Endor, before the battle of Gilboa where Saul and his sons died.

After Saul's rash act of disobedience at Gilgal, where he assumed the functions of the priest, Samuel, following the leading of the Lord, anointed David, the son of Jesse, a shepherd boy, to become Saul's successor. Some years afterward, while Saul was hunting for David in the wilderness of Engedi to destroy him who he thought was a contender for the throne of Israel, Samuel died. The Scripture says, "And all the Israelites were gathered together, and lamented him, and buried him in his house at Ramah" (I Samuel 25:1).

After David's accession to the throne of Israel the borders of the kingdom were widely extended. Practically all of the nations adjoining Palestine were forced into submission and were brought under the rule of his expanding empire, which finally attained the limits promised to the Israelites when they entered Canaan:

Every place whereon the soles of your feet shall tread shall be yours: from the wilderness and Lebanon, from the river, the river Euphrates, even unto the uttermost sea shall your coast be (Deuteronomy 11:24).

These were the boundaries of the kingdom over which he acquired and maintained control during his long reign of forty years.

David's rule was marked with wisdom and his achievements were not limited only to matters that had to do with governmental or military affairs and activities. His literary genius found its expression in the Psalms and he became known as the "sweet singer of Israel." He depended not only on his own sagacity. His ear was attuned to the voice of the prophets. They were his counselors. Already during the years of his wanderings, when he sought to escape the vengeance of Saul, the prophet Gad was his adviser. I Samuel 22:5. Later during his reign this same prophet rebuked him fearlessly for his sordid affair with Bathsheba. II Samuel 12:1-15. This prophet was also his counselor in the matter of building the temple (I Samuel 7:1-17), and was influential in getting Solomon installed as David's successor to the throne (I Kings 1:8).

Solomon, it seems, was not so much concerned with extending the borders of the kingdom as he was with internal developments and improvements. His building plans included the temple complex at Jerusalem, his palace of justice, his own palace, and housing for his large and expanding harem. His stables at Megiddo, fortifications, vast building and commercial enterprises called for a host of laborers, skilled workmen, and materials, much of which had to be secured from other countries. The defense works at Jerusalem were rebuilt and those at Hazor and Megiddo in the north were strengthened. Gezer, lower Bethhoron, Baalah, and Tadmor were enlarged and reconstructed. The copper mines at Arabah on the Gulf of Aqaba were developed and Ezion-gaber was made a port city. Ships sailed from there to Tarshish, South Arabia, Abyssinia, and India and returned with merchandise and treasures of those far countries.

Administrative changes were also made. The realm was divided into twelve regions or districts, the borders of which cut across the former tribal boundary lines. This was probably done intentionally for the purpose of breaking up the old tribal loyalties and bringing the outlying, non-Israelite centers under control.

Funds to finance this vast program of construction and expansion had to be secured largely by the imposition of taxes upon the population. Much of the manpower was requisitioned from the people of Israel themselves. One can well imagine that there would, in the course of time, develop much discontent and dissatisfaction among the people.

The territorial holdings which were acquired during David's reign and were held under the strict military rule of his administration now, under the new regime, showed signs of weakening in their loyalty. A rebellion among the Arameans, led by Rezon, broke out in the north and Damascus won its freedom. Discontent flared up also in Edom and that province was lost to Solomon.

There were also other evidences of unrest and dissatisfaction within the empire. Oppressive taxation, forced labor, separation of husbands from their families, and governmental extravagance were then no more appreciated than they are today. Ahijah, a prophet from Shiloh, became the spokesman for this discontented group. He met Jeroboam, one of Solomon's overseers, who was then in charge of a building project at Jerusalem, tore his garment from him, and divided it into twelve pieces of which he gave ten to Jeroboam. I Kings 11:26-40. By this token he, Jeroboam, was informed that someday he would become ruler of ten of the tribes of Israel. When Solomon heard of this episode, he sought to forestall whatever eventualities might come out of this affair by having the young man executed. This design was thwarted when Jeroboam fled to Egypt, where he remained until after the death of Solomon. The rest of the acts of Solomon were recorded by Nathan the prophet, Ahijah the Shilonite, and Iddo the seer.

The Division of the Kingdom

At the close of Solomon's reign, the embers of discontent that had been smoldering during his latter years broke out afresh with renewed fervor. The dissatisfaction was not confined to the outlying conquered possessions only. It reached into the very heart of the empire proper. Rehoboam succeeded his father to the throne. Jeroboam returned from his Egyptian exile and championed the cause of the discontented element among the tribes. He led the delegation that petitioned the new king for relief from the heavy tax and conscripted labor burdens that had been imposed by Solomon, his father. The inexperienced crown prince, who had been so recently elevated to the high office of ruler over an empire, asked for time to seek counsel. II Chronicles 10:2-5. He rejected the advice of the older men, who had stood before Solomon's court, and now suggested leniency and moderation. "If thou be kind to this people," they said, "and please them, and speak good words to them, they will be thy servants for ever" (II Chronicles 10:6, 7). He then took counsel with the young men "that were brought up with him." Instead of consideration and moderation which the older men advised, they urged that the burdens should be increased. Their spirit is well reflected in their reply. "Thus shalt thou say unto them," they said, "My little finger shall be thicker than my father's loins. For whereas my father put a heavy yoke upon you, I will put more to your yoke; my father chastised you with whips, but I will chastise you with scorpions" (II Chronicles 10:10, 11).

The time of decision had come. The clock in the great tower of time had struck the hour! When the people received the young king's reply, they cried, "What portion have we in David? . . . to your tents, O Israel: and now, David, see to thine own house" (II Chronicles 10:16). The kingdom which David had so laboriously built up had fallen apart!

When Rehoboam was informed of the break that had taken place, he mustered an army of 18,000 men to put down the insurrection. It was at that juncture that the prophet Shemaiah came on the scene and warned the king against the shedding of fraternal blood in order that the unity of the kingdom might be preserved. I Kings 12:21-24. His decision to abandon his military operations and suffer the division indicates the respect and power which the prophets held among Israel. Their counsel frequently prevailed even though it conflicted with the designs and motives of those who solicited their services.

All of the tribes of Israel followed Jeroboam's leadership except Judah and Benjamin. During the years more and more of the Levites from the Northern Kingdom also drifted back into Jerusalem. Jeroboam set up his government at Shechem. Later it was moved to Tirzah. During the reign of Omri, founder of the third dynasty, 885, it was again moved, this time to Samaria, where it remained until the fall of the kingdom in 722.

It soon became evident that the line of cleavage would cut deeper than the political fabric and would reach into the religious and spiritual affairs of the state as well. Throughout their sojourn in Palestine all Israel had, with the exception of some lapses, been faithful to the religion and mode of worship that was established at Sinai. Jeroboam soon saw that it would be difficult, if not impossible, to retain the loyalty of his followers politically if they should maintain their connection with the temple worship at Jerusalem, where they would be exposed to the teaching and influence of the priests and prophets. Hence, he made the break complete by setting up a system of worship that was entirely separate from the one in the Southern Kingdom.

Jeroboam's sojourn in Egypt had evidently a great deal of influence on his thinking along religious as well as political lines. He adopted the religion and mode of worship which he had learned and in which he may have participated in Egypt. After having taken what he considered proper counsel, he made two calves of gold, one of which he set up at Bethel and the other at Dan. He selected a priesthood from among those who supported his cause, which the chronicler describes as having come from "the basest of men." The feast days were changed. The Feast of the Tabernacles was shifted from the seventh to the eighth month, but the manner of observing it was patterned after the traditional one at Jerusalem. The Southern Kingdom, however, remained the center of Israelitish orthodoxy throughout its history until the conquest of Jerusalem by Nebuchadnezzar in 586, although it was frequently influenced and corrupted by the introduction of pagan practices.

It is important here to evaluate, also, the geographical and economic results of the great rift. The Northern Kingdom held by far the larger part of Palestine proper. There were embraced within its area some 9,400 square miles, and in addition it retained the loyalty of the tribes of Reuben, Gad, and one half of the tribe of Manasseh whose possessions lay east of the Jordan. Judea or the Southern Kingdom held only some 3,400 square miles of territory. During their history both these kingdoms lost most of their territorial holdings east of the Jordan. From the standpoint of climate and fertility, the Northern Kingdom held the advantage. It had several very fertile valleys, and fresh-water seas, while the Southern Kingdom was bordered on both sides by salt water and its southern portion reached down into the hot wind-blown desert of Sinai. The trade route flowed through Samaria to the ports of Joppa, Tyre, and Sidon from which the merchandise and wares of trade were taken to other lands.

The problem that confronted the Israelites throughout the

centuries of their occupation of Canaan did, however, not all originate within their own borders or those of their conquered or subdued possessions. To the east lay the great world empires of ancient Babylonia, Assyria, Neo-Babylonia or Chaldea, and Medo-Persia, all of whom in the heyday of their glory and power had at times wholly or in part controlled the affairs of Palestine. To the southwest lay Egypt which never ceased to look with covetous eyes upon the people who centuries earlier left their borders and established themselves, strongly, in the land of hills and valleys that lay between the River Jordan and the Mediterranean Sea. Greece and Rome, nations that lay to the north and west, were destined in time also to influence and finally to take over and control all of these people. In 722 the armies of Assyria took possession of the Northern Kingdom, deported most of its people, and repopulated the country with a mixture of races drawn from other of their conquered nations. The deported exiles of Israel were taken to other lands, where they were intermixed with other nationals until they lost their identity.

The Southern Kingdom, having retained the worship of Jehovah and chosen their kings and priests from the lines ordained of God, was able for a longer time to resist the corroding influences of evil. But it, too, eventually paid the price for its apostasy and in 586 B.C. it suffered the destruction of its temple and "holy city." Long lines of its people went into exile from which only a remnant returned, in 538, during the dominion of the Medo-Persian Empire.

It was during this period of the divided kingdom that some of the greatest prophets of known history came on the scene. Elisha and Elijah ranked foremost among those who left no writings. They were followed by a long and notable line of able men, Amos, Hosea, Isaiah, Micah, Jeremiah, and others, who gave to the world, for all time, a collection of written orations, addresses, and other papers that shed a great deal of light on the religious, moral, and political conditions of their times. Through them, their experiences, their revelations, and observations, there has come to us also a knowledge and appreciation of God, His nature and character, and His ways of dealing with men and nations, that is always enlightening and ennobling.

The National and Political Framework in Which the Prophets Lived and Worked

1. *The early Babylonian Empire* existed with varying extent of territory and power from about 1830 to 1550 B.C. This was the home of Abraham and his family from which they migrated to Haran and Abraham to Palestine.

2. *The Northern Mesopotamian kingdoms, Assyria,* 1700-1550 B.C., and the *Assyrian Empire,* 1100-612 B.C., were prominent during the period when Israel returned from Egypt until after the fall of the Northern Kingdom in 722 and up to the ministry of Jeremiah, who was the last of the great pre-exilic prophets in Jerusalem. This was the period in which prophetism in Israel and Judah flourished and reached the height of its influence.

3. *The Neo-Babylonian* or *Chaldean Empire* under Nebuchadnezzar rose in 612 and continued until 538 B.C. Its life was brief, but its influence was great. Under the rule of its great King Nebuchadnezzar, Judah went into captivity and Jerusalem and its temple were destroyed. Jeremiah, the great prophet, remained in Jerusalem during this period and Ezekiel prophesied among the exiles in Babylon. It is during this time that Daniel came on the scene.

4. *The Medo-Persian Empire,* 538-33. Daniel, Ezra, and Nehemiah were the great Jewish leaders of this period. It was during this time too that the Jews were released from captivity to return to their homeland. The books of Esther, Ezra, and Nehemiah, and the prophetical books of Haggai, Zechariah, and Malachi came out of this era.

5 | Prophecy During The Period of the Dual Kingdom

The Oral Prophets
931-722 B.C.

The history of the dual kingdom divides itself naturally into three periods: the period of Mutual Hostility, 931-853; the Period of Mutual Alliance, or the *Entente Cordiale*, 853-842; and the Resumption of Mutual Hostilities, 842-722. With the exception of the second period this was a stormy epoch in the history of Israel and Judah. There was always more or less dissension and strife between the two nations. The turbulent times that followed the division of the kingdom at the death of Solomon called for great men, the supply of which was then, as always, pitifully meager.

The Southern Kingdom escaped much of the internal strife and discord that usually follows such upheavals and disruptions. It had an established form of government that was founded by Samuel, who under divine instruction had placed Saul upon the throne. This government was consolidated and strengthened by two of Israel's ablest kings, David and Solomon. It had a divinely designated family line from which to draw its kings. This was true also of its priesthood, and its instituted and established mode of worship, and its civil and criminal code, all of which was formulated and set in order by Moses while Israel encamped at the foot of Mt. Sinai. In spite of the confusion and disaster, when at the death of Solomon the kingdom fell apart, the nation held steadfastly to these traditions. However, in spite of this, their worship was not always free from the pernicious influence of the corrupt religions and social practices of their neighbors. As a result their faith and life suffered.

The Northern Kingdom lacked all of these stabilizing factors. By divine revelation Jeroboam had been designated to become their king but he had no established form of government and no cabinet of counselors. His priests were drawn from the "basest of men," who were evidently also men without experience in conducting an organized form or mode of worship, unless it might have been a pagan form. He had no capital or central seat of government, no temple, and no army, except such troops as he had hastily gathered together at the time of the insurrection when the kingdom was divided. He had to begin building from the bottom.

The government and the religious situation of the Northern Kingdom never became stabilized as were those affairs in the Southern Kingdom. By the time of Omri, one of the few able kings to occupy the throne of Israel, in 871 B.C., the dynasty had already been changed three times, and five different kings had occupied the throne during those sixty years. During its entire history of two hundred and nine years, the dynasty changed nine times. The throne was the prize for which army officers, politicians, and adventurers strove. When it was vacated through the death of the king, there followed a scramble for the position which rarely went to the most worthy, scrupulous, or ablest one of the contenders.

The more settled and stable state of affairs in the kingdom of Judah—the Southern Kingdom—could not entirely escape the consequences or effects of the tumult and confusion in the North. Its political and religious conditions were frequently colored by what took place among its stormy neighbors. But those who take into consideration only earth-bound authorities and powers to accomplish their ends and promote their projects have not reckoned with all the factors and forces that are available, or that enter into a situation that must be dealt with in order to succeed. Hidden away in quiet, often obscure, homes, among the masses and sometimes in lonely places, were those who were faithful, whose hearts beat in unison with the promptings of the divine Spirit. From them the Lord drew helpers in times of need. Among them were the prophets, God's spokesmen, to whom was delegated a power with which the apostate house of Israel, as well as the wayward king and princes and priests of Judah, had to reckon. They had always been there. Had they failed, the Lord would no doubt have breathed His spirit into other hearts and set them aflame, for the resources of God are never exhausted.

The case against Judah and Israel had been building up over the years and the day of accounting was in the offing. While this was in the process of materializing, great men appeared on the stage to turn the tide Godward; and if that were not possible, then to salvage such remnants in either nation as could be saved. These men, the prophets, played through the centuries an important role as counselors and advisers of kings and priests and figured prominently in the religious and political affairs of their day.

A prophet, an unnamed one, appeared on the scene during the final years of Solomon's reign and predicted the fall of the kingdom. Later, when the break came, Ahijah, a prophet, supported the revolt of the ten tribes when at the death of Solomon the movement came to its climax. In spite of the protests of Rehoboam, Judah's newly installed king, the division was made and a new kingdom was set up in the north country.

This schism was, however, not the full answer to the problem of the dissatisfied element that followed Jeroboam. A sacred unity had been broken. Jacob's people were divided into opposing camps, and a spiritual fellowship and kinship that had extended over centuries was severed. In his endeavors to find some religious anchorage for his people, Jeroboam turned to idolatry. He set up two altars, one at Dan and the other at Bethel, and molten calves became the objects of their worship. Idolatry became the religion of the state, wherein they worshiped their ancestral gods in a repulsive and degrading way. It was then that many of the Levites drifted back to Jerusalem, where a more favorable religious atmosphere prevailed.

But the prophets were not silent. They rebuked the erring monarch vehemently. One day when Jeroboam was officiating at the altar, which he had set up at Bethel, *a man of God*, a prophet who had come out of Judah, appeared on the scene and cried out against the altar. He predicted that the day would come when the bones of the priests who had officiated there would be burned upon it. As evidence to substantiate and verify the truth of his prediction, he said that the altar would be torn and the ashes poured upon the ground. I Kings 13:1-4. All of this came to pass that day. When Jeroboam, who had assumed the functions of a priest, saw that his purpose was thwarted, he grasped for the prophet but found his arm disabled and useless. His humiliation, however, did not change his spirit. But he did show kindness to this man of God in return for healing his disabled arm, and invited him to his house for refreshments and a reward. But these prophets were an independent group. A spirit born of conviction possessed them and they were not readily beguiled by royal favors, regardless of how attractive they were. Hence, the honor of dining with the king was not accepted.

Jeroboam, during his reign of some twenty-two years, succeeded in establishing a stable government and fostered good, or at least tolerable, relations with the surrounding nations. But the peace with the Southern Kingdom remained unsettled. The historian says that "there was war between Rehoboam and Jeroboam all the days of his life" (I Kings 15:6). Shishak, from Egypt, during the fifth year after the division of the kingdom had taken place, invaded Judah and captured Jerusalem, looted the temple, the palace, and the house of the forest of Lebanon, and carried their treasures away as plunder to Egypt. This left Rehoboam in a despairing and impotent financial condition. Jeroboam also suffered an invasion from Egypt during this period. Inscriptions on the walls of Karnak note that one hundred and fifty-six towns were taken, one third of which were located in Jeroboam's realm.

The uneasy peace between Rehoboam and Jeroboam continued throughout the lives of these two rival monarchs. During the years of his reign, Jeroboam depended, more or less, upon the counsel of Ahijah, the prophet, who encouraged him to carry through to a finish his plans for the division of the kingdom. Politically, he was an able ruler and administrator, but religiously his record was bad. A recent commentator describes him as being a "symbol of obliquity" for all the succeeding kings of Israel. When his son fell ill he again sought the counsel of Ahijah, his former counselor and friend. This visit, however, gave him small consolation. His wife, whom he had sent in disguise to consult the prophet, brought to her household sad tidings. Her son, according to the predictions of this man of God, died when she entered the gates of the city, and the kingdom, she was informed, would. at the death of Jeroboam, her husband, pass to a new dynasty. After a long reign of twenty-two years, he died and his son Nadab succeeded him. Rehoboam of the Southern Kingdom reigned seventeen years in Jerusalem, and at his death his son Abijam came to the throne. The chronicler says that the acts of Rehoboam, first and last, are written in the book of Shemaiah the prophet, and of Iddo the seer. II Chronicles 12:15.

The passing of these two monarchs brought new men into history. Abijam, as already noted, succeeded his father in the Southern Kingdom and during the three years of his reign he was at war with Jeroboam. At the death of Abijam, his son, who is known in history as "the good king Asa," came to the throne of Judah. It was during the first years of his reign that Jeroboam, king of the Northern Kingdom, died. After a brief reign of less than two years Nadab, his successor, was slain by Baasha, an army officer, who wiped out the entire house of Jeroboam, established himself on the throne, and declared war upon Asa. The writer of the Book of Kings says, "There was war between Asa and Baasha king of Israel all their days" (I Kings 15:16).

Asa, king of Judah, under the guidance of Oded the prophet, instituted greatly needed religious reforms in his kingdom. II Chronicles 15:1-19. Early in his reign he recruited a large army of five hundred and eighty thousand men. He soon became involved in a war with Ethiopia in which he was successful. During the sixteenth year of Asa's reign, ominous signs began to appear along the northern border of his kingdom. Baasha began to strengthen his position by building a wall at Ramah, only five miles from Jerusalem, in order to keep his own people from consorting with the inhabitants of Judah. Asa stripped the treasury of the temple to cement a league between him and Benhadad, king of Syria, and inspire an invasion from the North to withdraw the army of Israel from its southern border. This plan succeeded and Asa was enabled to strengthen his own barricades with materials he salvaged from Baasha's fortifications and wall.

The chroniclers say that the prophets watched closely Asa's operations and on the whole approved what he did until he made his costly treaty with Benhadad. Hanani, the seer, rebuked him severely for putting his trust in the Syrian army instead of Jehovah. This greatly angered Asa, who then had this faithful counselor arrested and put in stocks as a reward for his service. (See II Chronicles 15, 16.)

Things in the Northern Kingdom were not going well either. Baasha's problems were not all located beyond the borders of his domain. Following his accession to the throne of his father he slew all the remaining members of the house of Jeroboam. As a result, Hanani, a prophet, predicted for him a fate that for cruelty exceeded that which he had meted out to the family of his father. At his death, after his long reign of twenty-four years, the customary scramble for the throne ensued. Elah, his son, succeeded him; but after a brief reign of two years he was assassinated during a drinking carousal by Zimri, an officer in the royal chariotry. Zimri then proceeded to destroy all of the house of the king in order to make his position secure.

When word reached the army that was then on the field besieging the Philistine city of Gibbethon, the soldiers at once chose Omri, their commander, as king of Israel. He then at the head of his troops laid siege to the capital. When Zimri saw the hopelessness of his situation, he committed suicide by burning the palace after having occupied the throne for seven days.

Omri was one of the rulers of Israel that could be classed as a statesman. He, however, was not noted for his piety or his loyalty to Jehovah. During his reign of twelve years he is credited with having moved the capital of the nation from Tirzah to Samaria. His major accomplishments are confirmed by the archaeological discoveries of the more recent past. We learn from the records of the *Moabite Stone,* of his conquest of Moab, which he added to his kingdom and which was retained as a tributary for forty years. The annual tribute he collected from his possessions alone amounted to one hundred thousand lambs and one hundred thousand rams with wool. II Kings 3:4. His reputation for power and military prowess reached as far as Assyria, where for a century and a half after his death the kingdom of Israel was spoken of by Assyrian historians as the "Land of Omri." His reputation, however, from the standpoint of religion was not good. He is classified with Jeroboam I as one "who made Israel to sin." His diplomatic relations with Syria, and his neighbors to the north, were more or less unsettled during the greater part of his reign. At Omri's death, after a reign of twelve years, Ahab, his son, came to the throne of Samaria.

Omri's relationship with the Phoenicians had been successful and his commercial treaties were satisfactory. One of the stipulations of the agreement with the Phoenicians was that Jezebel, the daughter of Ethbaal, king of Astarte, should be given to Ahab, Omri's son and heir apparent, to become his wife. This provision was perhaps the most unfortunate and regrettable part of that contract. She was a high-spirited, capable, and imperious woman. She brought with her into Israel her corrupting, idolatrous, pagan religion, together with her priests and prophets, their ritual and paraphernalia of worship, their intolerance and persecutions. After she had established herself in her new position as queen of the realm, she sent forth her promoters throughout the kingdom to set up altars of Baal in Samaria and elsewhere. Ahab himself "reared up an altar for Baal in the house of Baal, which he had built in Samaria. And Ahab made a grove; and Ahab did more to provoke the Lord God of Israel to anger than all the kings of Israel that were before him" (I Kings 16:32, 33).

Jezebel initiated a crusade to uproot whatever vestiges of godliness and true worship there remained in Israel, including the destruction of the prophets of God. She, with her impetuous disposition and commanding personality, dominated not only the religious affairs of the nation but, in a large measure, the affairs of the state as well. Ahab became a tool in her hands to carry out her nefarious program.

But fighting against God or drifting without His guidance is in the long run precarious and hazardous business. Behind the powers of earth and the tragedies they occasion, there is always a great reservoir of strength and wisdom that is divinely provided for those who desire to do His will. It is available at all times, and especially so when spiritual interests are at stake. These resources were neither known nor wanted by Jezebel in her day. If they were ever known to Ahab, her consort, they had long since been neglected, abandoned, and perhaps forgotten. Nor were they known to pagan priests and prophets, who sought to secure their ends by such means as they knew.

The time for reckoning in Israel, it seems, had come. In spite of Jezebel's determination to uproot and destroy entirely all traces of Jehovah worship within the kingdom, some prophets and faithful worshipers still remained. The historians of that day say: "Yet I have left me seven thousand in Israel, all the knees which have not bowed unto Baal, and every mouth which hath not kissed him" (I Kings 19:18). In addition to this remnant, there was also Obadiah, Ahab's court chamberlain, and one hundred prophets of God whom Obadiah had hidden in caves and supplied with food, probably salvaged from the king's table. It must have appeared to the people of that day that the design of this evil woman would succeed and the worship of Jehovah, the God of their fathers, would be totally extinguished.

Elijah the Tishbite

But the resources of God are never depleted. The time when the issues would have to be faced was drawing near. Hidden away among the rocks and crags of Gilead was Elijah the Tishbite. We know nothing of his childhood or his family. We know him only as the rugged, fearless spokesman for God, whose sporadic ministry was to figure large in the affairs of the kingdom which Jeroboam had established and whose altars were now dedicated to Baal.

One day this messenger, uncouthly clad in a garment of skins or camel's hair, girded about with a leathern girdle, confronted Ahab suddenly with a startling message. He presented no letters of introduction or credentials of his office. He bore no prophetic insignia, if there were such in his day. He wore no priestly regalia and carried no documents of authority from king or court. Without introduction or formality, he delivered his message, which was as brief and concise as it was shocking and startling:

As the Lord God of Israel liveth, before whom I stand, there shall not be dew nor rain these years, but according to my word (I Kings 17:1).

Then this messenger, having accomplished his mission, disappeared as abruptly as he had come. The historian says that according to the word he had from the Lord he turned eastward and went into hiding by the brook Cherith that is before the Jordan. Here he lived on such food as the ravens left and refreshed himself from the waters of the dwindling stream.

His predictions came to pass. The skies became cloudless and barren as desert skies are. When the streamlet upon which he depended for refreshment dried up, he, the prophet, was directed to go to Zarephath "which belongeth to Zidon" where he was sheltered and fed by a widow whose stock of meal had been reduced to a mere handful and whose cruse of oil was almost empty, and yet never failed during his sojourn in her home.

The long arm of the drought reached also into the king's establishment. While the rains lingered and the dews failed, the fields became barren and the streams and wells dried up. Ahab then sent messengers, so Obadiah says, throughout all his domain, into all the country and the surrounding nations, to apprehend the man whom he held accountable for this nationwide calamity. Then one day when Obadiah, the governor of Ahab's house, and Ahab had gone by different routes in search of pasturage and water for the king's animals, Obadiah was suddenly confronted by the prophet who stood in his way and blocked his path. He insisted, over Obadiah's protest, that a meeting be arranged between him and the king. At the meeting that followed, recriminations and charges flew wildly. Ahab said: "Art thou he that troubleth Israel?" to which Elijah replied, "I have not troubled Israel; but thou, and thy father's house, in that ye have forsaken the commandments of the Lord, and thou hast followed Baalim" (I Kings 18:17, 18). He then demanded that a convocation be called at Mt. Carmel. This was to include all Israel, together with the prophets of Baal and the prophets of the grove, which ate at the king's table, numbering altogether eight hundred and fifty people.

This meeting at Mt. Carmel was one of the major crises in Israel's history. The God of Abraham and Isaac and Jacob, and the gods of Baal were put to the test. The historians (I Kings 18:17-39) describe the proceedings. The prophets of Baal were given every advantage, but all their incantations and prayers were unavailing. Elijah had suffered himself to be placed in a most disadvantageous position. He permitted the prophets of Ahab's court to select the animals for his sacrifices as well as those for their own. He built his own altar and made a trench around it which he ordered them to fill with water, which was poured also upon the wood and the animal which he had prepared for sacrifice. This was repeated three times, until the water ran about the altar and filled the trench. At the time of the evening sacrifice, he summoned the people, whose call for help from their gods had failed so miserably, to witness the response of the God of Israel. After a brief but impressive prayer the "fire of the Lord" fell and consumed, not only the sacrifice, but also the wood and stones and the dust and "licked up the water" that was in the trench. I Kings 18:30-38. The victory was the Lord's. Elijah's claims for Jehovah were vindicated. When the people saw what had happened, they fell on their faces and cried, "The Lord, he is the God." The prophets of Baal who had been so sure of success, but who had failed so miserably, were slain by the militant prophet by the brook Kishon. I Kings 18:40. Ahab was greatly humiliated but not changed. Elijah, who saw a cloud rising out of the sea "like a man's hand," said to him, "Get thee up, eat and drink; for there is a sound of abundance of rain" (I Kings 18:41).

The drought was broken, and the rains had come again! But Jezebel was still alive. When she learned of the fate of her prophets, she instituted measures to put Elijah out of the way. This sent him once again on the road, this time into exile. He was discouraged in spite of the tremendous demonstration of God's power on Mt. Carmel. His servant accompanied him as far as Beer-sheba, which belongs to Judah. From thence he went alone, a day's journey into the wilderness, where he found shelter under a juniper tree. People today would say that a great "emotional letdown" had set in, and he prayed God that he might die. I Kings 19:4. When he awoke, he found that prepared food and a cruse of water had been left at his head for him. After another day he set out on a forty days' journey to Mt. Horeb, where he took up his abode in a cave. Here in this great solitude, where Moses was schooled and prepared for his mission and where Israel centuries earlier had witnessed such fearful manifestations of the glory and power of God, Elijah was also to meet Him and learn of the ways by which He makes Himself known. He witnessed His power in nature—winds that broke the rocks and earthquakes and fire! He learned also that God speaks in other tones and that He was not in the earthquake and wind and fire. The voice of God is more often still and small but mighty to accomplish His purposes. The stormy session he had with Ahab on Mt. Carmel had its place to demonstrate the judgments of the Most High, but the "still small voice" is the redeeming and healing voice that penetrates deeply into the soul.

Elijah's work, however, was not finished. His assignments were not light ones. Within a short time he was on the road again—this time with a fearful commission, to go by the way of the wilderness to Damascus to anoint Hazael, king of Syria, and Jehu, the "furious driver," the son of Nimshi, to become king of Israel, and to call Elisha, the son of Shaphat of Abel-meholah, to become his successor in the prophetic ministry.

On the way back from Horeb he found Elisha, evidently the son of a well-to-do husbandman, plowing in the field with twelve yoke of oxen. He threw his mantle upon him as a token of his call. When he reached Israel, he found Ahab engaged in a war with Syria. He continued his stormy ministry, assisted in the later years by Micaiah. II Chronicles 18:12-27. The last record we have of him is a letter he wrote to Jehoram, king of Judah,

who had married Athaliah, the daughter of Jezebel, who at the
death of her husband established herself on the throne as the
ruling queen of the Southern Kingdom. II Chronicles 21:12-15.
She reigned with all the arrogance and spirit of her mother, until
her tragic execution at the horse gate of the king's palace, on the
day when she tried to interfere with the coronation of her seven-
year-old son when he was crowned king of Judah.

Elijah's rugged ministry was finished. He was a desert man,
an individualist, an uncompromising prophet of Jehovah. One
writer says: "He rose like a meteor from the sky and struck like
a thunderbolt at the immoralities, infamies, and degradations that
rose out of Baal worship." He was the defender and champion of
the cause of Jehovah, that was threatened with destruction by
Jezebel and the patrons of false religions, that were deeply
entrenched in the high places in the kingdom, from which the
contagion was being carried to other lands. But Elijah's day had
come to its close. He was on his way home.

Elisha the Son of Shaphat

On that last day when Elijah and Elisha walked alone by the
Jordan, Elijah asked his successor what gift he might bestow
upon him as a parting token of his good will and appreciation of
his faith and ministry. Elisha's request was that he might be
given a double portion of his spirit. It appears that while they
were yet talking, a chariot suddenly appeared and took Elijah
away. He left the world as he had lived in it—in a storm, a whirlwind, a chariot of fire! As he went, his mantle fell on Elisha,
who then went back to Jericho, where he tarried for a time with
the sons of the prophets. II Kings 2:18.

Again, the time for a change was at hand. The period of
alliance between the Northern and the Southern kingdoms had
come to its end with the fall of Ahab's dynasty in 842. During
the reign of Jehu, who had extinquished the house of Omri, the
Northern Kingdom was at the mercy of Syria. Israel's military
establishment had but a token of an army and was left with no
"increment" of value. But back beyond Syria there had risen a
vast empire, Assyria, that was even then overshadowing the world
between the Tigris River and the Mediterranean Sea with its

power and influence. It was during this twilight period of the *Cordiale Entente*, the period of peace between Israel and Judah, that Elisha was to perform his ministry.

The times called for new men. God had proclaimed His judgments through the "thunders" of Elijah. Now Elisha came and took up the role of his master whose mantle he had assumed. He, it appears, was not one who loved the solitude or the storms and rigors and loneliness of the desert. He lived and associated with people. He was companionable and approachable, a man among men. He was at ease with kings and princes and prophets, and from records of his life and activities one would judge that he had a special attachment to the sons of the prophets. His influence was far-reaching and potent in the affairs of human rights and loyalty to Jehovah.[1]

When Elisha left the sons of the prophets at Bethel, whither he had gone after leaving Jericho, he was accosted by a group of young ruffians at one of the villages along the way. He was avenged and his office was vindicated when two she bears emerged from the woods and attacked them. After having visited Mt. Carmel, the place of Jehovah's great manifestation of Himself on the day when the prophets of Baal were defeated, he returned to Samaria.

Meanwhile, changes had taken place in the political world. Jehoram, the son of Ahab, came to the throne in Israel. The Biblical record says that "he did that which was evil in the sight of the Lord," but not like his father, for he put away the image of Baal that his father had made. Nevertheless, he "followed the sins of Jeroboam the son of Nebat, which made Israel to sin; he departed not therefrom" (II Kings 13:2).

Mesha, the king of Moab, who had kept Omri so bountifully supplied with lambs and rams and wool, rebelled and renounced his treaty. Jehoram of Israel took an inventory of his military strength (II Kings 3:6) and proposed an alliance with Jehoshaphat, king of Judah, to bring the delinquent, tribute-paying sheepmaster to terms. Jehoshaphat accepted the proposition, for, said he, "I am as thou art, my people as thy people, and my horses as thy horses" (II Kings 3:7). Here Elisha had his first

---

1. Price, *The Dramatic Story of Old Testament History.*

recorded conference with representatives of the allied armies who sought his counsel before entering upon this campaign. He rejected the plea of Israel's king and gave his scant approval only for Jehoshaphat's sake. II Kings 3:13, 14.

He prevented, by his counsel, two wars with the Syrians which could well have been disastrous. One time he blinded the invading army and afterward fed the soldiers and sent them home. II Kings 6:18-23. Sometime later, when they returned to besiege the city of Samaria, during a time of famine, the army became alarmed by noises which they interpreted as coming from the combined forces of the Hittites and Egyptians that were on the march to the field of battle. As a result, they fled and left all their military stores behind. II Kings 7:1-7.

Elisha's acts were frequently accompanied by deeds of kindness. He showed great consideration of Naaman, the commander of the Syrian army, who was a leper. On the advice of a captive maid, whom they had taken from Israel, he visited the prophet to secure a cure for his malady. II Kings 5:1-19. He pleaded with the king for the restoration of the unfortunate Shunammite's property and multiplied the failing oil of the widow of one of the sons of the prophets. II Kings 4:18-37; 4:1-7. He assisted one of the sons of the prophets in recovering an ax which he had accidentally lost while working to secure beams to enlarge the living quarters of their institution (II Kings 6:1-7) and healed the "noxious pottage" which the residents had gathered during a food shortage (II Kings 4:38-41). He fulfilled God's injunction to Elijah by sending one of the sons of the prophets to anoint Jehu, king over Israel. II Kings 9:1-10. This marked the climax of his contest with Phoenician Baalism. He lived to see this "furious driver" overthrow the dynasty of Ahab and bring about the death of the imperious Jezebel. He lived, also, to see the day when Hazael became king of Syria.

His deep concern during his last illness had to do with Israel's future. To the east, great nations were rising in power and he had forebodings of the calamity that would befall his people years later. The events that took place at his bedside—his deathbed—are recorded in II Kings 13:14-19. His funeral was likely an unostentatious one. His obituary was brief. The recorder says merely, "And Elisha died, and they buried him" (II Kings 13:20).

It was during this period, filled with tragedies, warfare, and insecurity, that the great prophets, Elijah and Elisha, and others of less renown, laid securely the foundations for the worship of Jehovah. They saw thrones topple, dynasties fall, tragedies take place, and violence reign in high places. New men were now coming on the scene. New faces appeared and new voices were heard. The Golden Age of Prophecy was at hand and its dawn was breaking! Although Baalism had been dethroned, strange, new voices of apostasy were being heard and the contest between the representatives of God and His adversaries was destined to be continued throughout the remaining years of Israel's history and beyond, as it will be even to the end of time.

6 | The Golden Age Of Prophecy

The Literary Prophets

Baalism, which had threatened to engulf the spiritual life of the people of both the Northern and Southern kingdoms, lost its power with the death of Jezebel and her daughter Athaliah. That, however, does not mean that idolatry and other apostate forms of worship had ceased to exist or were permanantly banned from either or both of the kingdoms. Laxity in spiritual matters or worldly things constitute dangers that are always lurking near and threaten to break down or destroy the inner life of the people and nations of all times. Neither Israel nor Judah were in their day immune to the influence of any or all of these factors.

During the years the shortcomings of the priests of both Israel and Judah became more and more pronounced and the influence and authority of the prophets rose. One may almost read the history of both the Northern and Southern kingdoms, from the latter half of the eighth century B.C., in the messages which these spokesmen for God left in their writings. The great Assyrian Empire in the east had reached—perhaps passed—its zenith during this period, but its shadows still hovered over Palestine and the nations beyond. The rising Greek Empire, that later dominated the cultural and political affairs of the world, was taking form and began to color somewhat the affairs of the eastern nations. Archaeologists make reference to these people, who were later to so greatly influence the affairs of the world, in the Tell Amarna tablets, of the fourteenth century B.C. In 495 B.C. they fixed the border of Oriental supremacy by defeating the Persians at Marathon, which was one of the decisive battles of the world.

A new set of spiritual leaders, the literary prophets, arose in Israel and became active during this period and the centuries that followed. These men left some of their messages and sayings in written form which were preserved and handed down from generation to generation to our time. We do not mean to imply that they attempted to write a history of their lives or of the time in which they lived. They were first of all preachers of righteousness and spoke to the nations, the people, and the problems of their day. They dealt with the spiritual needs of the people and the political, social, and religious conditions and affairs of their time. They also proposed and advocated such remedial measures and counsels as would bring the nation and people back into a proper relationship with God. This latter was, in fact, their chief concern.

These writings, then, together with the historical records of the books of Samuel, Kings, Chronicles, Ezra, Nehemiah, and Esther, enable us to secure a reliable and trustworthy knowledge of the religious, social, and political conditions of their time. More important still, they made available to the people of all generations a knowledge of God, His nature, His character, His will, and His dealings with nations and people. They banned, for all time, the delusion that a people that continues to live in sin can survive. It is through these messages, too, that the promised Messiah, who was so dimly revealed to Eve on the day of her disobedience in Eden, was made more clearly and fully known. They upheld the law which grew out of the principles set forth in the Ten Commandments, and provided regulations for a way of life that would enable them to fulfill their divine mission in the world. They insisted, also, that the rites, ceremonies, and symbolism of their mode of worship were meaningful and helpful spiritually when they were interpreted correctly and observed faithfully.

The content of this literature, in fact, treats of the workings of God in history. While these prophets spoke first of all to the need and problems of their time, they were not limited to that period only. They dealt with eternal truths that are as unchangeable as the nature and character of God. When these messengers spoke to the people of their day, they spoke as ministers, preachers of righteousness. When they spoke of things yet in the future, they were "foretellers"—they unveiled future events. When they explained their messages, they were interpreters. In all these areas they were divinely qualified to act as agents of God. Eiselen, the author of *Prophecy and the Prophets,* says:

> These prophets were pure in character, strong in intellect, sincere in purpose, quickened through personal communication with God, enlightened by the divine Spirit, and were able to see facts and understand truths that were hidden from the eyes of those who did not live in the same intimate fellowship with Jehovah.

This is, however, true not only of the literary prophets, who were no more and no less prophets, but of those who left no written record of their sayings. Our knowledge of the work and ministry of all of these men, however, has been greatly amplified and enriched by the labors of those whose messages were committed to written form.

During the more recent years, scholars have raised questions regarding the authenticity of these writings and the genuineness of their ascribed authorship. To say that no problems exist would not be in accord with the facts. There are problems that have to do with authorship, date, and content. They are, however, not considered by competent scholars to be of such a nature as to invalidate the trustworthiness and usefulness of the material. John R. Sampey, a noted Hebrew scholar and former seminary president, has the following to say on the subject:

> The tendency in recent criticism of the Bible has been to reduce every book to fragments and multiply, unduly, imaginary authors and editors. Common sense will continue to discount the claims of an overconfident criticism.

In addition we may say that the solutions which the critical school offers to some of the problems of the Scripture are frequently less satisfying and no less questionable than the questions they try to solve. Hence, this author follows the tradition of a long line of commentators and Biblical scholars who accept the prophetical writings as a part of the Scripture which Paul, the apostle, says "is given by inspiration of God, and is profitable for *doctrine*, for *reproof*, for *correction*, for *instruction* in *righteousness:* that the man of God may be perfect, throughly furnished unto all good works" (II Timothy 3:16, 17).

Scholars have, throughout the years, divided the literary prophets into two groups: the Major Prophets and the Minor Prophets. We accept this classification and shall consider them, in this study, in their general chronological order and in the historical setting out of which the writings came. Not everyone will agree with this arrangement, because some of the writings are not definitely dated. Some contend, also, that a number of books, and parts of others, were not written by the prophet whose name they bear. Regardless of how this may be, it is still the author's conviction that it should be interpreted in the light of the time and place in which it was written. This, however, does not mean that all that was said had reference to the period in which the prophet lived and spoke. Many of them uttered thought that lay beyond the bounds of time within which they lived and they spoke of things that came to pass in the future—sometimes in the far distant future.

For the purpose of this study, then, we shall place these men in three major groups or divisions, as follows:

Section one: The Assyrian Period, 1100-607 B.C. Joel, *ca.* 830-810; Jonah, 800-780; Amos, 760; Hosea, 750-725; Isaiah, 744-695; Micah, 735-700; Nahum, 630; Jeremiah, 628-607.

Section two: The Neo-Babylonian or Chaldean Period. Jeremiah, 607-585; Zephaniah, 630-625; Habakkuk, 609-600; Ezekiel, 633-571; Daniel, 602-?.

Section three: The Medo-Persian Period, 538-533. Haggai, 520; Zechariah, 520-480; Malachi, 430.

During this period of the literary prophets there is mention made of two women who are spoken of as prophetesses. Isaiah speaks of his wife as a prophetess. Isaiah 8:3. There is, however, no record of her at any time having performed the functions of

5

that office. The only thing that is said about her is that she bore
Isaiah a son who was, by divine injunction, given a name that
had prophetical significance—Maher-shalal-hash-baz, i.e., "make
speed to the spoil, he hastens to the prey." The other prophetess
mentioned is Huldah. The author of II Kings 22:13-20 speaks of
her as the wife of Shallum, the son of Tikvah, who was the son of
Harhas, the keeper of the wardrobe. She is said to have lived in
Jerusalem "in the college" during the reign of Josiah, when the
temple was in the process of being repaired and made ready for
the resumption of Jehovah worship, following the evil reign of
Manasseh and his son Ammon. For their apostasy and wickedness
the Lord had threatened to "stretch over Jerusalem the line of
Samaria, and the plummet of the house of Ahab: and . . . wipe
Jerusalem as a man wipeth a dish, wiping it, and turning it upside
down" (II Kings 21:12, 13). However, because of Josiah's loyalty
the Lord relented this dire threat and assured the king through
the ministry of Huldah that he should have a peaceable reign.
(See also II Chronicles 34:22-28.)

7 | Joel, the Son of Pethuel

The date of Joel's ministry is not found in his writings, nor are there historical allusions or references that give scholars and students a definite clue as to the time his message or messages were delivered. It was at the time, however, when the Grecians were already in the slave markets of the world, for he speaks of children of Judah having been sold to the Greeks. One gathers from chapter 1:3-6 that it was Tyre and Sidon that sponsored this traffic in human beings. For what the people of these cities have done He, the Lord, threatened to recompense them by placing their own children into the hands of Judah, who then would sell them to the Sabeans, the people of Sheba. 3:6-8.

Joel deals mainly with four subjects: the sinfulness of the people; God's judgments by way of droughts and failing crops; followed by a plague of locusts that swept over the land like a devastating army and destroyed or consumed what the drought had left. He closes his message with a call to repentance, and the promise of restoration.

Such occurrences as religious apostasy, droughts, locusts, and plagues were not unusual in Palestine. This one had, however, attained proportions that bore the marks of divine indignation and judgment upon an errant generation that no longer responded to the ordinary methods by which people are recalled from their waywardness and sin.

The calamity of which Joel speaks must have been of such dimensions as the people then living had never witnessed, nor had those of the preceding generation. "Hear this, ye old men," he says, "and give ear, all ye inhabitants of the land. Hath this been in your days, or even in the days of your fathers? Tell ye your children of it, and let your children tell their children, and their children another generation. . . . Awake, ye drunkards, and weep; and howl, all ye drinkers of wine, because of the new wine; for it is cut off from your mouth" (Joel 1:2, 3, 5). It appears that the calamity was so widespread and destructive that there was not sufficient in the way of animals and drink offerings for the priests to carry on their temple service, for, says the prophet, "The meat offering and the drink offering is cut off from the house of the Lord; the priests, the Lord's ministers, mourn" (1:9).

Because of the heat and lack of moisture, the seed that had been sown degenerated under the barren clods of earth. The granaries were desolate—empty. Their barns were broken down, for the corn was withered. The prophet describes sadly the scenes:

How do the beasts groan! the herds of cattle are perplexed, because they have no pasture; yea, the flocks of sheep are made desolate. . . . For the fire hath devoured the pastures of the wilderness, and the flame hath burned all the trees of the field. The beasts of the field cry also unto thee: for the rivers of waters are dried up, and the fire hath devoured the pastures of the wilderness (1:18-20).

Only those who have lived on the fringe of the desert can visualize such a scene and know how hopelessly destitute a land can become when the skies are cloudless and barren for weeks and weeks and when the rains fail. The life of the plains, the cattle, the sheep, and the untamed animals become crazed with hunger and thirst, forsake their young, and wander with eyes wild and then lusterless until, famished, they sink and die. Such was the situation out of which Joel spoke in his day. But as though heat and drought were not a sufficient scourge, a plague more devastating yet was to follow. "A day of darkness and of gloominess, a day of clouds and of thick darkness, as the morning spread upon the mountains: a great people and a strong; there hath not been ever the like, neither shall be any more after it, even to the years of many generations" (2:2).

When this plague struck, the people stood helpless as they always do under such conditions. The country, the prophet says, became like a burned-over land. "A fire devoureth before them; and behind them a flame burneth." Before the drought and the plague of locusts came, the land was like the Garden of Eden; after they had passed, the country looked like a "desolate wilderness."

He describes the appearance of this scourge as being like "a great people," "and as horsemen, so shall they run" (2:4). The sound of their movement was said to have been like that of chariots upon the mountain. Their "leap," he said, is "like the noise of a flame of fire that devoureth the stubble." They move as a "strong people set in battle array." "They shall run like mighty men; they shall climb the wall like men of war; and they shall march every one on his ways, and they shall not break their ranks: neither shall one thrust another; they shall walk every one in his path: and when they fall upon the sword, they shall not be wounded. They shall run to and fro in the city; they shall run upon the wall, they shall climb up upon the houses; they shall enter in at the windows like a thief. . . . The sun and the moon shall be dark, and the stars shall withdraw their shining" (2:7-10).

Commentators generally agree that this has reference to a plague of locusts that frequently follows a series of dry years in desert countries, or in semiarid plains, or in lands adjoining them. Many people now living recall the invasion of grasshoppers during the third decade—the 1930's of the present century—when following a series of dry years they came out of the hinterland like an uncontrollable army, and in their flying stage filled the sky like a dark cloud, and with a sound that resembled the whirring of chariot wheels. When they disappeared, the land was barren. What had been fields of grain or garden plots in the morning were empty wastes by evening. People stood helplessly by and saw their crops consumed by the ravenous invaders.

In chapter 1:4 the prophet describes the stages by which

the "army" moved. He says that what the *gazem,* the old locusts, left, the *arbeh,* the newly hatched hopper, ate; what the newly hatched hopper left, the *yelek,* or crawler, ate; what the crawler left, the *hasil,* or mature flier, ate. Thus, through the stages of development from the *gazem,* the old locust, to the *hasil,* the mature flier, they lived upon the country. In the process of their migration, the females deposit their eggs at a proper depth in the soil where they are hatched when favorable conditions prevail, and are again marshaled for a new assault upon what is available with no regard for how or what it does to land or people.

Such occurrences are not unusual in Palestine, where nature has set the stage for such developments. An invasion of that kind was vividly described in the December, 1915, issue of the *National Geographic Magazine.* The author says that in less than two months after their appearance "not only was every green leaf devoured, but the very bark was peeled from the trees, which stood out white and lifeless, like skeletons. . . . Even Arab babies, left by their mothers in the shade of some tree, had their faces devoured before their screams were heard." It must have been just such a calamity that prompted Joel to call the husbandmen and vine dressers, the priests and drunkards of his day to repentance.

But why should Israel be made to endure such a holocaust of suffering? Had not God promised them, centuries earlier, when they left the well-watered delta of the Nile for the Promised Land, that their new home would not be like Egypt, from whence they came, where "they watered the land beneath their feet," but that they should have a good land, "a land of brooks of water, of fountains and depths that spring out of valleys and hills; a land of wheat, and barley, and vines, and fig trees, and pomegranates; a land of oil olive, and honey; a land wherein thou shalt eat bread without scarceness, thou shalt not lack any thing in it; a land whose stones are iron, and out of whose hills thou mayest dig brass" (Deuteronomy 8:7-9)? However, the people must have forgotten that He also gave them ample warning of what would happen if they should neglect God in not keeping His commandments and His judgments and His statutes. "And it shall be," He said, "if thou do at all forget the Lord thy God, and walk after other gods, and serve them, and worship them, I testify against you this day that ye shall surely perish" (Deuteronomy 8:19).

Now this had happened. The prophet Joel had the answer. The people had forsaken the Lord. The priests had failed not only the people; they had also failed God. Their altars were polluted; their religion had become formal; their sacrifices were no longer acceptable. What the nation needed was a great revival, but before that could take place the people had to be made to feel the need of it. It seems that the routine way of teaching and worshiping at the altar no longer accomplished this purpose. Then the crash came when God moved in judgment against the nation. That day the people stood helpless before forces that were beyond their control. They saw their fields fail, their crops devoured, and perhaps found their babies dead with their faces eaten away. But the Lord was still interested in the nation. The people were His people. The earnest plea for penitence came from Him through the prophet who pleaded:

Turn ye even to me with all your heart, and with fasting, and with weeping, and with mourning: and rend your heart, and not your garments, and turn unto the Lord your God: for he is gracious and merciful, slow to anger, and of great kindness, and repenteth him of the evil (Joel 2:12, 13).

In order to get the message to the people, the prophet Joel called for a mass meeting of what was left of the nation. He said:

Blow the trumpet in Zion, sanctify a fast, call a solemn assembly: gather the people, sanctify the congregation, assemble the elders, gather the children, and those that suck the breasts: let the bridegroom go forth of his chamber, and the bride out of her closet. Let the priests, the ministers of the Lord, weep between the porch and the altar, and let them say, Spare thy people, O Lord, and give not thine heritage to reproach, that the heathen should rule over them: wherefore should they say among the people, Where is their God (2:15-17)?

So important was this meeting and so urgent was the need for penitence that all people, old and young, were to assemble. Even weddings had to be postponed and children who were still nourished at the mother's breast were to be included, rather than that mothers should fail to hear what God had to say to the people in this emergency.

Judging from the conditions described, and the urgency of a great assembly, the formalism and apostasy among the people must have been deep-seated and widespread. It included the priests, whose duty it was, through their ministry of teaching and of performing the service at the altar, to make the congregation sensitive to the need of divine help and to make themselves worthy of the goodness of the God whom they served.

Relief came with the response of the people to the call for repentance. Because God is good and is jealous for His land and filled with pity for His people, He promised to restore to them the years that the locusts had eaten, and send them corn and wine and oil, and make them to be no more a reproach among the heathen. 2:19, 20. He promised, too, to remove the "army" that had swept the land. He said their "floors shall be full of wheat, and the fats shall overflow with wine and oil" (2:24).

The question, however, arises whether this was an actual locust plague, or whether it should be considered as an allegory. Some scholars and ministers insist upon the latter and say that the four stages in their development have reference to the four kingdoms of Daniel—the Babylonian, the Persian, the Greek, and the Roman—and that the wheat and wine of Joel 2:24 have reference to the body of Christ, the blood representing the new wine, and the oil as the Holy Spirit. Others apply it to the apocalyptic age and say that it has reference to the locust warriors at the end of time and still others as having reference to what was to take place from Nebuchadnezzar's time onward.

By far the best interpretation, says George L. Robinson, Professor of Old Testament at McCormick Theological Seminary for many years, is the historical-literal. Many statements within the Book of Joel itself indicate that he was talking or writing to the people of his own time. Why does he ask the elders, or to whom is he speaking when he says: "Hath this been in your days?" Or in our language, "Have you ever witnessed anything like this?" Or why does he admonish the people to "rend your heart, and not your garments" if he was speaking to people who were to live centuries in the future?

The classic statement of Dr. Newman, "Thoughts beyond their thoughts, to these high bards were given," cannot, however, be gainsaid. Joel does make statements that have futuristic connotations. His predictions, it appears, reached beyond the bounds of Joel's time. He speaks of bringing again the captivity of Judah to Jerusalem, and of pleading with the nations for His heritage Israel, who had been scattered among alien people. After the soul-shaking experience of the apostles on Pentecost, Peter apparently recognized what Joel had reference to in its fullest sense when he said: "I will pour out of my Spirit upon all flesh: and your sons and your daughters shall prophesy, and your young men shall see visions, and your old men shall dream dreams" (Acts 2:17). When Joel spoke these words, he likely knew little of all the implications that were involved. Nor did Peter, who evidently was familiar with the text, know what this meant until the promise was fulfilled and the experience became his own on the day of Pentecost. In the light of everything that has happened to the interpreters, who so minutely interpret the predictive elements of the Scripture, the old adage of the fathers still stands —that prophecies are best interpreted after they are fulfilled.

But the Lord has hard words for the rulers of the nations who imposed hardships upon their people, and made merchandise of children, i.e., that traded a boy for a harlot and sold a girl for wine to drink. 3:3. The Greek traders are accused of having participated in this unholy traffic and the Lord promised that their own sons would be sold to Sabean traders, a people afar off.

But what are the values of the teachings of Joel for our day, or do they have any? Perhaps the most important one is that a nation and people cannot escape the consequences of their sins. Just what does he mean when he speaks of the "Day of Jehovah"? Does he have reference to the great judgment of God at the end of time? Or does he have reference to judgments that are more immediate and have to do with the events of one's lifetime? A New Testament writer says: "Some men's sins are open beforehand, going before to judgment; and some men they follow after" (I Timothy 5:24). Certainly, teachings such as this assure us that all people will have to face the consequences and misdeeds of their lives eventually and eternally at the end of time. But is that what Joel had in mind? Some commentators think so; but it appears that in this case and all along throughout history nations and people have had to meet the results of their misdeeds in this life also. One commentator had this to say:

> The Day of Jehovah has reference to the time in history when in the life of a nation Jehovah grasps the reins, which He seems to have held slackly before, when the currents of His moral rule, which had been running sluggishly, receive a mysterious quickening, and the Lord's work upon the earth is again more fully performed.

That seems to have been the record throughout the history of mankind. But out of this great statement other teachings grew; namely, that the terrors or consequences of God's judgments may be averted by means of repentance. "For godly sorrow worketh repentance to salvation not to be repented of" (II Corinthians 7:10). This is true not only in our day; it was always true. How often people and nations throughout history have been saved from destruction and suffering when they in penitence approached the mercy seat and pleaded for pardon.

The other great teaching of Joel is that of the outpouring of the Spirit. Joel lived to see a fulfillment of it in his day, when penitent Israel went forth in a new spirit. But the great outpouring came on Pentecost, and "Joel is the one who begins to bridge the chasm to the kingdom of grace," says one commentator.

8 | Jonah, the Foreign Missionary

The Book of Jonah is one of the controverted books of the Old Testament. The problem rises out of the episode that took place when the prophet fled from his commissioned duty and was swallowed by a sea monster that later disgorged him unhurt. This unusual and seemingly impossible incident poses a problem for those who do not accept the possibility of miracles. In the light of the supernatural occurrences that are recorded again and again in the Bible and are accepted without question, this should not be considered impossible, nor should it in itself constitute sufficient ground for the rejection of the entire book.

There are, however, also other questions that add to the problem of the authenticity and genuineness of the narrative. It is written in the third person, and the writer uses words which some scholars hold were not in use until a much later date. They question the existence of the person whose name is ascribed to the book as its author and also the truth of its content. They maintain that the story was built up to correct the false idea that had developed among the Hebrews that salvation was for the Jews only, and hold that the Jonah story was created to refute this view and show that God's mercy and salvation are for all people regardless of who they are. It was written, they say, to show also how God broke through the superstitions of that time and opened wide the heathen world as a mission field in which were included people that were notorious for their wickedness, barbarity, and cruelty wherever they were known and wherever their name was heard.

This view, however, raises more questions than it solves. There is no reason why the existence of Jonah as a person should be doubted. That he was accepted as a historical figure by other writers of the Old Testament is clearly stated in II Kings 14:23. The historian of that day has this to say about him: "In the fifteenth year of Amaziah the son of Joash king of Judah Jeroboam the son of Joash king of Israel began to reign in Samaria, and reigned forty and one years." Jeroboam's reign began, according to Price, a noted Old Testament historian, in 785 B.C. This marks the date when the writer of II Kings 14:25 says that this king, Jeroboam, one of Israel's ablest rulers, "restored the coast of Israel from the entering of Hamath unto the sea of the plain, according to the word of the Lord God of Israel, which he spake by the hand of his servant Jonah, the son of Amittai, the prophet, which was of Gath-hepher." This was a village located in the territory of Zebulun not far from where the city of Nazareth was later built. This description of Jonah corresponds identically with that of the Jonah of the whale episode, and there seems to be no good reason why it should not be accepted.

The book is written in the third person. This, however, does not preclude the possibility of its having been written by Jonah himself. It is altogether possible, even probable, of course, that someone else may have written this narrative, but even that would not necessarily invalidate the authenticity of the book, nor would the fact that it was written at a much later date necessarily do so. It could be possible that some person other than the prophet gathered up the facts of his life and ministry as it was handed down from the day in which he lived and put them into the form in which the book appears today. We are not sure who wrote the Book of Ruth or of Esther, nor are the writers of the Kings and Chronicles named, and yet they are accepted by capable and competent scholars as being authentic.

There is also the problem of words from other languages which are held to belong to a later period. Pusey, in his volume on the Minor Prophets, insists that all of the unusual words in the Jonah narrative were terms that are found in the records of the prophet's day, although they do not appear to have been widely used at that time.

Perhaps the chief barrier to the acceptance of the historicity of the Jonah story is the episode that took place on the sea when Jonah was running away from his duty. The confession of his delinquency does not reflect a good spirit on the part of the prophet. His experience of having been swallowed by some sea monster and of having spent three days and three nights in the belly of the fish is something so unusual and seemingly so impossible as to cause many people, scholars included, to relegate the whole affair to the realm of myth rather than that of reality. All kinds of explanations have been offered to offset the skepticism which this unusual and seemingly impossible event has occasioned. Dr. George L. Robinson, a noted Presbyterian scholar, has the following to say about this affair:

The details of a comparatively trivial incident have been unduly magnified, supreme emphasis being placed on things in which supreme values do not exist. Some expositors have been so ill-advised as to make belief in the marvel of a fish story a test of orthodoxy. But it was probably the last purpose of the author, that we should pore over the whale and forget God. In a very true sense the intrusion of "the fish" into the solemnities of the story is no ridiculous thing, for that fish was the making of a prophet!

This same author and scholar insists that the question is not whether a fish can be found that is large enough to swallow a person without mutilating him. There are records of incidents in existence where sea monsters were captured that were large enough to swallow not only a man but a horse. One such was captured off the coast of Florida in 1912 that weighed fifteen tons and had in his stomach at the time of his capture a fish that weighed fifteen hundred pounds. Incidents are also on record where *men* were swallowed by sea monsters.

But the question of whether there are denizens of the seas

that are large enough to swallow people is not the important one. The more important one is, Could a person be sustained alive in the belly of a fish for seventy-two hours? Responsible scholars declare that "all apologetic explanations and phenomena are trifling and unworthy. Either the story of Jonah is true and therefore a genuine miracle, no greater than others which God performed through the ages, or it is an Oriental story with no foundation in fact." They insist, however, that the one who wrote the story of Jonah's experience intended that the prophet's preservation from death was supernatural.

The experience of Jonah in the Mediterranean Sea is, however, only incidental in the history of this man's life and ministry. The important part of the narrative is that a people—sinful, ungodly, and unmerciful—had come to the place in their history where in the providence and wisdom of God they were found to be ready to respond to the call for repentance. God, at that time, needed a messenger to perform the task of bringing these people to their knees. He recognized in Jonah the man who could do so. His person, his bearing, his voice, and his message, brief and simple but probably dreadful and frightening, were needed. One wonders why the prophet hesitated to undertake this task, for one would suspect that nothing would have pleased him and his people more than to see the city with all its inhabitants destroyed. But after his experience in the sea and his mission to Nineveh and his period of pouting under the shadow of the gourd, he acknowledged his reluctance to carry out his commission, and confessed to the Lord and said, "I pray thee, O Lord, was not this my saying, when I was yet in my country? Therefore I fled before unto Tarshish: for I knew that thou art a gracious God, and merciful, slow to anger, and of great kindness, and repentest thee of the evil" (Jonah 4:2).

That was it. He wanted Nineveh and its host of people destroyed. Its reputation, its record in warfare and in dealing with captive warriors or with the restive people in its conquered possessions, was notoriously bad. The nation is even now credited with having been a hard master and one that dealt unmercifully with its enemies. One can readily see why Jonah would not relish a commission such as the one that was assigned to him. Much rather would he have seen the city and all its people destroyed.

At the time when he came on the scene, Assyria was suffering a period of decline. A line of three weak kings in succession had lowered its prestige and power among the nations. In the lower regions of the Tigris-Euphrates valley Babylon was again gaining strength and was threatening to become a power that would have to be reckoned with. In the northwest Urartu—ancient Armenia—was also becoming a threat to Assyria's supremacy. Naturally, the western nations were more or less relaxed because of the declining strength of the despotic power at whose hand they had seen their armies defeated, their captives impaled, their women ravished, and their children killed or taken into captivity. Damascus and Arpad, dependencies on the west, resisted the attempt of the Assyrian monarchs to subdue them. This resulted in a succession of calamities that left the empire in a greatly impoverished state.

This seemed to be an appropriate time for the Spirit of God to move on Nineveh. For He was then, as now, more interested in the spiritual welfare of people than in a nation's political affairs or its elimination. If the Jews had ever caught the vision of their opportunity or responsibility to be bearers of the knowledge of the nature, the goodness, and the desire of God to redeem all people, regardless of race, color, or nationality, it appears that they had lost it and had come to feel that His bounties, love, and goodness were intended only for His chosen race to enjoy. They were not for other nations and people—especially not for the Assyrians under whose dominion their captives and other conquered people suffered horrors that beggar description.

Hence, however faithful and devoted Jonah may have been when the welfare of Israel was at stake, one can see why he would hesitate to risk an evangelistic tour through Assyria and especially Nineveh, the stronghold of the nation and the center of prejudice against people whom they had reason to suspect of being antagonistic to their political policies and aspirations.

When, therefore, the call came to the prophet to go to Nineveh with a message, proclaiming its destruction when it might result in its conversion, he shrank from the task and attempted to flee from the country. He held the opinion, which was undoubtedly held by the majority of his countrymen, that it would be well to let Assyria go to its doom. What all the factors were that entered into his decision and how he planned to reconcile his actions with the call he had received from God, the Bible does not say. It only says:

But Jonah rose up to flee unto Tarshish from the presence of the Lord, and went down to Joppa; and he found a ship going to Tarshish: so he paid the fare thereof and went down into it, to go with them unto Tarshish from the presence of the Lord (1:3).

Then he retired to the hold of the ship and was soon asleep. He was on his way to land's-end, beyond which, according to the prevailing opinion of that day, lay the abode of the dead, the place from which no one ever returns. That was as far as he could go.

He, however, had not reckoned with all the factors that enter into a call such as he had, nor is it likely that he had considered it was from God, not Nineveh, that he was running away. Neither is it likely that he realized that God's mercy is not limited and extended to Israel only, but that it is intended for all people and that this was the day of grace for Nineveh. The props that had given that nation strength and ability for its crusades of conquest in the past were falling away and it was uncertain of its ability and unsure of its position in the world. So often what appears to be man's calamity is God's opportunity. This was His day for the Assyrians!

Then followed the episode in Jonah's career that has given critics material for ridicule and criticism. There is no question raised about the storm—they are frequent enough on the Mediterranean Sea. Neither is there any question raised about the action of the sailors. That was not unusual either. Jonah was considerably subdued and humiliated when he was awakened and evidently realized at once that God was following him and that his conduct was the cause of the storm. After he was thrown overboard and safely deposited in the "belly of the fish," the storm subsided and the sea became calm.

This episode, which has led many students, scholars, ministers, and others to discredit the whole affair, is not the main or important part of the story. Here was a man running away from an opportunity that comes perhaps once in a lifetime and more rarely yet in the history of a nation to bring a people to repentance, and now the messenger who was called to represent God in this mission was unwilling to face the issues, whatever they may have been, and assume the responsibility which the opportunity afforded.

After the return of Jonah, his commission was renewed and the writer says, "So Jonah arose, and went unto Nineveh, according to the word of the Lord. Now Nineveh was an exceeding great city of three days' journey." There are times when one person can become exceedingly impressive and it appears that Jonah was one of them. Without armor or arms, without retainers or bodyguard, he walked a day's journey into the city with only one brief message which, it appears, he periodically repeated without comment, explanation, or elaboration. It was repeated over and over as he went. "Yet forty days, and Nineveh shall be overthrown." The people were overwhelmingly stirred. When the message reached the king's house, he rose from his throne, laid aside his regal robe and trappings, and put on the garb of humiliation, the sackcloth, and sat in ashes. He proclaimed a day of penitence and fasting which man and beast were made to share. Then God heard and honored the prayers of a nation whose heart was touched, as He always does, and the city was spared.

In the meantime, the messenger who should have rejoiced went outside of the city, erected a booth for himself where he could be sheltered from the heat of the desert sun, and waited to see what would happen. When he realized that God heard and honored the cry of penitence that rose from the city, "it displeased Jonah exceedingly, and he was very angry." He asked that God should take away his life, "for it is better," he said, "for me to die than to live" (4:3).

This is not only the story of Jonah's experience, but also a record of God's dealings with a sin-laden people and a corrupt nation. When the prophet strode through the great city and proclaimed its destruction, he delivered a message that is a model of simplicity, directness, and brevity. There were no ideas lost in the maze of words! The people did not ask for a sign.

Christ referred to this incident twice during His ministry to a
skeptical nation, that continually asked for signs to confirm His
sayings. He evidently accepted the genuineness and authenticity
of the Jonah story (Matthew 12:38-41 and 16:4), for He told
His critical audience that the people of Nineveh had no sign but
the preaching of Jonah and they repented, while the Jews who
saw Jesus heal the sick, make the blind to see and the lame to
walk, continued to ask for one.

One writer says that the author of the Book of Jonah strikes
the high-water mark of Old Testament theology. In all the literature of the Old Testament there is no portion that more clearly
sets forth the character of God. His love for mankind is shown in
His forgiveness of a people as sinful as were those of Nineveh
when the king in response to the voice of His messenger repented
in sackcloth and ashes. In that respect, it is the most Christian,
because the mercy He extended was not based on race or creed
or ritual and sacrifices, but upon faith and repentance. It enables
people to understand that God always "so loved the world" that
He forgives those who accept His promises on faith and repent
of their evil deeds. Jonah, then, was the first foreign missionary!

What lesson, then, does the Book of Jonah have for our day?
First, his call was clear as to place, people, and their need. Neither
the mission nor the message was one that the prophet would have
chosen for himself. He could have glossed or toned down the
content of what he was instructed to say in order that animosities
might not be raised against him. He could also have done the
people no greater disservice than to have failed in carrying out
his commission. His message was directed to their need and
the consequences of their sinful way of life and dealings with
their enemies. This he could, no doubt, express with great
vehemence. To have been an effective preacher in Jonah's time,
in the early church, the middle ages, or in modern times, one like
Jonah must die to the lusts, the attractions, allurements, emoluments, and rewards which man has to offer and be content with
the compensations that God has to give. When Paul the great
apostle met the Lord at the gates of Damascus, he must have
felt much as Jonah felt when he met Him in the sea, and each
one at his rendezvous learned that:

> ". . . the love of God is broader
>   Than the measure of man's mind;
>   And the heart of the Eternal
>   Is most wonderfully kind."

And as the ancient saying goes, "God is not obliged to fulfill His threats, but He is obliged to fulfill His promises."

9 | Hosea, the Prophet of the Broken Home

Hosea had a significant name which comes from the same root as the word "salvation." He probably lived in the Northern Kingdom about 750 to 725 B.C. Some commentators, however, place him in the Southern Kingdom. The chronicler of that period says that he was called to his ministry during "the days of Uzziah, Jotham, Ahaz, and Hezekiah, kings of Judah, and in the days of Jeroboam the son of Joash, king of Israel." This would make him a contemporary with Isaiah. His messages, however, have to do largely with the affairs of the Northern Kingdom. The prosperous reign of Jeroboam was drawing to its close, and was followed by a period of anarchy, lawlessness, and lewdness during which the morals of the nation sank to their lowest level. The prophet ascribes this collapse to the evils of idolatry and religious apostasy.

Hosea was a poet and makes much use of figurative language. His writings are sprinkled with name places such as Lebanon, Tabor, Samaria, and others which are located in the upper part of Jeroboam's domain. One would judge from his use of rural terminology and illustrations that he was probably a child of the open country rather than of the city. He speaks of a "backsliding heifer" (4:16), which has meaning only to those who have had the experience of trying to lead one, and likens Israel to a "cake not turned" (7:8). "They shall be as the morning cloud, and as the early dew that passeth away" (13:3). Though "he [Israel] be fruitful among his brethren, an east wind shall come, the wind of the Lord shall come up from the wilderness, and his spring shall become dry, and his fountain shall be dried up" (13:15). "They that dwell under his shadow shall return; they shall revive as the corn, and grow as the vine: the scent thereof shall be as the wine of Lebanon" (14:7). His writings are filled with these beautiful, apt, and fitting illustrations, allusions, and figures of speech which are drawn from the fireside, the field, and the countryside. With them he tells the story of Israel's apostasy and doom, as well as the story of his own tragic life.

Hosea was to Israel what Jonah was to Nineveh—a missionary whose heart was made to feel the consequences of sin as the result of his own personal experience, as Jonah was made to feel his responsibility to Nineveh through his experience in the sea.

The period of his prophetic ministry was a stormy and tragic one. Following Jeroboam's death in 740 B.C., the orderly processes of law largely ceased to function and the struggle for the throne followed. During the following eighteen years, six different kings wielded the scepter in Israel. All too frequently the throne fell into the hands of opportunists and soldiers of fortune. Most of them were military men with no experience in statecraft. In 722 B.C. the Assyrian hosts swept over the country and practically emptied the land of its inhabitants and scattered them so widely among the nations that they are spoken of in some quarters as the "lost tribes of Israel." The remnant that was permitted to remain in the homeland was replenished with "outlanders" drawn from other areas of the conqueror's possessions. These aliens intermarried with what was left of Israel and brought forth a new people, the hated Samaritans, of whom a handful survive today.

Hosea viewed the situation with deep concern which at times seems to have bordered on despair. He sees sin and adultery everywhere. His mission to a lustful people and a decaying nation was a heartbreaking one. Words seemed to fall on heedless ears and the prophet by means of his own experience was made to feel in a real sense, as much as is humanly possible, what God must feel when a people whom He had espoused prove faithless and choose to follow their own lewd and selfish ways that lead only to destruction.

The Bible says that in the "beginning of the word of the Lord by Hosea" he was instructed: "Go, take unto thee a wife of whoredoms and children of whoredoms: for the land hath committed great whoredom, departing from the Lord" (1:2). This was a command to do what would ordinarily be considered a terrible thing. Hence, commentators do not agree as to what all the implications of this command were. The question is raised, Did the prophet actually marry a lewd woman from the street where she solicited patronage to satisfy the base desires of evil men? Many commentators think so. Dr. Elmer A. Leslie, Professor of Hebrew and Old Testament Literature in Boston University School of Theology, however, thinks that she was a temple prostitute and consequently in that setting she was considered, by the devotees of Israel's apostate religion, as a holy woman. In fact, the Hebrew word for prostitute also means "holy woman." Leslie speaks of her as "the maiden of the 'fig-cakes,' an Israelite sanctuary maiden, one of the sacred harlots, such as thronged the Canaanite high places as votaries of the Goddess Ashtarte." Dr. Frederick Eiselen, formerly professor and later president of Garrett Biblical Institute, thinks that she was at the time of her marriage a woman whose character was unstained, but that the evil tendencies were within her and had not yet manifested themselves openly, and that she finally yielded to the allurements of her time and the drive of her passions, and abandoned her husband for her paramours or perhaps for the licentious rites connected with Baal-worship. John Calvin, the great reformer, considers the whole affair as being allegorical and as having no connection with reality in any way except that it is symbolical of Israel's sinfulness in general. Others think that she was a "woman of the street" before Hosea married her and later tired of the restraints of home life and returned to her former profession.

Such a union would, in our Christian way of thinking, be abhorrent, as it must also have been in the minds of the people who were loyal to Jehovah in Hosea's time. If she was a temple prostitute, then she was considered by the devotees of Baal, whom Israel had chosen to follow, as a holy woman and in their minds such a marriage as that of Hosea and Gomer would not only have been considered allowable but also laudable.

Regardless of what the situation was, Hosea did what God had commanded him to do. He married Gomer, the daughter of Diblaim. During the time they lived together, she bore him two sons and one daughter. He gave to each one a significant name. He called the first-born son, Jezreel, meaning *God sows.* The daughter was named Lo-ruhamah, meaning "uncompassioned" or "*not having obtained mercy.*" The significance of this was, "I will no more have mercy upon the house of Israel; but I will utterly take them away." The second son was named Lo-ammi, meaning "*not my people,*" which assumes the concept, "*I will not be your God.*" Then she deserted the tenderhearted prophet who had espoused her at the command of God and whose love for her, in spite of her waywardness and debauchery, proved to be constant and unfailing.

But her fortunes turned to ashes as do those of all individuals who tread the primrose path to shame, or of apostate nations who replace in their worship and ways of life the God-given ideals that draw people heavenward, and adopt instead those that debase and satisfy only natural desires. When heaven-ordained principles are set aside and human pleadings fail, then the hand of God reaches in and in some way forestalls the devices of men. Then sin bears its bitter fruit. In chapter 2 the prophet forecasts the thorny path of such a one as Gomer. The course she followed was downward until even those who lured her away no longer desired her.

But God is good. His visitations are not so much punitive as they are remedial and redemptive. When the soul responds to His call, no matter from what depth, the Lord is ready to receive and restore. When Gomer had come to the end of herself and was left destitute and forsaken, her husband, whose love was constant and redeeming, found her for sale, perhaps on the auction block in the market place, and bought her for fifteen pieces of silver and for a homer and a half of barley. 3:2. He took her to his home again, for he said: "Thou shalt abide for me many days; thou shalt not play the harlot, and thou shalt not be for another man: so will I also be for thee" (3:3).

This is the story of a tragic marital experience which would hardly have found its way into the sacred writings of the Jews, except that it was symbolic of a wider and deeper tragedy that threatened the life and existence of a whole nation. The experience of Hosea is set up as an allegory by which is illustrated the relationship of God to a people whom He had chosen to be His own. Through them He and His will was to be made known to the nation. When this people proved faithless, forsook God, followed the ways of sin and unrighteousness, and chose their gods, together with their lewdness and debased way of life and worship, they assumed also the consequences that go with it. This affected their whole way of life, socially, morally, economically, and spiritually.

The writings of Hosea do not readily or easily yield themselves to an orderly analysis. One commentator says very appropriately that this book has been described as "one long impassioned monologue, broken by sobs." Chapters 1–3 tell us of the messenger. Chapters 4–14 tell of his message. The outrageous conduct of the prophet's spouse could have broken his spirit had it not been for his deep faith in the God of his fathers. Her conduct was symbolical of the condition within the kingdom which bore deeply the marks of a degenerate and decaying social, religious, and political order that was drifting toward disaster.

The reign of Jeroboam II was marked by an era of economic prosperity. He stood at the head of a military despotism that made him master of the political situation of his time. But even then evidences of moral and spiritual decline, so fatal in any social order, were not only condoned and tolerated but were supported by the state. Ephraim, the Northern Kingdom, was prematurely aging. With the death of Jeroboam, the decline was accelerated. Internal feuds and rivalries took place between the contenders for the throne. Hosea says that kings were swept away as "foam upon the water." Of the last six kings who had occupied the throne, only one died a natural death. Ephraim had become old without knowing what was wrong. The prophet says that "strangers have devoured his strength, and he knoweth it not" (7:9). The aging process was not due to the years, but to debauchery and profligacy.

The priests joined in the immoral, politico-religious revelry and took part in its sinful practices because it replenished their revenue and income. Hosea in describing the conditions of his time says, "There is no truth, nor mercy, nor knowledge of God in the land. By swearing, and lying, and killing, and stealing, and committing adultery, they break out, and blood toucheth blood" (4:1, 2). The religion of the nation was shot through with immorality and sensuality. Family life was corrupted with the harlotry that was committed at the altar. "They are," the prophet said, "as an oven heated by the baker" (7:4). The nation was treading the "primrose path" downward toward disaster and it was not long, indeed, after Hosea's ministry that the crash came. The Assyrian hosts under the leadership of Sargon came and in 722 B.C. they carried the larger part of the population of the Northern Kingdom into captivity—an exile from which they never returned.

As one attempts to set forth, categorically, the reasons for Israel's decline and fall, he need not look beyond the writings of Hosea for information. He saw all too clearly what the source of the trouble was. First of all, he says, "My people are destroyed for lack of knowledge" (4:6). "The pride of Israel doth testify to his face" (5:5). "Your goodness is as a morning cloud, and as the early dew it goeth away" (6:4). "Ephraim . . . hath mixed himself among the people" (7:8). "They have deeply corrupted themselves, as in the days of Gibeah" (9:9). "My people are bent to backsliding from me" (11:7). "And now they sin more and more, and have made them molten images of their silver, and idols" (13:2).

What an array of evidence against a people whose mission was to make known the holiness and goodness and greatness of God whom their ancestors had met in such a fearful and impressive way at Sinai, at the time of their deliverance from the house of bondage! And now, after these centuries in the good land which God hath given them, they either lost or built up a perverted sense of their mission. There really was no excuse for their ignorance—lack of knowledge—except that they had become so obsessed with their success, their freedom, and so enamored with the attractions within their surroundings, that the restraints which godliness imposes had become too drab, uninteresting, and confining, and they chose to follow the "paths of Gomer" and enjoy the pleasure of life by adjusting their code of righteousness to their lustful and wanton desires.

But God follows the affairs of nations as Hosea followed Gomer. Ephraim, the Northern Kingdom, the ten wayward tribes who descended from Jacob, were yet given the opportunity which by divine love and grace is open to all. God does not easily cast people aside. One of the great hymns of the church of the eighteenth century contains the following lines:

> O love that will not let me go,
> I rest my weary soul in Thee.

He had strewn Ephraim's thorny path with obstacles—invasions of hostile armies, droughts, famines, personal illnesses, and deaths. He sent to them prophets, Elijah, Elisha, and others, and gave them manifestations and demonstrations of Himself that should have rocked them out of their sinfulness and turned them to ways of righteousness and peace. The old proverb says: "If a man sin against the law, he will be maimed, but if he sin against love, he will be lost." While this may seem, at times, to be slow in materializing, it is yet always true. It is mercy that triumphs over judgment, as everyone knows who has once stood condemned by his own deeds at the bar of justice and was spared the penalty which the law required because of the mercy of the court. Hosea says that "When Ephraim spake trembling, he exalted himself in Israel; but when he offended in Baal, he died" (13:1).

God spoke through Hosea in His final appeal and said: "O Israel, return unto the Lord thy God; for thou hast fallen by thine iniquity. Take with you words, and turn to the Lord: say unto him, Take away all iniquity, and receive us graciously" (14:1, 2). In return, the Lord promised to "heal their backsliding" and "love them freely." "I will be as the dew unto Israel: he shall grow as the lily, and cast forth his roots as Lebanon. His branches shall spread, and his beauty shall be as the olive tree" (14:5, 6).

Historians tell us of the lamentable tragedies that followed the fall of the kingdom in 722. The Assyrian invaders took the people, who, after they had built themselves goodly houses and had filled their garners with plenty, had forgotten the Lord their God who had brought them out of the house of bondage. They were scattered among the nations because they had failed to keep His commandments and statutes which He commanded them that day. Deuteronomy 8:11.

What meaning, if any, does the message of Hosea have for our time? Today the world is filled with conflicting ideologies, discoveries, inventions, and programs. Nations are battling for the lives and minds of the people and for positions of power. Personal and national integrity is not always strong enough to resist the forces of destruction and evil. There are, within nations who are striving to maintain ideals of justice and principles of righteousness, subversive groups that seek their own welfare regardless of what that will do to others or to the nation as a whole. Too frequently the powers that were divinely instituted to act as guardians of the spiritual life of a people and to stimulate and promote a proper relationship to the same God that Hosea dealt with are drifting along the lines of least resistance in the enjoyment of pleasures which their means and the condition of times make possible. At the same time, the norm by which greatness and goodness, holiness and righteousness are measured is passed by and a nation's strength is judged by its weapons and missiles, its wealth and physical products.

Prosperity is desirable, but it never was, nor is it now, an unmixed blessing. Years ago when James Russell Lowell, one of America's outstanding poets, essayists, critics, and diplomats, spoke at the two hundred and fiftieth anniversary of the founding of Harvard University, he said:

> I am saddened when I see our success as a nation measured by the number of acres under tillage or of bushels of wheat exported, for the real value of a country must be weighed in scales more delicate than the balance of trade. The Gardens of Sicily are empty now, but the bees of all climes still fetch

honey from the tiny garden plot of Theocritus. On the map
of the world you may cover Judea with your thumb, Athens
with your finger tip, and neither of them figures in prices
current, but they still live in the thought and action of every
civilized man. Did not Dante cover with his hood all there
was of Italy six hundred years ago? And if we go back a
century, where was Germany unless at Weimar? Material
success is good, but only as the necessary preliminary of
better things. The measure of true success is the amount
that it has contributed to the thought, the moral energy, the
intellectual happiness, the spiritual hope and consolation of
mankind.

So it was in the days when Lowell spoke; so it was in the
days when Hosea wrote and when the prophets preached. So it is
today and shall ever be.

10 | Obadiah, Worshiper Of God

Historians tell us nothing of the parentage, birthplace, home, location, or the life and work of Obadiah. All we know about him is what we can glean from his brief message, which consists of one chapter containing twenty-one verses. The Old Testament is spotted with men of more or less prominence who bore the name Obadiah. Some of them were closely identified with the prophets and may have, on occasions, performed the functions of that office. Such was the case of the Obadiah who served in Ahab's palace and provided for a group of prophets whom he had hidden in a cave to save them from Jezebel's designs upon their lives. We read also of one who was a teacher of the law during the reign of Jehoshaphat. He is listed among the princes whom the king delegated as messengers to teach the law in the cities of Judah. II Chronicles 17:7. There was also another Obadiah who lived during the reign of Amaziah, ca. 799-787 B.C. He was the one who protested against the coalition of the armies of Israel and Judah during their campaign against the Edomites. II Chronicles 17:7. Then there is still another one who is listed as one of the overseers when the temple was renovated and repaired during Josiah's time. II Chronicles 34:12. Since the recorded activities

of these men cover a period of practically two and a quarter
centuries, it is impossible to identify any one of them as the
prophet who gave us this brief message concerning Israel.

The date of Obadiah's ministry is obscure. Writers and commentators have through the years placed him anywhere from the
reign of Jeroboam of the Northern Kingdom, 785-750 B.C., to the
fall of Jerusalem in 586 B.C. Eiselen, formerly of Garrett Biblical
Institute, makes him a contemporary with Jeremiah, 598-586.
Sampey, of the Southern Baptist Theological Seminary, places
him as the first of the literary prophets, but admits that a strong
case can be made for the later date—a justifiable caution. Other
scholars of equal standing agree with either of the above authorities or locate him at various dates between the two.

Such stirrings of hatred as Obadiah mentions were not by
any means infrequent throughout the entire history of the
Edomites, the children of Esau. Nor was the assault on Jerusalem
by Nebuchadnezzar the only one that befell that city. During the
reign of Pekah of the Northern Kingdom, *ca.* 750 B.C., Jerusalem
was besieged and Judah lost part of its territory to the Edomites.
A score or more years later, Ahaz, king of Judah, was forced to
strip the temple of its treasures to pay the tribute which the
king of Assyria demanded. Other incidents could be cited of the
struggle of Judah and Jerusalem for their existence against the
designs of their covetous neighbors.

There are, however, some things that are clear. Such
manifestations of hatred toward their kinsmen as Obadiah describes existed throughout the history of the Edomites. Hence
their conduct is not limited to any one occasion. Since this is
possible, it is not necessary that the date be known. Nor does the
lack of this knowledge invalidate the trustworthiness of the
message.

Obadiah's treatise deals altogether with the age-old feud
that existed between the descendants of Jacob and his brother
Esau. Long centuries had passed since the incident had taken
place in their ancestral home when Jacob in connivance with his
mother had, through deceit and fraud, dealt his brother out of
his birthright. This event was never forgotten, even though the
old grievance had apparently been settled at Peniel (Genesis

32:24-33), where Jacob had met God, and Esau, on his way back from Haran to the land of his fathers. In spite of that treaty, it still remained a festering sore that broke out again and again through all of Israel's history and was never fully or entirely forgiven.

The blessing and heritage which Isaac bestowed upon Esau was actually better suited to the nature and disposition of his son than the one that he coveted so much but lost. He no doubt hoped to become ruler of the clan and perhaps, most of all, to come into possession of a double portion of the estate which, according to the custom of the times, went to the first-born son. Instead, this was given to his twin brother, and to Esau was given a heritage that was in keeping with his natural abilities and his wild temperament. Isaac said:

Behold, thy dwelling shall be the fatness of the earth, and
of the dew of heaven from above;[1]
And by thy sword shalt thou live, and shalt serve thy brother;
And it shall come to pass when thou shalt have the dominion,
that thou shalt break his yoke from off thy neck.
                                                   —Genesis 27:39, 40.

There, in southern Arabia, in the deep gorges and canyons and clefts in the rocks, a place almost impenetrable and impregnable to outside foes, Esau's people found their home and carved dwellings and temples out of the solid rock that remain today as marvels of their time and ours. Surrounding this place, away from "the fatness of the earth," there were grazing lands that provided pasturage for their herds and flocks. From the records of Israel's sojourn in these surroundings during their forty years of wandering in the desert, we learn of fields and vineyards, and wells and highways in that or adjoining areas. Numbers 20:17-19. Even then, some eight hundred years after Israel's death, the descendants of Esau, their ancestor, remember well the concluding part of Isaac's pronouncement: "Thou shalt have the dominion [over him]," and "shalt break his yoke from off thy neck."[2]

They seem through all the years to have been diligent to

---

1. Away from the fat of the earth shall your dwelling be,
   Away from the dew of heaven on high.—American translator, J. Powis Smith.
2. Genesis 27:40.

bring this promise to fulfillment. When the Israelites on their way to Canaan asked for permission to pass through his territory, they were rudely forbidden to do so, even though they offered to follow in the king's highway and compensate Edom for the water their cattle might drink. The memory of Jacob's trickery no doubt accounted for this unkind treatment as well as for the numerous uprisings of the Edomites and their invasions and plundering expeditions that were so frequent during Israel's occupation of Palestine.

It was one of these forays or alliances with Judah's enemies that called forth Obadiah's proclamation of Edom's doom for this, as well as for all of his unbrotherly acts and attitudes toward his fraternal kinsmen. It appears from verse one of the prophet's message that a messenger—an ambassador—had been sent to stir up trouble. Obadiah warns him—Edom—that even though he dwells "in the clefts of the rock" and his "habitation is high," his boast of security is vain. The prophet assured this nomad of the desert who dwelt in the deep gorges and canyons of the mountains that he is not beyond the reach of the Almighty, who is not limited nor circumscribed by heights or depths, nor is He hindered by wide and empty spaces. "Though thou exalt thyself as the eagle, and though thou set thy nest among the stars, thence will I bring thee down" (Obadiah, verse 4).

The prophet, in his summary, blames them for being worse than robbers. "If thieves came to thee, if robbers by night, . . . would they not have stolen till they had enough? if the grape-gatherers came to thee, would they not leave some grapes" (verse 5)? These folks to whom he writes did not steal and plunder to satisfy their needs, as many of the impoverished inhabitants of that time did and still do. They plundered because they hated and because they wanted to punish and destroy their enemies.

But now it appears from Obadiah's message that this boastful foe was deserted by his confederates, who abandoned him at the "border." He finds now that those who had been in league with him were traitors and those who were at peace with him had overpowered him.

God does not stand idly by and permit people to violate His laws and precepts constantly and unendingly, without some recompense for their sins and misdeeds. At the time of Obadiah's ministry it seems that the Edomites took advantage of Israel's calamity to satisfy their deep-seated hatred of them. The prophet states clearly what the trouble was.

For thy violence against thy brother Jacob shame shall cover thee, and thou shalt be cut off for ever. In the day that thou stoodest on the other side, in the day that the strangers carried away captive his forces, and foreigners entered into his gates, and cast lots upon Jerusalem, even thou wast as one of them (verses 10, 11).

He then becomes specific as he enumerates the offenses of the Edomites. He says:

You should not have gloated over your brother,
    on the day of his adversity.
You should not have rejoiced over the Judeans,
    on the day of their ruin.
You should not have made a wide mouth,
    on the day of trouble.
You should not have entered the gate of my people,
    on the day of their calamity.
You should not have gloated over his misfortune,
    on the day of his calamity.
You should not have put forth your hand upon his goods,
    on the day of his calamity.
Nor should you have stood at the breach,
    to cut off his fugitives,
Nor have delivered up his refugees (verses 12-14).[3]

For the day of the Lord is near upon all the heathen: as thou hast done, it shall be done unto thee: thy reward shall return upon thine own head. For as ye have drunk upon my holy mountain, so shall all the heathen drink continually, yea, they shall drink, and they shall swallow down, and they shall be as though they had not been (verses 15, 16).

The divinely designed law of retribution, in due time, begins to function and the penalty for personal or national sins and transgressions, sooner or later, turns to rest on the transgressor's

3. Taken from the *American Translation of the Old Testament*, edited by J. Powis Smith.

head. But with the threat of divine justice comes also the promise of blessing to the oppressed and pardon to the penitent transgressor. The prophet, looking down through the ages, was given to see that the plan of God will not fail. The hope of the ages for mankind, throughout the centuries, has ever been in what lies beyond. Obadiah, who spoke out of a time that was filled with omens of hardship and suffering, caught the vision of the glories of the future and said:

> But upon mount Zion shall be deliverance, and there shall be holiness; and the house of Jacob shall possess their possessions. And the house of Jacob shall be a fire, and the house of Joseph a flame, and the house of Esau for stubble, and they shall kindle in them, and devour them; and there shall not be any remaining of the house of Esau; for the Lord hath spoken it. And they of the south shall possess the mount of Esau; and they of the plain the Philistines; and they shall possess the fields of Ephraim, and the fields of Samaria; and Benjamin shall possess Gilead. And the captivity of this host of the children of Israel shall possess that of the Canaanites, even unto Zarephath; and the captivity of Jerusalem, which is in Sepharad, shall possess the cities of the south. And saviours shall come up on mount Zion to judge the mount of Esau; and the kingdom shall be the Lord's (verses 17-21).

What meaning does this message have for our day? The one sustaining hope, and the only hope of mankind, lies in God, who can overrule and bring to nought all the devices of evil men. As God broke and scattered the foes of Israel with a rainstorm at the brook Kishon in the days of Deborah, and laid low the hosts of Napoleon at Moscow with so simple and commonplace an occurrence as a snowstorm, so can He ever bring to nought the devices of nations that threaten to impede His way and block His designs for the welfare of mankind.

11 | Amos, the Shepherd Prophet of Tekoa

Amos was a native from the sun-baked, wind-blown region that bounded the fringe of the desert south of Jerusalem. The "rolling hills" stretched southward from his village, Tekoa, to the "howling wilderness" of which the Biblical writers speak. Here in this stern environment Amos grazed and shepherded his flock of sheep, which are designated as "Noked," an ungainly breed, small and ugly in appearance and not of much value for meat, but highly esteemed for the fine quality of their wool. His livelihood was drawn from the sale of wool in the markets and was supplemented with the fruit of the sycamore trees, which grew in the oases of the valley by the Dead Sea and in the low places between the hills of the Negeb, the dry southland of Judea.

Here in these primitive surroundings he lived the simple, rugged life of a shepherd, a man of the wide open spaces, a brother of the wind and weather, the heat and cold. He followed his flocks across the semidesert landscape, under skies that were often unclouded and barren. He lived close to the heart of nature. He was a man of granite make-up, stern and fearless, unspoiled by the conventionalities and the social-religious-political movements of his time. He may have come from a poor family—

certainly not from one of great wealth and prominence. He received his schooling under the harsh tutorship of his surroundings, although one may well assume that he was influenced by the home from which he came. Here in this environment he was trained for the ministry he was to perform as a prophet. He saw in the markets of Samaria, where he probably went year after year to dispose of his wool, the evils, social, moral, and religious, as well as all the unrighteousness and corruptions that flourish in a decaying socioreligious order. He carried with him on his return from this carnival of ungodliness memories of what he had witnessed, and during his lonely vigils by the sheepcote he no doubt meditated with deep concern on what the outcome of such a situation would eventually be.

He dates his prophecies from the days of Jeroboam, king of Israel, and Uzziah, king of Judah, two years before the earthquake which was of such severity that it became a point from which reckonings were made for several hundred years. Zechariah says that when the day of the Lord comes, the great day of reckoning, people will "flee to the valley of the mountains; . . . like as . . . [they] fled from before the earthquake in the days of Uzziah king of Judah." It appears, too, that there was an eclipse of the sun at about this same time. Zechariah 14:5-7. According to the calculations of astronomers this took place in 763 B.C. If this is correct, then the ministry of Amos took place in *ca.* 765, perhaps in the early summer when he was in Samaria to dispose of his wool.

Amos had no formal training for his prophetic ministry. But he was evidently a vigorous man of the country, "morally noble and fundamentally spiritual." His faith was cultivated by the surroundings within which he lived and likely based on a foundation that was laid in a godly Jewish home. When Amaziah, the priest of Bethel, sent to Jeroboam, the king, a report of what he called "a conspiracy of Amos," he also at the same time counseled Amos to flee the country and go to his own land if he wished to preach. 7:10-13. Amos defended himself on the ground that this was not his own doings but that it was God who took him from the flocks and authorized him to preach in Israel. He insisted that he had no connection with the prophets nor the sons of the

prophets. 7:14, 15. His call had come from a higher authority
and led him with unshakable steadfastness to perform his mission.
One commentator says, "There in the lonely wilderness . . .
the shadow fell upon his soul, which made him aware of God's
coming judgments and forced him to lift his voice in lamentation
over his people." That is where he received his commission.

He saw, in the markets of Bethel, within the shadow of the
royal palace, the injustice, the immorality, and the ungodliness
of a people who had broken with their ordained mission and had
lapsed into forms of sin and ways of life that affected their homes,
their business, and their worship. All of this was going on at the
time when one of Israel's ablest kings, Jeroboam, was on the
throne and when the country was in one of its most prosperous
periods. The nation, though it bore the name of Israel, the
honored father of a people with a great mission, had descended
to the level of paganism and heathendom in its life and practices.
The evils, luxury, feasting, banqueting, extravagance, and oppression of the poor were evident on every hand.

Amos was, as far as we can ascertain, not learned in the
schools of his time, but he was by nature and experience gifted in
the use of words. His style, says one commentator, was of the
purest and most classical Hebrew in the entire Old Testament.
He was an orator, and who knows what orations his flocks may
have heard after his return from the markets of Samaria, when
his heart was burning with the things he had seen during his stay
in the center of Israel's apostasy. His sentences are brief and
uninvolved. His first discourse is addressed not alone to Israel,
but to the nations surrounding Israel. In it he poured out his
soul in condemnation upon them for their evil deeds. This was
a clever way of getting an audience and it may be assumed that
he soon had the street or market place filled with people who
were thrilled with what he said about the nations round about
them.

One can well imagine the impression this crudely clad desert
man made when he stood in the market place amid the din of
merchandise and the clamor of tradesmen and their prospective
clients who were engaged in bargaining for sales. His voice must
have risen above the confusion of his surroundings and startled

the masses to attention when he cried that *"The Lord will roar from Zion* . . . and the habitations of the shepherds shall mourn, and the top of Carmel shall wither."* Then followed the classical phrase with which he began a series of denunciations upon the surrounding nations.

For three transgressions of Damascus, and for four, I will not turn away the punishment thereof; because they have threshed Gilead with threshing instruments of iron: but I will send a fire into the house of Hazael, which shall devour the palaces of Benhadad (Amos 1:3, 4).

Gaza was to share in this judgment because it carried away the whole captivity to deliver them up to Edom. Tyre and Edom and Ammon and Moab and Judah were all included in the dramatic denunciations of this desert orator.

No doubt this oration was appreciatively accepted by the motley audience in the market place. Then the blow fell!

For three transgressions of Israel, and for four, I will not turn away the punishment thereof; because they sold the righteous for silver, and the poor for a pair of shoes (2:6). That pant after the dust of the earth on the head of the poor, and turn aside the way of the meek: and a man and his father will go in unto the same maid, to profane my holy name: and they lay themselves down upon clothes laid to pledge by every altar, and they drink the wine of the condemned in the house of their god (2:7, 8).

He charges that they gave the Nazarites, whom God had raised up, wine to drink and ordered the prophets whom he had sent to "prophesy not." He says that they overloaded God with their sins until He is "pressed under you, as a cart is pressed [perhaps overloaded] that is full of sheaves" (2:13).

The first and part of the second chapters are introductory, in which the prophet came in this roundabout, well-planned, or perhaps divinely directed way to "Israel's incurable sin," the subject that lay as a burden upon his heart. The next section, chapters 2–6, consists of several discourses in which he discusses Israel's sin and the pending judgments of God.

Hear this word that the Lord hath spoken against you, O children of Israel, against the whole family which I brought

up from the land of Egypt, saying, You only have I known
of all the families of the earth: therefore I will punish you
for all your iniquities (3:1, 2).

Hear this word is the formal opening of a series of discourses
that continue through chapters 3—6. He illustrates the effects of
Israel's sin upon its relationship with God by the use of short,
crisp illustrations in chapter 3:3-7:

Can two walk together, except they be agreed? Will a lion
roar in the forest, when he hath no prey? will a young lion
cry out of his den, if he have taken nothing? Can a bird
fall in a snare upon the earth, where no gin [trap] is for him?
shall one take up a snare from the earth, and have taken
nothing at all? Shall a trumpet be blown in the city, and
the people not be afraid?

But the Lord is just in dealing with His people. He assures the
multitude that God will do nothing without making it known to
the prophets, but when the lion roars, he says, who will not fear?

The Lord had roared out of Zion, but the people did not seem
to be much moved. Because of this an "adversary there shall
be even round about the land; and he shall bring down thy
strength from thee, and thy palaces shall be spoiled" (3:11).
No doubt Amos frequently found on his grazing ground a piece
of an ear or some leg bones of one of his sheep which a lion had
taken. So, he says, will Israel be when her adversaries will have
finished with her. They will be lucky to have the corner of a bed
or a couch left when their winter homes and their summer houses
and their palaces of ivory will have been destroyed.

It was, however, not only the men that had gone astray.
The women were involved also. The word "kine" in chapter 4:1
is feminine and the prophet likens them to the wild cattle that
roam on the plains of Bashan and in the mountains of Samaria.
They were to the pasture lands of northern Palestine what the
"longhorns" were to the great plains of the United States that
some of us so well remember. Amos accuses them—the ladies of
Samaria—of oppressing the poor and crushing the needy and of
demanding that their "lords" bring them drink. The Lord, he says,
has sworn by His holiness that they will be taken away with
hooks and their posterity with fishhooks.

The Lord, the prophet said, had given them warning. It was He that withheld the rain and caused the want of bread in their cities and blasted their fields with mildew and sent pestilence among them and overthrew some of them, like Sodom and Gomorrah, and yet they have not turned unto Him. Therefore he urges them to prepare to meet their God. In other words, "Get ready for what is coming." He challenges those "that are at ease in Zion, and trust in the mountain of Samaria" to consider what happened to erring nations such as Calneh and Hamath and Gath, upon whom judgment fell because of their sins.

While Amos was orating in the market place and crowds were no doubt gathering, Amaziah sent word to King Jeroboam that Amos was conspiring against him. Strangely enough, he also warned Amos to flee into the land of Judah and "eat bread, and prophesy there: but prophesy not again any more at Bethel: for it is the king's chapel, and it is the king's court" (7:12, 13). The prophet's reply was, no doubt, considered an ungracious one, for he declared that he was following the command of God, and because of the priests' presumption his family would meet with disaster.

The prophet's message was largely one of doom. He evidently saw little hope of a reformation in Israel. Their way of life was too deeply rooted for any change. The last discourse grew out of a vision of "summer fruit" which the Lord showed him, which meant that the end has come. The Lord said, "I will not again pass by them any more" (8:2). The "fruit" of their ungodliness was ready to be garnered. He recounts once more some of the evils he saw. They could hardly wait, he said, until the new moon, the first day of the month, which was a holy day, was gone so that they could engage in buying and selling with their deceitful weights and scales and measurements. They wanted to "buy the poor for silver, and the needy for a pair of shoes; yea, and sell the refuse of the wheat." But for all this, he warned, they shall be held accountable. Their trouble will come as a flood, he said; the sun will go down at noon, their feasts will be turned into mourning and their songs into lamentations. There will come a famine in the land more dreadful than a famine of bread and water—a famine of the Word of God. "And they shall wander from sea to sea," he said, "and from the north even to the east, they shall run to and fro to seek the word of the Lord, and shall not find it" (8:12).

The final predictions of chapter 9 in which the doom of Israel is portrayed are perhaps the most terrifying of all. He speaks of the normally devised provision the people had made for their security. They had set their nest on high, in the top of Mount Carmel, or hidden themselves in the bottom of the sea beyond the reach of men, but they shall not escape. "Though they dig into hell," the Lord said, "thence shall mine hand take them; though they climb up to heaven, thence will I bring them down" (9:2). In other words, there is no such thing as an impenitent person hiding himself from God and escaping the consequences of his sins.

Like the great orator that he was, Amos sprinkled or concluded his orations and addresses with climactic statements that attain sublime heights.

Therefore thus will I do unto thee, O Israel: and because I will do this unto thee, prepare to meet thy God, O Israel. For, lo, he that formeth the mountains, and createth the wind, and declareth unto man what is his thought, that maketh the morning darkness, and treadeth upon the high places of the earth, The Lord, The God of hosts, is his name (4:12, 13).

❖   ❖   ❖

Seek him that maketh the seven stars and Orion, and turneth the shadow of death into the morning, and maketh the day dark with night: that calleth for the waters of the sea, and poureth them out upon the face of the earth: The Lord is his name (5:8).

❖   ❖   ❖

It is he that buildeth his stories in the heaven, and hath founded his troop in the earth; he that calleth for the waters of the sea, and poureth them out upon the face of the earth: The Lord is his name (9:6)!

❖   ❖   ❖

The eyes of the Lord God are upon the sinful kingdom, and I will destroy it from off the face of the earth; saving that I will not utterly destroy the house of Jacob. . . . For, lo, I will command, and I will sift the house of Israel among all nations, like as corn is sifted in a sieve, yet shall not the least grain fall upon the earth (9:8, 9).

❋   ❋   ❋

But Amos was not a defeatist. He was a man of faith. He looked forward to the time when, in keeping with the promises of God, a purged nation will be raised up and established upon the ruins of the past. The Lord said:

In that day will I raise up the tabernacle of David that is fallen, and close up the breaches thereof; and I will raise up his ruins, and I will build it as in the days of old: that they may possess the remnant of Edom, and of all the heathen, which are called by my name. . . . Behold, the days come . . . that the plowman shall overtake the reaper, and the treader of grapes him that soweth seed; and the mountains shall drop sweet wine, and all the hills shall melt. And I will bring again the captivity of my people of Israel, and they shall build the waste cities, and inhabit them; and they shall plant vineyards, and drink the wine thereof; they shall also make gardens, and eat the fruit of them. And I will plant them upon their land, and they shall no more be pulled up out of their land which I have given them, saith the Lord thy God (9:12-15).

12 | Isaiah, Orator and Statesman

Isaiah was the son of Amoz. Beyond that, we know nothing of his family connections except that there is a tradition that he was a cousin of Uzziah, king of Judah. He was a gifted orator and one would judge from his writings that he was educated in the best institutions and under the best conditions his day provided. His prophetic ministry extended over a period of thirty-nine years, from 740 to 701 B.C., which covers Uzziah's latter days and the reigns of Jotham, Ahaz, and Hezekiah, kings of Judah. It also includes the period covered by the rule of a succession of weak kings, military leaders, and political despots that followed the regin of Jeroboam II in the Northern Kingdom. He must have come from a family of considerable prestige and standing because of his ready access to kings and priests.

He was married and spoke of his wife as a prophetess (8:3), a status which she probably acquired as a prophet's wife, for there is no record of her ever having performed the functions of the prophetic ministry. He had two sons to whom he gave significant names. He named the older one Shear-jashub, which translated means "a remnant shall return." The second was called Maher-shalal-hash-baz, which means "hastening to the spoil hurrying to the prey."

No prophet since the days of David and Solomon had lived at a time when Israel's horizon was as widely extended as it was during Isaiah's time. The reign of Uzziah, king of Judah, runs roughly parallel with the reign of Jeroboam II of the Northern Kingdom. Both these monarchies had developed into military powers of such importance as to merit serious consideration by the surrounding nations and figured prominently in the affairs of that day. They had also formed commercial ties and alliances that reached afar into other lands and had attained a degree of prosperity that was exceeded only by the early days of the monarchy under David and Solomon. The political, social, moral, and religious conditions in Judah coincided with those that prevailed during the years when Amos and Hosea spoke to the soul needs of its population.

Isaiah received his call while he was in the temple "in the year that king Uzziah died." The visions he saw concerning Judah and Jerusalem include also conditions that existed in the days of Uzziah. 1:1. During the years of that monarch's reign, the natural resources of the country were being developed. Trade and commerce with other nations was being extended. A seaport was built at Elath on the eastern arm of the Red Sea. The trade routes to southern Arabia were brought under control and merchandise from other lands found its way into the markets of Judah. On the whole, the country was in a high state of prosperity.

This situation may not have been entirely due to the astuteness of Judah's reigning monarchs. The surrounding nations were weak. Uzziah annexed part of the territory of the Philistines to his own domain. The Ammonites, Edomites, and Arabians were reduced to the state of vassals and were put under tribute. In the Northern Kingdom there reigned, after Jeroboam II, a succession of adventurers who finally brought about the dissolution of the kingdom and the deportation of the greater part of its population in 722-721. After the death of Uzziah his son Jotham, who had been coregent with his father during the last few years of his reign, came to the throne and reigned for the brief period of four years. He was at his death succeeded by his son Ahaz, who reigned seven years. It was during the reign of the latter that an alliance was made between Damascus and the Northern

Kingdom to resist the designs of Assyria upon them. Ahaz was invited to join the coalition in order to protect himself against the aggressor. When Ahaz refused to do so, they, Israel and Syria, planned to dethrone him and put Tabeal, his son, on the throne. This, together with the frequent forays of raiding parties into Judea, brought on the Syro-Ephraimite War, one of the crises of Isaiah's day.

Isaiah sternly opposed this alliance. He, together with his son Shear-jashub, met Ahaz at the end of the conduit of the upper pool, in the highway of the fuller's field, where the women brought their newly woven cloth to wash and "full" (shrink) it. He urged the king to be quiet. "Fear not," he said, "neither be fainthearted for the two *tails of these smoking firebrands*," for the stand they have taken to go up and vex Judah and place Tabeal on the throne. "It shall not stand," the prophet declared, "neither shall it come to pass" (Isaiah 7:7). But Ahaz was frightened and refused to accept the prophet's counsel. Instead, he called upon Tiglath-pileser, the great warrior of Assyria, for help. The Assyrian monarch eagerly grasped this opportunity. He not only delivered Ahaz from the Syro-Ephraimite menace, but by the time the war was over Judah was humiliated and stripped of the revenue it collected from its tributaries, Ashkelon, Ammon, Moab, Edom, and the Arabians, which thenceforth went to Assyria.

But this alliance cost Ahaz more than the annual revenue from his tributary possessions. He went to Damascus to take part in the celebration of Tiglath-pileser's triumphs. While there he saw a pagan altar which caught his fancy, of which he had an exact duplicate made, which he set up in the temple in Jerusalem to replace the brazen altar of Solomon. Along with this, he introduced the religion of Assyria. The writer says that he caused his own sons to pass through the fire. II Kings 16:10-16.

In the midst of the upsurge of ungodliness that took place in Judah, Ahaz died and Hezekiah his son came to the throne. The new king saw the calamity which had befallen the Northern Kingdom. Shalmaneser had become king of Assyria. The new monarch ruled with a heavy hand. He imprisoned So, king of Egypt, because he had failed to bring the annual "present" as

he had done year by year. II Kings 17:4. Hoshea of the Northern
Kingdom was imprisoned in the third year of his reign. In the
seventh year the Assyrians laid siege to Samaria. The city fell to
Sargon II in 722 and twenty-eight thousand of its people went into
exile and were distributed among the nations of the east.

Hezekiah reigned twenty-nine years in Judah. He came to
the throne at a very critical time. Two thirds of the people of the
Northern Kingdom had gone into captivity and the vacated lands
and cities were repopulated with colonists brought from the
eastern tributaries of Assyria. Hezekiah began his reign in
Judah with a reformation. The paraphernalia of pagan worship
was removed from the temple and the "groves" and high places
throughout the land were destroyed. The worship of Jehovah
was re-established. His godly generosity led him to invite the
remnants of northern Israel to join in celebrating the Passover.
II Chronicles 30:5-27. Posts (messengers) were sent throughout
the country with invitations which were unkindly received by
many, although the chronicler's records show that a few came
to Jerusalem and joined in the festivities.

Hezekiah's reign was not free from problems. Assyria was
spreading its wings, both eastward and westward. Sargon II
and Sennacherib are ranked among that nation's ablest kings,
and Judah's security was repeatedly threatened. One of them
boasted that he had gathered the treasure and riches of the subdued or conquered countries: "as one gathereth eggs that are
left, have I gathered all the earth; and there was none that moved
the wing, or opened the mouth, or peeped" (Isaiah 10:14). Isaiah,
however, took a different view of Assyria's conquests. To him
this was a device in the hands of God to bring a wayward people
to repentance. Centuries earlier He had adopted them as a people through whom He would make Himself known to the nations
who had forsaken Him. Therefore Isaiah said,

Shall the axe boast itself against him that heweth there-
with? or shall the saw magnify itself against him that shaketh
it? as if the rod should shake itself against them that lift it
up, or as if the staff should lift up itself, as if it were no
wood (10:15).

Therefore, the prophet says, the Lord will send leanness and under His glory He will kindle a flame that will devour the "thorns and . . . briers" in one day. In that day, he says:

The remnant of Israel, and such as are escaped of the house of Jacob, shall no more again stay upon him that smote them; but shall stay upon the Lord, the Holy One of Israel, in truth (10:20).

Down in the lower part of the Tigris-Euphrates Valley, Abraham's former home, trouble was even then brewing for the Assyrians. The people of that region were again becoming a power that, during the next few centuries, had to be reckoned with. The Babylonians had again won their freedom during the reign of Sargon II of Assyria, in 721, which they maintained until 709 B.C. Six years later, in 703, after Sennacherib came to the throne of Assyria, they again had a brief interlude of independence for a period of six months.

Such is the brief sketch of the political framework of the world in which Isaiah lived and served during the thirty-nine years, 740-701, of his service as a prophet and counselor of kings. The religious, moral, and spiritual conditions that existed in Judah at the beginning of his ministry are set forth in chapters 1–5 of the writings that bear his name. In the opening paragraph of chapter one there are recorded the following startling words:

Hear, O heavens, and give ear, O earth: for the Lord hath spoken, I have nourished and brought up children, and they have rebelled against me. The ox knoweth his owner, and the ass his master's crib: but Israel doth not know, my people doth not consider (1:2, 3).

He declares that except for a small remnant the situation was no better than that of Sodom and Gomorrah. He does not accuse the people of having forsaken altogether the formalities of their religion, but he raises the question of the purposes of the "multitude of . . . sacrifices" (1:11), and declares that their feast days, new moons,[1] and appointed feasts are a trouble to the Lord, and

When ye spread forth your hands, I will hide mine eyes from you: yea, when ye make many prayers, I will not hear: your hands are full of blood. Wash you, make you clean; put away the evil of your doings from before mine eyes; cease to do

1. The Jewish month began with the new moon and was set apart as a holy day.

evil; learn to do well; seek judgment, relieve the oppressed, judge the fatherless, plead for the widow (1:15-17).

Then follows the statement of God's abounding mercy and goodness. He says:

Though your sins be as scarlet, they shall be as white as snow; though they be red like crimson, they shall be as wool. If ye be willing and obedient, ye shall eat the good of the land; but if ye refuse and rebel, ye shall be devoured with the sword: for the mouth of the Lord hath spoken it (1:18-20).

He likens the "faithful city" to a harlot, that was full of judgment but which is now full of murderers. 1:21. And yet, at the same time, the country was in a highly prosperous state. "Their land," he says, "is full of silver and gold, neither is there any end of their treasures; their land is also full of horses, neither is there any end of their chariots" (2:7). "Jerusalem," he says, "is ruined, and Judah is fallen: because their tongue and their doings are against the Lord. . . . The shew of their countenance doth witness against them; and they declare their sin as Sodom, they hide it not" (3:8, 9). Social corruption, moral degradation, and sin reached into every area of their society.

Moreover the Lord saith, Because the daughters of Zion are haughty, and walk with stretched forth necks and wanton eyes, walking and mincing as they go, and making a tinkling with their feet: therefore the Lord will smite with a scab the crown of the head of the daughters of Zion, and the Lord will discover their secret parts (3:16, 17). All of their jewelry and headbands, changeable suits of apparel, mantles, crisping pins, cauls and round tires like the moon, glasses, linens, hoods, and veils will be confiscated. Where there was a girdle will be a rent, instead of well set hair, there will be baldness, instead of a stomacher, a girding of sackcloth, a burning instead of beauty. 3:21-24.

In that time of distress, when the fruit of their sin had come to maturity, seven women, he said, will lay hold of a man and pledge to support themselves if he will but permit them to be called by his name, to take away the stigma of their unmarried state and unchaste life. 4:1.

The prophet pretty well summarizes the conditions of the times by the 6 woes of chapter 5.

Woe unto them that join house to house, that lay field to field, till there be no place, that they may be placed alone in the midst of the earth (5:8)!

❖   ❖   ❖

Woe unto them that rise up early in the morning, that they may follow strong drink; that continue until night, till wine inflame them (5:11)!

❖   ❖   ❖

Woe unto them that draw iniquity with cords of vanity, and sin as it were with a cart rope (5:18)!

❖   ❖   ❖

Woe unto them that call evil good, and good evil; that put darkness for light, and light for darkness; that put bitter for sweet, and sweet for bitter (5:20).

❖   ❖   ❖

Woe unto them that are wise in their own eyes, and prudent in their own sight (5:21)!

❖   ❖   ❖

Woe unto them that are mighty to drink wine, and men of strength to mingle strong drink (5:22)!

This section contains also the elegant *Song of the Vineyard* (5:1-6), in which he proclaims the goodness and favor of God in making provisions for His people. He selected the choicest seed, prepared well the seedbed, set up barriers against the intrusion of despoilers, and made provision for taking care of the crops. But when he looked for grapes, he found only wild grapes. The people could readily understand this figure or illustration. Many of them were husbandmen or owners of vineyards and knew very well what an intelligent and sensible grape culturist or farmer would do under such conditions. Besides that, they no doubt grasped the meaning of the parable and discerned that it applied to them. They were the offspring of Abraham, whose seed, God promised, should become as numerous as the stars of the sky and the sands upon the seashore. They were planted in a fruitful land surrounded by safeguards, moral and spiritual teachings, to keep them out of evil and promote and preserve the good. Now that He looked for righteousness, He found a cry—the bitter fruit of a degenerate seed!

But even within the unpromising surroundings in which they lived, Isaiah saw signs of hope for a future.

> It shall come to pass in the last days, that the mountain of the Lord's house shall be established in the top of the mountains, and shall be exalted above the hills; and all nations shall flow unto it (2:2).

The great experience in Isaiah's life that qualified him for the ministry he was to perform came in the year that King Uzziah died, *ca.* 740. Whether the pronouncements, promises, and visions (chapters 1—5) came prior to Uzziah's death cannot be definitely determined. Conditions were such that the ultimate consequences could well be comprehended without any supernatural revelations. The experience that prepared him for the great place he was to occupy among the people came while he was in the temple following the accession of Jotham to the throne, which his father had so ably occupied during his long reign. The prophet needed no supernatural vision to see and comprehend what was wrong with the people, but he evidently did not realize what was wrong with himself, until he was made conscious of his nature in the presence of the holiness of God. There is more required of a prophet than an eloquent tongue and the gift of speech. One that is skilled in the use of words may make a good showing among his fellow men, but the nation needed more than eloquence and oratory. It needed messages white hot from the altar fires of God that came from clean lips. Superior ability and greater knowledge alone are not sufficient. Paul, a later writer of the Scripture, says that they that compare themselves among themselves are not wise. II Corinthians 10:12. That was always true but is too seldom recognized.

On that day when he was in the temple he met the Lord as he had not met Him before. He saw the *holiness of God* and, in comparison, his own righteousness must have looked shoddy and cheap. He discovered there what it was that he lacked—he was "a man of unclean lips." There at the altar in the presence of his Maker he became a cleansed person. Regardless of whether the cleansing process, which is so graphically described in chapter

6:6, 7, is literal or figurative, it has in it the element of humiliation and suffering which so often goes with a deep cleansing of
the soul. A "live coal taken from the altar of God may be painful
when applied to unclean lips or sin-laden hearts, but it is always
good." Hence, in that year when an able king, who had guided
the nation to greatness, died, a new leader was reborn to assume
the spiritual leadership of a people that was frittering away its
life at the shrines of worldliness, self-indulgence, vanity, and
pleasure. Then followed a ministry to kings and nations as well
as to his own people, Judah, that for "understanding, eloquence,
elegiac rhythm, beautiful phrasing, and comprehension of the
divine will," places him high in the order of the realm of the
prophets. Jerome, one of the great scholars of the early church,
called him the *Demosthenes of Israel.*

The Book of Isaiah is, as a whole, not one that is easy to
interpret. It deals with religious, moral, and political issues and
people that are far removed from us in time. It contains also a
large element of predictive prophecy that deals with events, some
of which were distantly removed in time from Isaiah's day and
which Jesus Himself applied to His own time. Many incidents
can be chronologically dated, but even so they do not always
follow in chronological order. The following, which is largely
based on Robinson's studies in Isaiah, is an attempt to bring
together the material and subject matter in an order that is related to the tenure of the kings who ruled in Judah from the
beginning of Isaiah's ministry in 740 to its close in 701 B.C.

From the close of Uzziah's reign to the death of Jotham.
740-736. Chapters 1–6.[2]

The Reign of Ahaz. 736-722 B.C.

Chapters 7–12 and 17 deal with the period of the Syro-
Ephraimite War. 736-727 B.C.

Chapters 13, 14, 23–27. Oracles against various nations.

The Reign of Hezekiah. 722-701 B.C.

Chapters 15, 16, 19–22, 38, 39 deal with events during
the reign of Sargon II, king of Syria.

Chapters 18, 28–37 deal with events that took place
prior to and during the siege of Jerusalem in 701 B.C.

2. George L. Robinson, *The Book of Isaiah.* Baker Book House, 1954.

Chapters 40–66 deal with the crisis of 701 B.C., and following period.

Ahaz came to the throne following the death of his father, Jotham, in 736 B.C. and continued his reign until 722 B.C. The kingdom continued in a state of prosperity, but portents of trouble were beginning to rise on the northern horizon. Rezin, king of Syria, and Pekah, king of Israel, had entered into a confederation to invade Judah. When news of this movement reached Jerusalem, Isaiah says, the heart of the house of David "was moved, and the heart of his people, as the trees of the wood are moved with the wind" (7:2). They were in a dangerous place and in an evil time and, as it were, between two millstones— Syria, Assyria, and Israel in the north and east, Egypt on the south and west. Physically and spiritually, Judah was poorly prepared for a war with either of these four powers. Isaiah, however, knew that the strength of a nation is not always measured by the size of its armies nor the number of soldiers it can put in the field. He insisted, again and again, that their security rested upon their relationship with God. He met Ahaz, the king, in the highway at the fuller's field, along the upper pool, and assured him that the move would come to nought. He went so far as to challenge him to ask God for a sign, but the king refused under the pretension that he did not want to tempt the Lord. 7:12. Therefore, the prophet replied, the Lord will give you a sign: "Behold, a virgin shall conceive, and bear a son, and shall call his name Immanuel," and assured him that before such a child would be old enough to know right from wrong, the land which he abhorred would be forsaken of its king. 7:16.

Isaiah spoke to the needs of his own day, but while doing so he spoke also to the ages. He constantly found his hope and consolation in God and refused to be carried away by the spirit of his times. He remained undaunted even when the shadow of the great Assyrian monarch, the incarnation of ruthlessness, brutality, efficiency, sensuality, and power, hovered over the nation and threatened its destruction. He warned the erring Judah of the Assyrian invasion that "shall overflow the land like a wild stream that has overflowed its banks," and that any alliances or confederations Judah may make with other nations will be of no avail but will be broken in pieces. 8:7-9. In the meantime, a son was born to Isaiah and he predicted that before the child was old enough to cry, "My father, and my mother," both Damascus and Samaria would be overthrown by Assyria.

He admonished Judah that Assyria was after all "the rod of . . . [His] anger" and the staff in their hand is His indignation.

I will send him against an hypocritical nation, and against the people of my wrath will I give him a charge, to take the spoil, and to take the prey, and to tread them down like the mire of the streets (10:6).

But this boastful tyrant who said, "By the strength of my hand I have done it, and by my wisdom; for I am prudent: and I have removed the bounds of the people, and have robbed their treasures, and I have put down the inhabitants like a valiant man" (10:13), did not realize that he had God to reckon with. Isaiah tried to calm the fears of Judah with the assurance that the high-handed Assyrian was but an instrument in the hands of God to punish the wayward nations.

Therefore shall the Lord, the Lord of hosts, send among his fat ones leanness [a wasting sickness]; and under his glory he shall kindle a burning like the burning of a fire. And the light of Israel shall be for a fire, and his Holy One for a flame; and it shall burn and devour his thorns and his briers in one day (10:16, 17).

Ahaz's reign was drawing to its close. He followed the counsel of the majority, and refused the admonition and advice of the prophet who spoke for God and the minority and kept alive among them a hope for the future. The prophet said:

The people that walked in darkness have seen a great light: they that dwell in the land of the shadow of death, upon them hath the light shined. . . . For unto us a child is born, unto us a son is given: and the government shall be upon his shoulder: and his name shall be called Wonderful, Counsellor, The mighty God, The everlasting Father, The Prince of Peace (9:2-6).

Throughout a large part of his ministry, Isaiah's hope rested in the minority—the remnant of which he frequently speaks. During all history this group was pitifully small, but it exercised and wielded an influence that was altogether out of proportion to its size. Robertson Smith calls this a significant development. He says:

> Till then no one had dreamed of a fellowship of faith, dissociated from all national forms, maintained without the exercise of ritual service, bound together by faith in the divine word alone. It was the birth of or the conception of the church, the first step in the emancipation of spiritual religion from the forms of political life.[3]

In line with this great conception, the church is set in the midst of an unregenerate, worldly social order to serve as a leaven to transform the whole. Whether this remnant was completely dissociated from the organized forms of religion of its day may be open to question, but it was still in line with the idea of a church that is free from all political connections and bonds, as well as from the ties of a "worldly social order."

We have no way of knowing whether Isaiah understood all the implications of his Messianic pronouncements and forecasts. But those who are consecrated and committed to the divine will, have an inner light and assurance which frequently transcend the knowledge and security that derive from human history and give them a faith that is steadfast when human reason would dictate otherwise. This remnant has been, in every age, a steadying influence in the social order of its day. It rarely, if ever, constituted a large and popular segment of society, but time has vindicated, again and again, the faith, the wisdom, and the judgment of these faithful few.

The reign of Ahaz had come to an inglorious end. God sets limits to the bounds of iniquity, and when people or nations reach that border, they fall under the weight of their own corruption. The Northern Kingdom paid the price of its revelry, its humanly devised way of life, and its devotion to false gods. It was on its way to lose itself among the nations. Judah, too, suffered humiliations and losses, perhaps without being conscious of the significance of what was happening. Hezekiah, who inherited the throne, inherited also the social, political, and religious problems which his predecessors, Jotham and Ahaz, had created. The

3. Robertson Smith, *The Prophets of Israel*, pp. 274-5.

writer of the Book of Kings tells us that he was twenty-five years old when he assumed the duties of his office as king of Judah, and that he reigned for twenty-nine years. He further says that "he did that which was right in the sight of the Lord" (II Kings 18:3). He instituted a revival of Jehovah worship and removed the high places, broke the images, cut down the groves, and broke the brazen serpent which Moses had made and which the people now worshiped. II Chronicles 29:3; 31:1-21. He says, also, that he trusted in the Lord God of Israel so that after him was none like him among all the kings of Judah, nor any that were before him. II Kings 18:5.

Isaiah, it appears, had become the king's court counselor, and stood faithfully for the cause of Jehovah when even external circumstances seemed utterly hopeless. To the north lay Assyria, strong, ruthless, and godless, governed by one of its ablest sons, Sennacherib. To the south and east lay Egypt—a nation that had its eye on the prosperous folk, who had one time occupied some of the rich lands along the Nile and the broad grazing area that stretched from the doorstep of Egypt to the Arabian desert. The politicians of Judah played between these two world powers and catered first to one and then to the other as the situation demanded in order to maintain their existence or security.

Following the results of Ahaz's alliance with Assyria, and the deportation of a large part of Israel's population, they began to look to Egypt for help. Isaiah was strenuously opposed to any alliance with any foreign power. He said:

Woe to them that go down to Egypt for help; and stay on horses, and trust in chariots, because they are many; and in horsemen, because they are very strong; but they look not unto the Holy One of Israel, neither seek the Lord (31:1)!
. . . Now the Egyptians are men, and not God; and their horses flesh, and not spirit. When the Lord shall stretch out his hand, both he that helpeth shall fall, and he that is holpen shall fall down, and they all shall fail together (31:3).

But the prophet's faith was unshaken and in spite of this gloomy outlook he pointed to a more secure power. He said:

Behold, a king shall reign in righteousness, and princes shall rule in judgment. And a man shall be as an hiding place from the wind, and a covert from the tempest; as rivers of water in a dry place, as the shadow of a great rock in a weary land (Isaiah 32:1, 2).

However, instead of taking the prophet's advice, King Hezekiah broke diplomatic relations with Assyria and proposed an alliance with Egypt. When the annual tribute failed to come through from Hezekiah, the wrath of the Assyrian monarch broke out afresh and an invasion was planned to bring his delinquent tribute-paying ally to time. What happened is graphically described in Byron's poem. "The Assyrian came down like the wolf on the fold," he says. Hezekiah was smitten with fear. Negotiators from Assyria were pressing for the surrender of Jerusalem, while the haughty monarch from the north and his hosts were at Lachish, the gateway to Egypt, trying to prevent the Egyptian army from coming to the rescue of Jerusalem. In order to appease Sennacherib, Judah's king met his proposal for peace by stripping the temple and its treasury of its gold, even to the "overlay" of its doors and panels and other equipment, which he then covered with burnished brass known as "Hezekiah's gold." Sennacherib repudiated his offer as soon as the treasures were delivered to him and annulled his promise to withdraw from Judea. His demand for the surrender of the city was renewed. When this word reached Jerusalem, Hezekiah dispatched his servant Eliakim with a delegation from the scribes and priests to Isaiah for counsel. Isaiah's reply was brief and decisive:

> Thus shall ye say to your master, Thus saith the Lord, Be not afraid of the words which thou hast heard, with which the servants of the king of Assyria have blasphemed me. Behold, I will send a blast upon him, and he shall hear a rumour, and shall return to his own land; and I will cause him to fall by the sword in his own land (II Kings 19:6, 7).

Hezekiah then went to the temple and laid his case before God in the beautiful prayer recorded in Isaiah 37:14-20. His own glory was laid aside, and the greatness of his character is shown in the concluding verse:

> Now therefore, O Lord our God, save us from his hand, that all the kingdoms of the earth may know that thou art the Lord, even thou only.

In the meantime, startling things had happened at the border of Egypt. A plague had wiped out, in a single night, the entire Assyrian army. A messenger of God had intruded and the might of the Assyrian monarch was broken. Sennacherib made his way to Nineveh, where, while worshiping at the shrine of his god, he was slain by his sons, who escaped into Armenia. Esarhaddon, one of them, took over the affairs of state and reigned in his stead. 37:38.

Misfortune still dogged the steps of Hezekiah. Isaiah tells us that the king was smitten with a disease and was "sick unto death." The prophet counseled him: "Set thine house in order: for thou shalt die, and not live" (38:1). In response to the king's earnest plea, he was granted another fifteen years to live.

But in the east, down in the lower part of the Tigris-Euphrates Valley, the new power that was rising became alert to the events that had taken place in the west. Merodach-baladan, the son of the king of Babylon, having heard of Hezekiah's illness and recovery, sent letters and a gift to him. The king, evidently flattered by this attention, showed the bearers of these gifts through his entire establishment, including his treasury, and his army and military establishment. Isaiah severely reprimanded him for his indiscretion and lack of judgment. He predicted correctly, as history tells us, that the time would come when all this treasure, together with the people, would be taken away into a strange land where his descendants would become eunuchs in the palace of the kings of Babylon. One wonders at the reply of Hezekiah: "Good is the word of the Lord which thou hast spoken. He said moreover, For there shall be peace and truth in my days." Did he actually mean that he had no care or concern for what happened to the kingdom or to his posterity so long as he had peace in his day?

Hezekiah reigned for another fifteen years in Jerusalem after he recovered from his illness. His son Manasseh succeeded him and proceeded at once to undo all the reforms and good works of his father. He restored the groves and the altars of Baal worship and built altars in the Lord's house for the worship of all the hosts of heaven. But Isaiah's voice was heard no more. Historians tell us nothing about him after the death of Hezekiah.

There is a tradition that he was murdered by Manasseh. One can hardly visualize the prophet as having been silent had he lived in the midst of the upsurge of the new apostasy that was rising under the tolerance and with the support of the new king.

Chapters 40–66 nowhere bear the name of Isaiah. There is, in fact, no historical character named in the entire section, except Cyrus, king of Persia, who lived a century and a half after Isaiah's time. This has given rise to serious questions regarding the authorship of these chapters, even though compilers evidently considered them as having been written by him. John R. Sampey, in commenting on this problem, says that "nothing but the unique call and splendid genius of Isaiah would prevent anyone from questioning the critical position of those who ascribe these writings to writers of a later date." In other words, the "unique call and splendid genius" of Isaiah would justify one's belief that the gifted prophet wrote the chapters of this section. George L. Robinson maintained steadfastly his acceptance of Isaiah's authorship. When the Dead Sea scrolls were discovered, scholars hoped that the answer to this problem would be forthcoming, but nothing new was found. When the scrolls were examined, it was discovered that the beginning of the section at chapter 40 was connected with the preceding chapter in the same way as it is in the later manuscripts from which our modern translations are made. The question now rests where it always did and to many it is an unsolved problem.

The large predictive element in this section contains some of the most inspiring portions of the Old Testament. If truth could not, in that day, be made known by divine revelation, then the great fifty-third chapter must have been written at the beginning of Christian history, or it must be considered that it has no reference to Christ at all. It is true, however, that the question cannot be settled by so simple a formula; hence, the large part of Christendom continues to accept by faith, not only this isolated chapter, but the entire section as having come by inspiration of God from the mind and hand of the great prophet Isaiah, whose name it bears. Multitudes will continue to draw from it the consolation and comfort it has to offer.

This section is by some writers and commentators spoken of

as the *Book of Comfort*. It derives its name from the first verse
of the first paragraph, "Comfort ye, comfort ye my people." This
seems to be the thread that runs through the whole book. For
convenience in study, it may be divided into three parts.

I. God's Preparation for the Deliverance of His People.
   Chapters 40–48.
   The main theme of this section seems to be to assure the
exiles of Israel of their deliverance from the captivity.

> Speak ye comfortably to Jerusalem, and cry unto her, that
> her warfare is accomplished, that her iniquity is pardoned:
> for she hath received of the Lord's hand double for all her
> sins (40:2).

Thus spoke the prophet in his opening address. Then follows his
matchless dissertation on the greatness and grandeur of God. Perhaps no one of his time was so qualified for the task of making
Him known as was Isaiah, because of his great experience in the
temple when he saw Him "high and lifted up." He gathers
figures and illustrations from the surroundings within which he
lived in order to impress upon his people the greatness of God—
the stars of the sky and the uncharted spaces of the universe
whose measurements only God knows! This is one of the great
chapters of the Bible in which the full genius of the prophet
comes into play as he gathers words and illustrations to impress
a dissolute and wavering people with the greatness of Him who
was the God of their fathers.

   This is the redemptive section—the message of the Redeemer.
His manifesto is clearly stated in chapters 43–45. Such promises
may have seemed empty to people who were hopelessly in bondage in strange lands, or whose freedom was frequently interrupted
by alien armies or unfriendly neighbors. But the reassuring words
of comfort have been fulfilled, and have come down through the
centuries for inspiration to the oppressed of our day, and of all
time.

> But now thus saith the Lord that created thee, O Jacob, and
> he that formed thee, O Israel, Fear not: for I have redeemed
> thee, I have called thee by thy name; thou art mine. When
> thou passest through the waters, I will be with thee; and

through the rivers, they shall not overflow thee: when thou walkest through the fire, thou shalt not be burned; neither shall the flame kindle upon thee (43:1, 2).

A new name comes into the record here; "the righteous man from the east" is thus made known.

Thus saith the Lord to his anointed, to Cyrus, whose right hand I have holden, to subdue nations before him; and I will loose the loins of kings, to open before him the two leaved gates; and the gates shall not be shut (45:1).

*   *   *

That they may know from the rising of the sun, and from the west, that there is none beside me. I am the Lord, and there is none else. I form the light, and create darkness: I make peace, and create evil [calamity or adversity] (45:6, 7).

*   *   *

Hearken unto me, O house of Jacob, and all the remnant of the house of Israel, which are borne by me from the belly, which are carried from the womb: and even to your old age I am he; and even to hoar hairs will I carry you: I have made, and I will bear; even I will carry, and will deliver you (46:3, 4).

It is possible that these glowing words filled with hope for the day of redemption may have penetrated the abodes of the exiles of Israel who were already at that time scattered among the nations and, years later, brought comfort to the exiles of Judah who wept as they sat with empty hands by the rivers of Babylon.

II. The Suffering Servant and Redeemer. Chapters 49–55.

The main theme of this section appears to be that of the suffering Servant, through whom the redemption is to be accomplished. One would judge from the records of the Scripture that those who occupied the lands that were vacated through deportations when the Northern Kingdom went into captivity were never fully resettled nor their cities rebuilt. When, years later, Nehemiah was appointed governor of Judah, he found the city still largely a heap of rubble. But when Isaiah looked into the future he admonished the exiles to

Break forth into joy, sing together, ye waste places of

Jerusalem: for the Lord hath comforted his people, he hath redeemed Jerusalem (52:9).

This redemption, however, was not to come by the might of men, but by one whose "visage" centuries later "was so marred more than any man" (52:14), and who is so graphically described in the great Messianic chapter of Isaiah 53. Does this mean that through all the ages the redemptive work of God was accomplished through Him who centuries later was born in Bethlehem's manger—the one who not only taught but showed people what God is like in His character and holiness and refreshed the world's concept of what constitutes true righteousness and sin? Throughout all history this servant of which Isaiah speaks has "[dealt] prudently" and taught people so. The wasting of resources for "that which is not bread," and things that become burdensome instead of satisfying has even been the lot of mankind because they never learned to delight in "that which is good."

This section closes with the "Great Invitation," which is phrased in the great literary master's finest language:

Ho, every one that thirsteth, come ye to the waters, and he that hath no money; come ye, buy, and eat; yea, come, buy wine and milk without money and without price. . . . Incline your ear, and come unto me: hear, and your soul shall live. . . . Seek ye the Lord while he may be found, call ye upon him while he is near: let the wicked forsake his way, and the unrighteous man his thoughts: and let him return unto the Lord, and he will have mercy upon him; and to our God, for he will abundantly pardon. . . . For as the rain cometh down, and the snow from heaven, and returneth not thither, but watereth the earth, and maketh it bring forth and bud, that it may give seed to the sower, and bread to the eater: so shall my word be that goeth forth out of my mouth: it shall not return unto me void, but it shall accomplish that which I please, and it shall prosper in the thing whereto I sent it (Isaiah 55:1, 3, 6, 7, 10, 11).

III. Promises and Warnings. Chapters 56—66.

The first three chapters of this section are given to ethical

instructions. The years of Israel's apostasy were years of decadence. During the time of their servitude in foreign lands and
among alien people, they were exposed to pagan cultures, much
of which was in conflict with their faith and principles by which
they should have lived. The promises that follow are found in
the opening words of chapter 56.

> Keep ye judgment, and do justice: for my salvation is near
> to come, and my righteousness to be revealed. Blessed is the
> man that doeth this, and the son of man that layeth hold on
> it; that keepeth the sabbath from polluting it, and keepeth
> his hand from doing any evil (56:1, 2).

The promise was not limited to exiles only. It included the
son of the stranger that hath joined himself unto the Lord and the
men who had been mutilated and made barren. To the latter He
promised a place within His house and His walls that is better
than sons and daughters and an everlasting name that shall not
be cut off. In the years of their exile they had seen the righteous
perish and "no man . . . [laid] it to heart." But the Lord did,
and promised that they should "enter into peace: they shall rest
in their beds, each one walking in his uprightness," and that
in spite of their having been the sons of a sorceress, the seed
of the adulterer and the whore, the seed of falsehood, who in-
flamed themselves with idols, under every green tree, slaying
their children in the valleys, under the cliffs of the rocks. (See
Isaiah 57:1-5.)

To such depths will their redeemer reach to redeem people
from their evil ways. Therefore, he says,

> Cry aloud, spare not, lift up thy voice like a trumpet, and
> shew my people their transgression, and the house of Jacob
> their sins (58:1). Behold, the Lord's hand is not shortened,
> that it cannot save; neither his ear heavy, that it cannot
> hear (59:1). Arise, shine; for thy light is come, and the
> glory of the Lord is risen upon thee (60:1).

The same line of thought pervades the remaining chapters,

61—66. It is from this section, 61:1, that Jesus drew His text for the first sermon He preached in the synagogue of His home town after His return from the temptation in the wilderness and declares definitely that it refers to Himself. As one reviews the history of God's dealings with His people, he is forced to the conclusion that:

"There's a divinity that shapes our ends,
Rough-hew them how we will."

Isaiah believed this deeply. Others before and after him shared this belief. David, Israel's great king, said, "The wicked shall be turned into hell, and all the nations that forget God" (Psalm 9:17). The great Bismarck of modern Germany spoke as though he knew when he said, "The chief thing to be considered in national affairs is the character of the cards providence holds." People of our day still want to believe that God guided the founding fathers who landed on the shores of a new, untamed continent centuries ago, to make this a home for the oppressed and unwanted of many lands. Their aims, though fundamentally laudable, were not always free from taints of bigotry and injustice, but out of it came our homeland. We still quote the precepts and teachings of the divine Word, as well as the motives and purposes of the fathers, with perhaps taking little note of how deeply the corrosions of selfishness and sin ("respectable sins") have eaten into our way of life, our ideals, faith, and purposes. Isaiah spoke not only to the people of his day but also to those of our day. Righteousness is a personal matter and evil is a personal problem. It always was. It is high time that every person from the head of the nation to the most humble one on the field or street or in the countinghouse should become concerned with the things that have to do with our relationship to our Maker and the age-old and time-honored principles that have to do with life and faith and character, rather than with economic resources, armaments, amusements, shorter hours, and higher economic levels. The God who "[roared] out of Zion" is still on the throne and His voice is not stilled. Nor is His arm shortened nor His hand withdrawn from the affairs of men and of nations!

13 | Nahum, the Master of Invective

Historians have not been able to find out much about Nahum, except what may be gleaned from his message. Even his name is almost unknown and does not occur in the Bible except in the genealogy of Joseph, the husband of Mary, who became the mother of Jesus. His name, like that of many Jewish persons, is meaningful. His message, though filled with invective, so much so that one commentator called him the "master of invective," in reality bears the significance of comforter.

We know even less about his home than we do about his name. He introduces himself as "Nahum the Elkoshite" (1:1), which no doubt has reference to his place of residence or perhaps the place of his birth. Commentators differ widely in their opinion as to the location of Elkosh, from which the title "Nahum the Elkoshite" derives. One writer locates it at Ol-Kush, a village which lay some distance north of Mosul. The Nestorian Church, which maintains a monastery at that place, has identified what it considers the location of the village. There is something to be said in favor of this location because of Nahum's knowledge and graphic descriptions of the city of Nineveh. If this assumption is correct, it is possible that he belonged to the Northern King-

dom and shared with his people the rigors and loneliness of the
Great Deportation when the ten tribes were taken into captivity
by Tiglath-pileser in 734, or twelve years later when Sargon II
practically emptied the land and repopulated it with a mixture of
people and races drawn from various parts of his broad empire.
Others, however, differ. Ain-Japhata, a town located near
Babylon, has a tomb that tradition says is the place of Nahum's
burial. Still others hold that Caphar-nahum (Capernaum), which
interpreted means "The City of Nahum," in Galilee is the home
of the prophet. Still others designate a village south of Jerusalem
as his home. There is something to be said in favor of each or
any of the numerous places that claim the eloquent prophet as
one of their distinguished sons, even though they did not adhere
too closely to his teachings in his day, nor do they now.

The date of his ministry is more easily determined. The city
of No-Ammon, now Thebes in upper Egypt, had already fallen
to Assyria in 663 B.C. and Nineveh was still in existence at the
time Nahum was active. The date would then fall somewhere
between 663 and 612 B.C.

One has to understand the attitude and character of the
Assyrian people, especially their kings, in order to understand
the messages of the prophets of their day. They had, as a nation,
a long record of atrocities and cruelty that exceeds all the bounds
of human decency and honor. As far back as the ninth century
B.C., Ashurnasirpal, their king, made clear the object of his conquests and his treatment of the people whom he had subdued.

Then, I approached, he said, the slopes of Lebanon. To the
great sea of Akarri—the Mediterranean—I ascended. In the
great sea I purified my weapons and offered sacrifices to the
gods. Tribute of kings on the shores of the sea, of Tyre,
Sidon, Biblos, Makhallata, Maica, Kaica, Akharra, Arvad
in the midst of the sea, silver, gold, lead, copper, copper
vessels, variegated and linen garments, a large and small
pagutu, ushu and ukarinu wood, tusks of the nakhiri, the sea
monster, I received in tribute. They embraced my feet.[1]

When one reads how the subjugated nations and people were
treated, he can readily see why they handed over their treasures

1. Breasted, *A History of the Babylonians and Assyrians*, pp. 193-4.

with the hope of securing some consideration from the hands of the conquering hordes that had subdued them. The method of reducing the revolting people of his possessions and bringing them under control is related in a paragraph taken from the record of his conquests of Tela, whose inhabitants had rebelled against the tyranny of the Assyrian monarch.

> The inhabitants trusted in their strong walls and numerous soldiers. They did not come down or embrace my feet. With battle and slaughter I took the city. Three thousand warriors I slew in battle. Their booty and possessions, cattle and sheep, I carried away. Many captives I burned with fire. Many of their soldiers I took alive. Some of them I cut off hands and limbs, of others their noses, ears, and arms. Of many soldiers, I put out their eyes. I reared a column of the living and a column of heads. I hung high their heads in the trees of the city. Their boys and girls I burned in the flames. I devastated the city, dug it up, in fire burned it. I annihilated it.[2]

Such was the character of the Assyrian rulers, who struggled for the mastery of the world during the centuries when they were in power, which began around 1200-1100 B.C. and continued, more or less successfully, until 607 B.C.

But it would be only fair to say that the lords of Assyria, in spite of their gory conquests, made some useful contributions to their day and ours. The great city of Nineveh, the seat of their government, capital of their empire and home of their kings and war lords, was located in a fertile valley on the banks of the Tigris River, whose waters brought life to the barren hills and plains. It was noted for its elaborate buildings, its large palace and equipment. Its great library was probably founded by Sennacherib and further replenished by the succeeding monarchs. Tens of thousands of clay tablets were classified and systematically arranged on shelves where they were readily available for consultation and use. Its material consisted, in content, of official documents and dispatches, religious, historical, and scientific materials of the Assyrians and the Babylonians. Included in the collection were translated copies of the ancient sacred classics of

2. Breasted, *op. cit.,* p. 197.

early Babylonian lore. Much of the material found its way into the libraries of Europe and other lands where it is accessible to scholars and students of the history of those early lands and people. The result is that from this material one may glean a satisfying knowledge of the life and thought of those early years. This body of literature is noted not only for its content, but also for its full and free descriptions, its style and good literary quality.[3]

The miles of walls that encompassed the city were paved on top and were broad enough to enable three chariots to drive side by side. Its palace was a marvel of architecture, surrounded with groves of trees and garden, pools of water and whatever would contribute to royalty's comfort and pleasure. Highways from the east and west led to this metropolis of the eastern world. Great caravans from the ancient countries, from Babylon and other marts of trade in the east to Egypt and other countries that bordered on the eastern and northern coast of the Mediterranean Sea, brought merchandise and wares to supply the wants and needs of the Assyrian kings and people, and along highways and lanes of trade moved its armies in their ventures of conquest.

Here, in this center of literary culture and military might, were gathered the treasures of the ancient world. Her galleries were filled with the art, statuary, and carvings of their times. Ashurnasirpal, from the ninth century B.C., gives the following description of his palace:

A palace for my royal dwelling place, for the glorious seat of my royalty, I founded forever and splendidly planned it. Sculptures of the creatures of the land carved in alabaster, I made and placed them at the doors. Lofty doorposts of wood, I made, sheathed with copper, and set them up in the gates. Thrones of costly woods, dishes of ivory containing silver, gold, lead, copper, and iron. The spoil of my hand I deposited there.[4]

Such briefly was Nineveh, "the capital of the most powerful, sensual, ferocious, and diabolically atrocious race of men that per-

3. Breasted, *op. cit.*, pp. 315-16.
4. Breasted, *op. cit.*, p. 200.

haps ever existed in all the world. They were great besiegers of
men, ever crying, 'siege, siege, siege!' "[5]

But every nation has its day! Nineveh had its dark days as
well as its heydays of victory and glory. The disaster that befell
Sennacherib's army at the threshold of Egypt in 701 was serious,
but it did not bring the nation's heartless career to an end. Around
625 B.C. its fortunes began to wane, and in 607 B.C. the empire
that had survived for centuries fell to the Chaldeans, the "swamp-
people" from the lower part of the Tigris-Euphrates Valley. This
was a blow from which Assyria never recovered and marked the
beginning of the end of its history. The roads that were once
filled with moving armies and merchandise for her markets were
empty or led to other marts of trade along the way. Her conquest
had hardly been paralleled at that time. Her treasures were
among the most lavish and her libraries among the wonders of
the world. The nation that had built up its greatness upon the
ruins of those it had destroyed had reached its end, and other
nations and people rejoiced in its fall.

What then has this to do with Nahum's ministry? He must
have lived at a time when the security of his people was in
danger of becoming involved with the designs of this warrior
who boasted of his skill and success in subduing or destroying
the nations whose wealth and resources he coveted. Nahum, the
Elkoshite, well knew what the consequences would be if an
invasion of the Assyrians should take place. But he also knew
that there were other factors which could influence any situation
that such an undertaking could create or bring to pass. He knew
that the Lord though "slow to anger, and great in power . . . will
not at all acquit the wicked" (1:3). He knew, too, that God is a
jealous God, in the highest and best sense of that term, and that
He will take vengeance on His adversaries. His way is not to war
with weapons of man's devising. He deals with elements and
forces that are far beyond the control of man. "The Lord hath
his way," the prophet says, "in the whirlwind and in the storm,
and the clouds are the dust of his feet. He rebuketh the sea, and
maketh it dry, and drieth up all the rivers" (1:3, 4). The Assyrian monarchs and warriors saw armies melt before them and

5. G. L. Robinson, *The Twelve Minor Prophets*, p. 110.

all their armaments fail, but they stood helpless like everyone else before the storms that swept across the land and the seas that dashed against its shores. Even the mountains, he said, quake at the presence of Him and the hills melt and the earth is burned. The theme of his discourse seems to be that Assyria, an untamed and unrestrained power, has to finally reckon with God who deals with sin in judgment.

The people needed a vision of the greatness and holiness of God. The prophet knew the strength of Nineveh. For centuries its armies swept across the world and appeared to be invincible and unconquerable. Opposing hosts melted before them and nations fell; their wealth was devoured and confiscated, and the people were annihilated or placed in bondage and servitude. But God, Nahum said, is not only master of mankind. He controls the wind and weather and brings the elements of nature into play against those who override His purposes and get beyond control of mankind. "The mountains quake at him, and the hills melt, and the earth is burned at his presence, yea, the world, and all that dwell therein."

Nahum, like most of the prophets, looks for help from a source beyond that which the world has to offer. He sees a future for Israel, and says:

Behold upon the mountains the feet of him that bringeth good tidings, that publisheth peace! O Judah, keep thy solemn feasts, perform thy vows: for the wicked shall no more pass through thee; he is utterly cut off (1:15).

Somehow and somewhere all the prophets received a knowledge of a Redeemer, which sustained them in their time and throughout their all too frequently troubled history.

Chapter 2 is generally considered a forecast, or perhaps a historical description of Nineveh's fall. It opens with a very graphic review of the attack upon their city. Orders were trumpeted across the wide spaces from the military headquarters: "Keep the rampart, watch the road, brace your loins, strengthen your forces!" But the battle raged in the streets where charging chariots gleamed in the sunlight like flaming torches. In addition to the hosts of the attacking army, there is a tradition that the Tigris River went wild as the result of the unusual and excessive rains in that area and caused a great and uncontrollable flood which swept through the city and broke down its massive walls. Nineveh's end had come. Its glory and might were gone and its name is now but a record on history's pages.

Today this great center of the Assyrians' might, before which the nations of the world once trembled, is covered with dust which the winds of the centuries have blown in from the desert. Its palaces lie in ruins; its glory is gone! Huzzab, according to tradition, "was led away with the maids tabering upon their breasts, cooing like mourning doves." Its excellent library is gone. What fragments have been rescued by excavators are now found in the great libraries of the world where they continue to tell the story of the life and culture of millenniums that have gone by. One "gruesome memorial" of the battle that raged is a fractured skull which is now in the British Museum. It is supposed to be that of a soldier who was on duty as guard in the royal palace.[6]

When people begin to compare themselves with other people and measure their greatness with other nations, they engage in a very questionable exercise. Long ago the sacred writer said that they, "measuring themselves by themselves, and comparing themselves among themselves, are not wise" (II Corinthians 10:12). Often in history, nations, whose military power and equipment excelled that of their enemy, went down to defeat because a *strong arm,* unknown and unseen, reached into their affairs and turned the tide of victory into defeat. As Nineveh sowed, so it also reaped, in spite of the strength of its armies, because its inner life was corrupt. Nahum said it came about

> because of the multitude of the whoredoms of the well-favoured harlot, the mistress of witchcrafts, that selleth nations through her whoredoms, and families through her witchcrafts. Behold, I am against thee, saith the Lord of hosts. . . . And it shall come to pass, that all they that look upon thee shall flee from thee, and say, Nineveh is laid waste: who will bemoan her? whence shall I seek comforters for thee (3:4, 5, 7)?

6. Breasted, *op. cit.,* pp. 325-6.

Perhaps the saddest of all funerals is the one where there are no mourners! When Nineveh died, it seemed that no one wept!

There comes a time in the life and experience of nations that have recklessly reckoned without God when they will find that "there is no healing of their bruises," and that their wounds are deeper than they thought. This may happen in times of prosperity as well as in times of depression. It may even happen to those who "multiplied . . . merchants above the stars," that the cankerworm that works silently "spoileth, and fleeth away."

Nahum's message becomes especially poignant to the nations of today, when they are measuring their strength by their military might. Two global wars have been fought and won, and still the problems of the nations and their interrelated situations and conditions lie smoldering and threaten to break into another holocaust of proportions that one fears to conjecture. There was a time when Nineveh was reveling in her glory and power and indulging in her sensual lusts when an unwilling prophet brought her to her knees in sackcloth and ashes. She finally failed in *ca.* 612 B.C., perhaps because the prophets were strangers to the sackcloth. Perhaps, too, she had gone to the point of no return where only one thing could happen—she must suffer the consequences of her sins!

There are three great truths that come out of Nahum's message. First, God's government is universal. He is not limited by the bounds of time. He is the same yesterday, today, and forever. His tenure does not expire. Second, nations as well as persons will eventually reap what they have sown. That has been repeated over and over throughout the centuries and in a way people believe it, but somehow it does not receive too much consideration when it becomes involved in people's or a nation's own affairs. Third, "The wicked shall be turned into hell, and all the nations that forget God."

Nahum's message teems with fierce denunciation and prophecies of doom. His descriptions are graphic, realistic, and impressive, but it is after all a message of consolation and comfort. For it is always consoling to know that He who spoke worlds into existence and gave to man his life and being, is eternal in His existence and power and is never on leave of absence, but always

alert to the needs of those who are worthy. Perhaps if nations
and people were more concerned with their own sins and shortcomings, rather than with those of their foes, their own situation
would clear up and become more tolerable and secure.

14 | Micah, Prophet of The Poor

Micah was a native of Moresheth, a dependency of Gath, a village located some twenty miles southwest of Jerusalem, known as Moresheth-Gath, near the border of the Philistines. Like Amos, he was a child of the country. Unlike Isaiah, his great contemporary, who was at home among the royalty, kings, princes, and priests, and the moving masses of the city, Micah was a village man in the country districts of Judah. He, according to his own statement, was a man of deep conviction and corresponding courage. He says:

> But truly I am full of power by the spirit of the Lord, and of judgment, and of might, to declare unto Jacob his transgression, and to Israel his sin (3:8).

He was the champion of the cause of the poor and oppressed. One writer says that "Amos had a passion for justice, while Hosea had a heart of love." Micah seems to have had both. He was not afraid to say what had to be said.

The political, sociological, and religious situations in Micah's time were well known. They were the same as those described in Isaiah's day. Jotham, Uzziah's son, spent his time enjoying the prestige and emoluments of his position while building palaces in

Jerusalem and fortresses to guarantee his security while he reveled in the "delights of sin." The sufferings of the poor were, seemingly, of small concern to him. Ahaz led Judah into an unfortunate alliance with Assyria which eventually resulted in burdensome conditions that reached into every stratum of society, the rich as well as the poor. Grasping landlords dispossessed the peasants of their property and evicted widows from their homes with apparently no thought or concern for their welfare. Hezekiah attempted reforms but was handicapped with concessions and treaties which his predecessor had made. One commentator describes the situation as follows:

> The custodians of the law abused their powers; nobles fleecing the poor, judges accepting bribes, prophets flattering the rich, and priests teaching for hire. Lust of wealth ruled on all sides. The mongrel tyrants laughed at possible judgment. Commercialism and materialism were supplanting almost the last vestige of everything ethical and spiritual.

At that juncture great voices were heard on the village streets and in the cities. Among them was Micah, the servant of God, from an obscure village. While Isaiah was facing the issues of his day in the high places of the kingdom, the city and the court of kings, Micah was preaching religious reforms and social justice among the village people. "His unfeigned sincerity," one writer says, "stands out in sharp contrast with the flattering teachings of his contemporaries, whose chief concern was their own pecuniary welfare." Micah said:

> Thus saith the Lord concerning the prophets that make my people err, that bite with their teeth, and cry, Peace; and he that putteth not into their mouths, they even prepare war against him. Therefore night shall be unto you, that ye shall not have a vision; and it shall be dark unto you, that ye shall not divine; and the sun shall go down over the prophets, and the day shall be dark over them (3:5, 6).

People in that day were not much different from the people of our day. It appears that many felt that they were good if they were considered respectable by the social order in which they lived. Micah refuted this fallacy and insisted that righteousness is a personal matter that has to do with morals and ways of living. His ethical standards were high and consequently were in conflict with much that was accepted as righteous and good in the society of his time.

The content of the book falls definitely into three sections, each one of which is introduced with a formula which indicates that it may be the opening or beginning of an address. "Hear ye," he says, in chapters 1:2; 3:1; and 6:1. The first section, chapters 1, 2, is loaded with pronouncements of doom against the political and religious leaders of his time. He was the first prophet to threaten or predict the downfall of Jerusalem. The dooms element of this section is, however, tempered by promises of restoration after Judah had paid the price of its folly in exile.

Section I: One almost fancies he hears the voice of the prophet crying above the confusion of the market place:

Hear, all ye people; hearken, O earth, and all that therein is: and let the Lord God be witness against you, the Lord from his holy temple. For, behold, the Lord cometh forth out of his place, and will come down, and tread upon the high places of the earth. And the mountains shall be molten under him, and the valleys shall be cleft, as wax before the fire, and as the waters that are poured down a steep place (1:2-4).

This terrifying threat was made necessary in the divine plan because of Israel's and Judah's sin. The prophet says:

For the transgression of Jacob is all this, and for the sins of the house of Israel. What is the transgression of Jacob? is it not Samaria? and what are the high places of Judah? are they not Jerusalem (1:5)?

That was the problem. The ungodliness of Samaria and the idolatry with all its corruptions, which were introduced and established in Judah and Jerusalem following the death of Uzziah, were responsible for this message of divine displeasure. Little did the people realize how deep-seated and damaging their iniquity was. One can well see why they would counsel the prophet to cease his prophesyings. The life of a degenerate nation was being weighed in the balances by measurements more sensitive than those of man's devising. Its fate is clearly stated in the following lines:

... I will make Samaria as an heap of the field, and as plantings of a vineyard: and I will pour down the stones thereof into the valley, and I will discover the foundations thereof. And all the graven images thereof shall be beaten to pieces, and all the hires thereof shall be burned with the fire, and all the idols thereof will I lay desolate: for she gathered it of the hire of an harlot, and they shall return to the hire of an harlot (1:6, 7).

*   *   *

For her wound is incurable; for it is come unto Judah; he is come unto the gate of my people, even to Jerusalem (1:9).

Micah's account of Judah's sinfulness is continued in chapter 2. The most demoralizing practices, he declares, are carried on in broad daylight. 2:1. They covet the fields, even of a man's inheritance, and take them by violence. This, the prophet declares, cannot be overlooked.

Therefore thus saith the Lord; Behold, against this family do I devise an evil, from which ye shall not remove your necks; neither shall ye go haughtily: for this time is evil (2:3).

So covetous had they already become in the time of Amos that he declared that they "pant after the dust of the earth on the head of the poor" (Amos 2:7). So jealous had they become of their way of life that Micah said if a prophet dared to raise his voice in protest they warned him to prophesy not. 2:6. But if one coming in "the spirit and falsehood do lie, saying, I will prophesy unto thee of wine and of strong drink; he shall even be the prophet of this people" (2:11).

But there were, no doubt, still in Judah and Jerusalem many pious souls who had not bowed their knees to Baal, nor worshiped at his shrine and longed for better days. Micah, like Isaiah, his contemporary, speaks of them as the remnant. They may have constituted a small minority, but they were the hope of the nation—then as they always are. To them the prophet had something to say that came as a ray of light in a dark time.

I will surely assemble, O Jacob, all of thee; I will surely gather the remnant of Israel; I will put them together as the sheep of Bozrah, as the flock in the midst of their fold: they shall make great noise by reason of the multitude of men.

The breaker is come up before them: they have broken up, and have passed through the gate, and are gone out by it: and their king shall pass before them, and the Lord on the head of them (2:12, 13).

Section II: Once again the people heard the voice of the prophet ringing through the city as he called for their attention.

Hear, I pray you, O heads of Jacob, and ye princes of the house of Israel; It is not for you to know judgment: who hate the good, and love the evil; who pluck off their skin from off them, and their flesh from off their bones; . . . and chop them in pieces, as for the pot, and as flesh within the caldron (3:1-3).

One may well imagine what thoughts came to the prophet's mind as he saw the poverty-ridden people who lined the streets of the city and the byways of the countryside. But there always comes a time of reckoning. To the oppressed it may seem a long time in coming, but the Master of man's destiny knows the appropriate hour. Micah, in spite of the people's disregard of his ministry, insists that he is "full of power by the spirit of the Lord, and of judgment, and of might, to declare unto Jacob his transgression, and to Israel his sin." He warns the "heads of the house of Jacob, and princes of the house of Israel, that abhor judgment, and pervert all equity . . . [that] judge for reward, and the priests thereof teach for hire, and the prophets thereof divine for money: yet will they lean upon the Lord, and say, Is not the Lord among us? none evil can come upon us" (3:9, 11). He tells them that Zion will become "plowed as a field, and Jerusalem shall become heaps, and the mountain of the house as the high places of the forest" (3:12). The prophets that prophesied falsely and the oppressors that took advantage of their situation to enrich themselves will receive no mercy because they showed none, the prophet said.

But he has a word of consolation to those who were steadfast in their faith. The present situation appeared irredeemable. Their hope of redemption lay in the future.

In the last days it shall come to pass, that the mountain of the house of the Lord shall be established in the top of the mountains, and it shall be exalted above the hills; and people shall flow unto it. And many nations shall come, and say, Come, and let us go up to the mountain of the Lord, and to the house of the God of Jacob; and he will teach us of his ways, and we will walk in his paths (4:1, 2).

Then the nations "shall beat their swords into plowshares, and their spears into pruninghooks." There will be an era of peace when "they shall sit every man under his vine and under his fig tree. . . . For all people will walk every one in the name of his god, and we will walk in the name of the Lord our God for ever and ever" (4:4, 5). In this gathering will be the nation that was driven out and was afflicted, and the Lord will reign over them forever. 4:6, 7.

Why dost thou cry out aloud? is there no king in thee? . . . For now shalt thou go forth out of the city, and thou shalt dwell in the field, and thou shalt go even to Babylon; there shalt thou be delivered; there the Lord shall redeem thee from the hand of thine enemies (4:9, 10).

But before redemption and restoration can take place, people must learn their lesson in the hard school of adversity. This will not be accomplished by sitting, weeping, on the banks of the rivers of Babylon and yearning for their homeland. Psalm 137:1. Many of them finally became so well established in what was at first the "land of their sorrows" that they did not return to Zion when the way was open. But others had retained their loyalty, and when a half century later news spread throughout their villages that they could go home, the Psalm writer said that the news was to them like a dream.

But deliverance from physical bondage is not of greatest importance. There is a bondage yet more serious—the bondage of sin. This was at the bottom of all their troubles. That is why they were taken into exile. It was the cause of their suffering and sorrow. Relief from the world's burden of sin was not accomplished when they returned to Jerusalem. It did not come about through military might or through intellectual achievements in the large centers of population. But in a little village—Bethlehem Ephratah.

Though thou be little among the thousands of Judah, yet out of thee shall he come forth unto me that is to be ruler in

Israel; whose goings forth have been from of old, from everlasting (5:2).

This man, who was to be born centuries later, Micah says, shall be our peace. When the Assyrians shall come into our land, "the remnant of Jacob shall be in the midst of many people as a dew from the Lord, as the showers upon the grass, that tarrieth not for man, nor waiteth for the sons of men" (5:7).

Section III: The Great Assize. The words at the opening of this chapter bear the familiar ring of the voice of the bailiff whose duty it is to call the court of justice to order that the plaintiff might have his cause adjudicated. It is, in fact, the Lord that brings His own cause before the tribunal of justice, the "everlasting hills," and pleads for consideration. In His summation He rehearses His work of redeeming Israel, the defendant, from Egypt, the house of bondage, from which centuries earlier they could not deliver themselves. He cites His care and guidance throughout their wanderings in the wilderness, until their arrival at Gilgal, the very gate of their homeland, in order that they might know the righteousness of the Lord. Now again, after many years in their own land, there is confusion. The very people whom He so faithfully delivered worship again at strange shrines and glory in the "delights of ungodliness." Their reply or answer before the high court implies a feigned ignorance. They plead:

Wherewith shall I come before the Lord, and bow myself before the high God? shall I come before him with burnt offerings, with calves of a year old? Will the Lord be pleased with thousands of rams, or with ten thousands of rivers of oil? shall I give my firstborn for my transgression, the fruit of my body for the sin of my soul (6:6, 7)?

Then the Judge of the high court speaks. The verdict is clear and decisive:

He hath shewed thee, O man, what is good; and what doth the Lord require of thee, but to do justly, and to love mercy, and to walk humbly with thy God (6:8)?

The sins of the nation must have been deep, for the prophet asks, "Are there yet the treasures of wickedness in the house of the wicked, and the scant measure that is abominable? Shall I count them pure with the wicked balances, and with the bag of deceitful weights" (6:10, 11)?

All of these practices, which were in conflict with the principles by which God's people should live, were the ones that governed their lives and determined their conduct. As a result, they were destined to suffer the consequences of their willful ways of life. He says:

Thou shalt eat, but not be satisfied; and thy casting down shall be in the midst of thee; and thou shalt take hold, but shalt not deliver; and that which thou deliverest will I give up to the sword. Thou shalt sow, but thou shalt not reap; thou shalt tread the olives, but thou shalt not anoint thee with oil; and sweet wine, but shalt not drink wine. For the statutes of Omri are kept, and all the works of the house of Ahab, and ye walk in their counsels; that I should make thee a desolation, and the inhabitants thereof an hissing (6:14-16).

One would conclude from Micah's closing chapter that there was no evidence of a change among the people. The whole situation looked like a vineyard in which there were only the gleanings left. 7:1. To him it appeared that "the good man is perished out of the earth: . . . they all lie in wait for blood" (7:2). The prominent man states his desire, the prince and the judge ask for reward; so they "wrap it up" (7:3). Not even one's friends were to be trusted, and a person had to keep the doors of his mouth from her that "[lay] in . . . [his] bosom." Family life was broken down and a man's enemies were those of his own household.

It is small wonder, then, that the prophet looks beyond the bounds of earth for relief. The Lord's heritage had reached the level where admonition and teaching were no longer of any avail—they needed to be taught with sterner measures—the rod in the hands of God. Israel, the ten tribes, had then already felt the weight of God's indignation, and were now among strangers in far lands because the gods whom they had adopted could not save them from the hands of the aggressor. But there is a pardoning God who in mercy passes by the transgressions of the "remnant of his heritage." When transgressors meet Him in penitence at the mercy seat, "he retaineth not his anger for ever, because he delighteth in mercy, . . . [and] wilt cast all their sins into the depths of the sea" (7:18, 19).

Lessons from Micah for Our Time

In the reading room of the Congressional Library in Washington, D.C., there stands inscribed the following motto:

He hath shewed thee, O man, what is good; and what doth the Lord require of thee, but to do justly, and to love mercy, and to walk humbly with thy God (Micah 6:8)?

Little did Micah think when he spoke those significant words that he was speaking to the nations and people of all time. These simple words constitute the fundamental principle of the Sermon on the Mount. Now and then writers since Micah's and Christ's time have phrased the same sentiment in language that has stood the test of the centuries. Hundreds of years later another writer wrote words that reflect something of the sentiment expressed by the ancient prophet. He says:

The quality of mercy is not strained;
It droppeth as the gentle rain from heaven
Upon the place beneath:
It is twice blest;
It blesseth him that gives and him that takes.
                              —Shakespeare's *Merchant of Venice*.

One of the great needs of our day is a change in the concept of what constitutes righteousness. An act is not righteous because it has legal sanction or not necessarily so because it has the sanction of the church, or of one's conscience. Nations, as well as lesser organized bodies, have at times given legal status to acts that were not only unmoral but even immoral. People in groups or as individuals have subordinated their consciences to justify evil in order to gain certain ends. This has no doubt been true throughout the history of mankind. It was true in Micah's day and it is still true in our time. The kingdom of peace is a kingdom within the kingdoms. The prophet says:

The mountain of the house of the Lord shall be established in the top of the mountains. . . . He shall judge among many people, and rebuke strong nations afar off; and they shall beat their swords into plowshares, and their spears into pruninghooks: nation shall not lift up a sword against nation, neither shall they learn war any more (4:1-3).

In the prophet's day, as well as in our day, the basis on which this was to be achieved was on law and justice. In an unregenerate society it can hardly be any other. But within the Christian order, a "nation within the nations," whose faith and way of life is rooted in the Gospel, the motive is Christian love, and the course of its action is *justice seasoned with mercy!*

15 | Habakkuk, Orator And Philosopher

Historians tell us nothing about Habakkuk. All we know about him is what we can glean from his writings. His reference to the Chaldeans gives us a clue as to the time in which he lived. Nebuchadnezzar's star was in its ascendancy and Neo-Babylonia under his leadership was becoming prominent in world affairs. Nineveh evidently had fallen or at least was reduced to the position where it no longer posed a major threat to the nations that were battling for positions of supremacy in world affairs. The battle of Carchemish was fought in 605 B.C., and the Assyrians were defeated. This event marked a turning point in history, for the Assyrians never again gained the position of power they had at one time held among the nations. The seat of political dominance and power in the east was shifted to Babylon in the lower reaches of the Tigris-Euphrates Valley.

But this also marked a turning point in the history of Israel. When Josiah in 640 B.C., at the age of eight years, came to the throne of Judah, he instituted a sweeping reformation under the leadership of Shaphan the scribe and Hilkiah the priest. The temple was completely renovated and repaired. All the paraphernalia of idol worship was removed and destroyed and Jehovah worship was restored. In the process of cleansing the house of Israel's God, a roll was found which greatly impressed Hilkiah the priest, who turned it over to Shaphan the scribe, who later read it before the king. This scroll of the law contained also references concerning the destruction of Jerusalem. This gave them grave concern. The king's body of counselors and advisers included also a prophetess named Huldah, whose counsel was then sought regarding the validity of these prophetic predictions. Her answer sustained the forecasts of the prophet and brought the king and his counselors to their knees in penitence and humiliation. This experience set off the great reformation that took place during Josiah's reign. He called a general assembly of the priests, prophets, and people in whose presence were read the words of the covenant which had been found in the temple. At this great gathering, the king made a solemn promise before Jehovah and his people to put into force all the requirements that were set forth in the book of the law.

This started the "cleanup" which reached its peak around 622. All the idols, images, and altars were ground to powder and strewn over the graves of those who had instituted them. The reformation reached even to Bethel and other places in Samaria. The false priests and prophets, witches and soothsayers were destroyed or driven out of the country. The priests of the Aaronic order were again placed in charge of the temple worship and the prophets of Jehovah were given a place at the king's council table.

But while these religious and social reforms were taking place under the benign rule of Josiah, things were happening also in other parts of the world that were later to greatly influence Judah's future. The power of Assyria was broken and the star of its destiny was on the way down. Chaldea or Neo-Babylonia was rising in influence and power and Media was giving it encouragement and support. Nineveh had fallen in 612, but a part of its army had escaped and established the seat of its new government at Haran in Mesopotamia. Necho, king of Egypt, decided in 609 to join what was left of the Assyrian army and move against the Medo-Chaldean coalition, whose rise to power posed a threat, not only to Assyria and the countries bordering

on the eastern and northern coasts of the Mediterranean Sea, but
to Egypt as well. The Egyptian monarch's attempt to secure the
support of Josiah had failed; hence he presumptuously undertook the venture to cross Palestine without the king's permission.
Josiah, at the head of his army, tried to block their way and in the
battle that ensued on the plains of Megiddo, he was mortally
wounded. His body was brought back to Jerusalem where, amid
great lamentation, he was buried. Judah's orators extolled his
virtues and lauded his good works while the people wept and
sorrowed. His long and benign reign, from 640 to 608, had come
to its end.

Josiah's defeat and death left Egypt master of the situation in
Palestine. The people of Judah placed Shallum, whose name was
changed to Jehoahaz, on the throne in 608. His attitude toward
Egypt evidently was not satisfactory to the Egyptians. After a
brief reign of three months, he was summoned before Necho,
who bound him with fetters and sent him into exile in Egypt,
where he disappeared from the scene. The Egyptian general
then put Eliakim, Jehoahaz's older brother, on the throne and
changed his name to Jehoiakim. This is rather significant because
of its meaning—"Jehovah establishes." Did the Egyptian war lord
actually recognize Jehovah as the God of Israel? The newly appointed king's lavish expenditures to provide a proper palace for
himself and maintain a suitable court, together with the heavy
indemnity he was forced to pay to Egypt, laid great burdens upon
the people and were the cause of no little dissatisfaction and
unrest.

It was during this period that new prophetic voices were
heard in Jerusalem and Judea. Among them was Habakkuk. The
date of his ministry is not definitely known. The only clue we
have is his mention of Chaldea.

. . . that bitter and hasty nation, which shall march through
the breadth of the land, to possess the dwellingplaces that are
not theirs. They are terrible and dreadful: their judgment
and their dignity shall proceed of themselves. Their horses
also are swifter than the leopards, and are more fierce than
the evening wolves . . . and their horsemen shall come from
far; they shall fly as the eagle that hasteth to eat. They shall

come all for violence: their faces shall sup up as the east wind, and they shall gather the captivity as the sand. And they shall scoff at the kings, and the princes shall be a scorn unto them: they shall deride every strong hold; for they shall heap dust, and take it (1:6-10).

Such was Habakkuk's view of the Chaldeans, and yet their good King Josiah had given his life in his attempt to block the way of the Egyptians that were en route to the embattled territory that finally transferred the seat of international power from Egypt and Assyria to the Medo-Chaldeans.

Habakkuk's message is, in one respect, different from that of his predecessors as well as of those who followed him. They spoke to the people in behalf of God. Habakkuk spoke to God. One commentator calls him the "man who scolded God." The situation in which Judah found itself must have seemed confusing to the prophet. Here was Judah, the remnant of a chosen race or nation, designated by Him throughout the centuries as His people. He had promised Abraham their father that He would make them a great nation. Centuries earlier while he still lived in ancient Babylonia, the land of his birth, the Lord said unto him:

> Get thee out of thy country, and from thy kindred, and from thy father's house, unto a land that I will shew thee: and I will make of thee a great nation, and I will bless thee, and make thy name great; and thou shalt be a blessing: and I will bless them that bless thee, and curse him that curseth thee: and in thee shall all families of the earth be blessed (Genesis 12:1-3).

Later, when this covenant was again confirmed, the Lord said:

> For all the land which thou seest, to thee will I give it, and to thy seed for ever. And I will make thy seed as the dust of the earth: so that if a man can number the dust of the earth, then shall thy seed also be numbered (Genesis 13:15, 16).

Israel's mother was the daughter of Bethuel, the son of Nahor, Abraham's brother, a wealthy stockman who lived in Syria. One day Rebekah, his daughter, met a stranger at the watering trough near her home. He was the servant of Abraham, who had been sent to find a bride for his son Isaac. When her brothers bade her farewell at the borders of their grazing grounds some days later, they bestowed upon her a final blessing whose echo has come down through the centuries and stands unmatched as a gem of its kind. They said:

Be thou the mother of thousands of millions, and let thy seed possess the gate of those which hate them (Genesis 24:60).

Now, however, the long arm of the oppressor from the east, from the land which the founder of Israel's race had left centuries before with such glowing promises for the future of his children and his children's children, was stretched out against them and purposed to bring them again into his fold. This was beyond Habakkuk's understanding. Therefore, he views the situation with alarm and begins his message with a complaint.

O Lord, how long shall I cry, and thou will not hear! even cry out unto thee of violence, and thou wilt not save (1:2)!

The land is filled with "spoiling and violence," he says. It appeared to him that those "that raise up strife and contention" have the advantage and are favored and prosper. He observes:

The law is slacked, and judgment doth never go forth: for the wicked doth compass about the righteous; therefore wrong judgment proceedeth (1:4).

The Lord had the answer. The spoiling and violence in the land was largely due to the moral and spiritual perversions of God's chosen people. Therefore, He says He will do something among the nations that will make him

. . . wonder marvellously: for I will work a work in your days, which ye will not believe, though it be told you. For, lo, I raise up the Chaldeans, that bitter and hasty nation, which shall march through the breadth of the land, to possess the dwellingplaces that are not theirs. They are terrible and dreadful: their judgment and their dignity shall proceed of themselves. Their horses also are swifter than leopards, and are more fierce than the evening wolves: and their horsemen shall spread themselves, and their horsemen shall come from far; they shall fly as the eagle that hasteth to eat (1:5-8).

But in the midst of his success, the prophet says that the

leader of this scourge shall change his mind and shall pass over
and offend, by imputing this power unto his god. 1:11. This
throws light on the prophet's problem. He sees that this invasion
has been ordained for judgment and was "established . . . for correction" (1:12). If this is true, then one would reason, Why does
God look upon them that deal treacherously and hold His tongue
when the wicked devour "the man that is more righteous than
he" (1:13)? It appears to him that his people have become as
the "fishes of the sea" which the invader catches with his snares
and nets and angles. Therefore, he says, "they sacrifice unto
their net, and burn incense unto their drag" (1:16). But he still
believes that God is righteous and just; therefore he says:

> I will stand upon my watch, and set me upon the tower, and
> will watch to see what he will say unto me, and what I shall
> answer when I am reproved (2:1).

Or, according to modern translators, "What answer I shall receive
concerning my complaint."[1] The answer of the Lord was apparently not long in coming. He said:

> Write the vision, and make it plain upon tables, that he may
> run that readeth it (2:2). Or as the modern translator says,
> "That he that runneth may read."[2]

"The vision," he said, "is yet for an appointed time"—an
advance warning. But in the end, at the proper time, it shall come
to pass. Even though God's plans may seem slow in materializing,
the people are warned to wait for them, for His predictions will
surely come to pass. The prophet had to learn a lesson in
patience. Man with his limited, human perspective often becomes impatient for results, but God knows the proper time. He
works in ages to accomplish His ends, while man works within
days and years—often hours. A poet of modern times says:

> Though the mills of God grind slowly,
>   Yet they grind exceeding small;
> Though with patience He stands waiting,
>   With exactness grinds He all.

The testings of time are as essential for the welfare of the
race as is the fire that separates the dross from the gold. Undue

1. The Berkeley Version.
2. *Ibid.*

haste as well as the lack of patience has forestalled the solution
of many a problem and brought to ruin many a well-laid plan.
The aggressor whose soul is lifted (puffed) up is not upright,
"yea also, because he transgresseth by wine, he is a proud man,
neither keepeth at home, who enlargeth his desire as hell [the
abode of the dead], and is as death, and cannot be satisfied, but
gathereth unto him all nations, and heapeth unto him all people"
(2:5). To these subdued and subjugated people he will become
the theme of their taunt-song and a song of derision saying:

Woe to him that increaseth that which is not his! how long?
and to him that ladeth [loads] himself with thick clay [i.e.,
pledges] (2:6)!

But in the sight of God he has brought shame to his own
house and sinned against his own soul. Those who suffered long,
the prophets declare, will rise up suddenly and strike back. There
is always a day of retribution. It is again a matter of a person
reaping what he has sown. This ancient proverb is not an empty
saying. History has verified its truth again and again. How often
has the oppressor been made to eat the "bitter meal" he ground
for others! This, Habakkuk predicts, will happen again. Because the oppressor has "spoiled many nations, all the remnant of
the people shall spoil thee; because of men's blood, and for the
violence of the land, of the city, and of all that dwell therein."

Thus was the first woe. The second woe is pronounced upon
"him that coveteth an evil covetousness to his house, that he may
set his nest on high, that he may be delivered from the power of
evil" (2:9)! But in doing so he has brought shame to his house
and "sinned against . . . [his own] soul." He had accomplished
his end "by cutting off many people" (2:10). For this, the very
stones "shall cry out of the wall, and the beam out of the timber
shall answer it" (2:11).

The third woe is pronounced upon him that "buildeth a town
with blood, and stablisheth a city by iniquity" (2:12)! A corrupt
municipal administration has so often, in the past as in the present
times, brought the wrath of an indignant population upon the
heads of local officials whose unjust practices had become un-
bearable. These local aberrations of justice, as well as the
tolerance of licentiousness, immorality, and the introduction of

idolatry, no doubt all contributed to Judah's problems, which in Habakkuk's time had become incurable.

It is well said that the stage of a nation's decadence may be determined by the place injustice in state as well as personal affairs—drunkenness, immorality, and illicit pleasure—holds among its people. Much of it may be considered respectable and still be wrong. The prophets of Israel appear to have held this view. They speak of these related evils as having been common practices in both Israel and Judah prior to their fall. These, together with the introduction of strange altars and alien gods, constitute the gauge by which they measure the rate of a nation's decline.

The pronouncement of the fourth woe is upon the drunkards of Judah. "Woe unto him that giveth his neighbour drink, that puttest thy bottle to him, and makest him drunken also, that thou mayest look on their nakedness" (2:15)! The sin of drunkenness is almost as old as the human race. It is not likely that Noah was the first one that had imbibed too freely of the product of his vineyard. But since that day references are frequently made to what became one of the besetting sins of humanity, and sexual impurity seems to have, through the centuries, become a counterpart of the drunkard's obsessions.

The next pronouncement is upon the maker of graven images, and the molten image, and the teacher of lies. What profit are these dumb idols that are made of gold and silver, and wood and stone? "Woe unto him that saith to the wood, Awake; to the dumb stone, Arise, it shall teach" (2:19)! Crowds may have surged around those altars and laid costly sacrifices upon them, but the gods to whom they were offered remained silent because there was not a "breath of life" in them.

Habakkuk was, in every sense, very human, even though he was one of the Lord's prophets. It appears from his writings that he thought God was moving too slowly. Then the revealing answer came. He found himself standing in the stream of time and saw the workings of God in human history. Chapter 3. He saw the Lord as He came from Teman and the Holy One from mount Paran. His glory covered the heavens. The earth, which the prophet may have considered doomed, was filled with praise.

God stood and measured the earth. He beheld and drove asunder the nations. The "everlasting mountains," which for ages had defied the ravages of time, were scattered and the "perpetual hills" did bow. He saw the tents of Cushan in affliction and the curtains of Midian trembling. The sea and rivers divided to make a way for the salvation of His people. He stayed the sun and moon in their course and marched through the land in indignation, threshed the heathen in His anger, and struck the head of the villages who went scurrying as the whirlwind to scatter "me" and devour the poor secretly. He walked through the sea, through great heaps of waters.

When the vision was finished, the prophet stood trembling, and he who had been impatient and critical now says, "My lips quivered at the voice: rottenness entered into my bones." Out of that experience came an expression of faith that rises like a tower in the annals of time.

Although the fig tree shall not blossom,
Neither shall fruit be in the vines;
The labour of the olive shall fail,
And the fields shall yield no meat;
The flock shall be cut off from the fold,
And there shall be no herd in the stalls:
    Yet I will rejoice in the Lord,
    I will joy in the God of my salvation.
    The Lord God is my strength,
    And he will make my feet like hinds' feet,
    And he will make me to walk upon mine high places.
                     —Habakkuk 3:17-19.

In facing the threats of his time, when the land was confronted with an invading army that appeared invincible and unconquerable, the prophet became assured that these forces were "ordained . . . for judgment" and "established . . . for correction." His own people had brought this scourge upon themselves. He knew, too, that the invader would not permanently survive the judgment of God. Jeremiah, Habakkuk's late contemporary, says of this occasion:

What is the chaff to the wheat? saith the Lord. Is not my

word like a fire? saith the Lord; and like a hammer that
breaketh the rock in pieces (Jeremiah 23:28, 29)?

Again today we stand in the "stream of time" and view with
concern the "goings on" in the world. Modern political conditions
and sociological and religious movements are no doubt responsible for the economic, social, moral, and religious situation,
which has become such that the peace and security of the world
stand in jeopardy. But such conditions prevailed, also, in
Habakkuk's time and have recurred again and again throughout
the history of the human race. Nations and people who have
founded a culture that is established on human reason and
modified by human wants and desires, without taking into account the higher laws of God, have always sooner or later fallen
under the weight of their own devisings. That is true now as it
was in the ages that have passed. The earth is a vast burial
ground where nations that were born and grew mighty in power
lie buried. The fascist state that flamed along the political
horizon for a brief season, like an erratic star that had gone out
of orbit, lies now in the ash heap and dust of fallen nations, while
the body of its boastful founder who tried to outdo the Caesars
hung for a time in the shambles. The Hohenzollerns and
Romanovs have vanished and the Nazi empire which Hitler
boasted would stand for a thousand years survived scarcely a
single decade. What will happen to the nations that follow the
philosophy of Karl Marx remains to be seen and what will become of other nations that are frittering away their spiritual and
moral energy at the shrines of philosophies and programs which
aim to make life easy instead of useful, self-reliant, and self-
sustaining, remains yet to be seen. Historians, some of whom
may have already been born, will write the story.

Time has not changed the outcomes of human conduct. It is
a well-stated axiom of the Scripture that "whatsoever a man
soweth, that shall he also reap." This is still true. Habakkuk
uses an expression that may have been old even before his day,
but which is applicable still. "The just shall live by his faith," he
said. It has lain, sometimes for centuries, covered with the
"must" and "dust" of ecclesiastical or political dogmas or pronouncements, but great souls have recovered it again and again.

Martin Luther found it in his time, made it the watchword of the Reformation, and lifted the church out of the stagnation that had collected through the centuries.

The people of each generation have prospered or suffered in accordance with the way they met the issues of their own time. They had to endure the disciplines imposed by corrective measures or endure the consequences of negligence and disobedience that are divinely devised and imposed. "The constant riddle of the Old Testament," says one writer, "is not the survival of the fittest, but the suffering of the best." This was true of the exiles in Babylon when the "fittest" adapted themselves to their alien environment, prospered, and remained in Babylonia when the way was opened for them to return to their homeland. But it was the "suffering . . . best" who trekked home to Palestine over the long miles, to rebuild their temple, reclaim their land, and re-establish their homes. This was true also in the Middle Ages when the "suffering . . . best" built anew the church around the mounds and ash heaps of those who did not survive. It was true also of those who left the lands of their birth and went to a newly discovered continent where they claimed untamed lands which they hopefully turned into islands of freedom in a troubled world. It will be so again, if need be, in order that the faith of the saints may survive. For saith the prophet:

The earth shall be filled with the knowledge of the glory of the Lord, as the waters cover the sea. . . . But the Lord is in his holy temple: let all the earth keep silence before him (2:14, 20).

16 | Zephaniah, the Eloquent Spokesman for God

Zephaniah is the orator, a man of straightforward speech, severe and uncompromising in his denunciation of the evils of his day and the sins of his countrymen. He prophesied in Judah around 630 B.C. He is careful to trace his genealogy back through four generations. He states that he was the son of Cushi, the son of Gedaliah, the son of Amariah, the son of Hizkiah. This, no doubt, gave him standing and influence among the people as well as among those who were occupied with the affairs of state and those who were responsible for the spiritual nurture and care of the masses. We know nothing about his life except what we are able to learn from his writings. He probably lived in Jerusalem as his familiarity with the place would indicate. The noise of the market at the fish gate, the Maktesh or bazaars (1:10, 11), was apparently well known to him.

The title of the book says that the word of the Lord came unto him in the days of Josiah, king of Judah. It is not clear, however, whether his ministry began before the great reformation of Josiah's reign had taken place. It appears that even before the king's death a reaction, which so marked Jehoiakim his successor's reign, had already set in. The idolatrous practices which

Zephaniah had so vigorously denounced are the same as those which Josiah had abolished. The reformation, according to II Chronicles, appears to have extended over a period of years. He says that in his eighth year he, Josiah, began to seek after God and to purge Judah and Jerusalem from their idols and places of idol worship. II Chronicles 34:3. He says also that the reforms reached into the regions of the Northern Kingdom. II Chronicles 34:6, 7. In the eighteenth year of his reign he began to repair the temple, during the process of which the book of the law was discovered, and the reforms were continued with renewed energy.

It was during this time that Zephaniah's proclamation of judgment began. For some reason, in spite of the reforms of Josiah, Zephaniah saw forebodings of trouble and an outpouring of Jehovah's indignation. 1:14, 15. It may be that the response to Josiah's cleanup movement had not been wholehearted and sincere, and the appearance on the horizon of the Scythians came as a "scourge of God" which drove the prophet into action. These wandering hordes came from beyond the Black and Caspian seas. They were a ruthless, filthy, and unwashed race "that neither plowed nor sowed," but lived upon the plunder they secured from the raided cities and people. They seem not to have been particularly attached to any place. They clothed themselves with napkins made from the scalps of their enemies and drank blood from cups made from the skulls of those whom they had slain. They broke through the Caucasus Mountains sometime between 630 and 625 and descended like a locust plague upon Syria and Media. They then moved across Mesopotamia and en route to Egypt they ravaged Syria. At Ashdod, they encountered the Egyptian forces under Psamtik who "cooled their ardor" with rich gifts and prevented an invasion of his own country. They, however, remained in Western Asia for a quarter of a century. A group of them is presumed to have settled at Scythopolis, on the west side of the Jordan River. Some commentators think that this invasion was in reality a manifestation of judgment upon the nations to call people from their evil ways to repentance.

This invasion coincided with the date that is ascribed to

Zephaniah's ministry and also with the beginning of Jeremiah's long and eventful service in Jerusalem. The spiritual, moral, and political situation in the Southern Kingdom was at that time much the same as that of which the prophets who had preceded him had spoken. There was religious apostasy which persisted in some quarters in spite of Josiah's effort to uproot it. Moral looseness, injustice, and the evils which grow out of similar situations also prevailed. The conditions which existed were in themselves such as would justify the warnings of the prophet, even though the Scythians and other threatening powers from the outside had not appeared.

Zephaniah opens his writings with a sweeping pronouncement of judgment upon all the land. "I will utterly consume all things from off the land, saith the Lord" (1:2). This included not only the people, but also man and beast, the fowls of the heavens, the fishes of the sea, and the stumbling blocks, i.e., the things that cause people to err. It included their black-robed priests and "them that worship the host of heaven upon the housetops" and swear by Ammonitish idols. It included also those who did not worship at the shrines of idolatry but neither did they seek the Lord God. This cleansing, he threatens, will reach into the king's house. There will, he predicted, be a "cry from the fish gate," a "crashing from the hills," and a "howling from the second [quarter]" (1:10, 11).

The moral corruptions and religious conditions were appalling, according to the prophet's view. The worship of Jehovah was re-established, but other religions were tolerated or, if not tolerated, they at least persisted. Incense was burned to Baal, and idolatrous priests were maintained. There were among them practical atheists who denied that God had any part in the affairs of the world. "The Lord will not do good, neither will he do evil," they said. 1:12. There were apostates who did not bother to seek Him at all. 1:5, 6. When one compares Zephaniah's condemnation of the inhabitants of Jerusalem with Nahum's complaint against Nineveh, he finds that they had much in common. "The unjust knoweth no shame" (3:5), he said. The people of Judah appear to have been a self-complacent, proud, merciless, shameless lot. For that reason their day of grace was passing and the clouds of judgment were gathering.

Zephaniah visualized this outpouring of justice upon an offending world to be as sweeping and wide in its scope as was the judgment in the days of Noah when the earth was swept clean.

That day [says the prophet] is a day of wrath, a day of trouble and distress, a day of wasteness and desolation, a day of darkness and gloominess, a day of clouds and thick darkness, a day of the trumpet and alarm against the fenced cities, and against the high towers (1:15, 16).

The storm was scheduled to hit Jerusalem first, for there it appears that the people had sinned irremediably against the Lord. Even the righteous, the prophet predicted, will be compelled to share in the hardships and sufferings when the blow falls. He says: "It may be ye shall be hid in the day of Jehovah's anger." This is the only hope that is held out to the meek in the land which had brought upon itself God's judgment. 1:15. The storm, it is predicted, will reach beyond the walls of Jerusalem. Its path sweeps westward to the land of the Philistines and eastward to Moab and Ammon, the descendants of Lot, and to Ethiopia, which lies far to the south.

My determination [saith the Lord] is to gather the nations, that I may assemble the kingdoms, to pour upon them mine indignation, even all my fierce anger: for all the earth shall be devoured with the fire of my jealousy (3:8).

Zephaniah has a broad view of the judgment which God visits upon the nations. Its purpose was not to be punitive, but redemptive. In that day it shall be said to Jerusalem,

I will bring you again, even in the time that I gather you: for I will make you a name and a praise among all people of the earth, when I turn back your captivity before your eyes (3:20).

The prophet's predictions cover a wider scope and include more people and nations than merely Israel. "The Lord," he says, ". . . will famish all the gods of the earth; and men shall worship him, every one from his place, even all the isles of the heathen" (2:11). "The fire of God's jealousy," says one writer, "refines while it consumes." It purifies the lips "that they may . . . call upon the

6

name of the Lord, to serve him with one consent. From beyond the rivers of Ethiopia my suppliants, even the daughter of my dispersed, shall bring mine offering" (3:9, 10).

The concept of a personal Messiah, such as Isaiah and other prophets had, does not appear in the writings of Zephaniah, but there is nowhere any intimation that such a one does not exist. He spoke to the situations and conditions that existed in his day and was concerned with what would happen to the people of his own time. He does not predict how the "purifying process" is to be accomplished, except that the judgment is near at hand and is to be unparalleled in terribleness, but through it, he says, shall come salvation to Israel and to all mankind.

The earlier prophets, such as Micah and Isaiah, indicate Zion or Jerusalem as the center from which the redemptive hope will spread. "And all nations shall flow unto it," they said. Zephaniah goes a step beyond that and says, "And men shall worship him, every one from his place, even all the isles of the heathen" (2:11). Centuries later when Christ, the "Hope of the Ages," had arrived, He said to the woman at the well at Sychar,

The hour cometh, when ye shall neither in this mountain, nor yet at Jerusalem, worship the Father. . . . But the hour cometh, and now is, when the true worshippers shall worship the Father in spirit and in truth (John 4:21, 23).

Zephaniah's judgment of Jerusalem which appeared so imminent and so near was averted, but its fulfillment began with the disasters that befell the surrounding nations. Great upheavals were taking place in the east. Neo-Babylonia, Media, and Persia were coming into prominence and beginning to figure in world affairs. New powers were raising their heads along the Mediterranean seacoast—powers that were later to challenge the supremacy of the nations of the east which had for centuries dominated the affairs of the world. The day of Judah's judgment was drawing near and culminated within the next half century in the overthrow of its kings and the destruction of Jerusalem, the seat of political authority and the center of its divinely instituted form of worship. These steps of progress led toward the end, says one writer. They constitute elements in the "fulness of times" in which the universal kingdom of God shall have its beginning.

Zephaniah, like all of the prophets, was not able to anticipate the time when his prophetic predictions would reach their consummation. It was given to these ancient spokesmen "to soar above the earthborn mists, which becloud human vision, and see God's purposes rising majestically against the clear firmament of His righteous sovereignty like the sunlit Alpine peaks against the azure sky." But they were not given the vision nor the ability to see or comprehend the many obstacles or barriers that had to be surmounted, or the disappointments that would need to be endured ere the hopes that grew out of their visions would be realized.

The prophets dealt with eternal truths, and have a message for our day. Regardless of what rational disposition people may make of the concept of God or the place the messages of the prophets have for our time, they must realize that they are dealing with forces that were beyond the control of man. God is still God. He is ever judging the world. Nations as well as individual persons or groups of persons are constantly confronted with His judgments. Whether or not they realize it, it is still true. Each generation must learn, so it seems, for itself that authority or power, violence or might are not the final forces that man has to deal with. Nor do man's rationalizations constitute the answer to his problems. Only the truth and righteousness that is of God abides.

Israel was never a world power. It was frequently victorious in battle, but its prowess and strength was drawn from a higher source than that which is merely human. It was a small nation that was tossed hither and yon, bruised and battered, often by the mighty powers of the earth—Assyria, Babylonia, Media, Persia, Egypt, Greece, and Rome. But it rose again and again, flayed and punished for its sins, to go on to the fulfillment of its heaven-ordained mission, and in the course of time it gave to the world at Bethlehem the wonder of "principalities and powers in heavenly places," the Saviour of mankind, Jesus Christ, King of kings, and Lord of lords! Out of this gift to a troubled and sin-laden world rose the Christian Church, which so often through the centuries has risen from what would ordinarily be considered sure defeat. Chastened and purified, it rose again and again to go forth conquering and to conquer. It survived through the ages because of the faith and labors of its greatest and ablest sons, Paul and Peter, Polycarp, Augustine, Luther, Calvin, Menno Simons, and a host of others "of whom the world was not worthy." Thus it was in the past; so it will, no doubt, always be until the end of time.

17 | Jeremiah, the Prophet Who Saw Judah's Fall

Jeremiah's Call

Jeremiah received his call to the prophetic ministry during the thirteenth year of the reign of the good King Josiah, in 627 B.C., and continued throughout the reign of his three sons and one grandson. The chronicler tells us that he was "the son of Hilkiah, of the priests that were in Anathoth in the land of Benjamin," a village some three miles north and east of Jerusalem. One would conclude from his statements in 11:23; 29:27, and 32:7, 8 that he probably continued to maintain a home at that place during his ministry.

He was apparently a young man when his call came. He gave his youthfulness and his timidity as cause for declining the responsibility which the duties of this office would involve and finally accepted the position reluctantly. 1:6 ff. The task that lay before him was a momentous one, and his natural disposition was such that he says he would rather have withdrawn to a lodge in the wilderness where he could have lived in peace (9:2) or that he might have died on the day he was born. 20:14-18. On the other hand, he possessed qualities and natural abilities that fitted him eminently for the work and responsibilities to which he was called and enabled him to fulfill his mission with honor and divine approval. He was deeply sympathetic and could share, as much as it was humanly possible, the sorrows and heartaches of the loyal minority among God's people who reflected the love and spirit of a heavenly Father whose chosen race was on the road to destruction. His deep faith in Him from whom he received his call enabled him to withstand the trials and endure the disappointments, hardships, and threats that fell to his lot. For the Lord had said, "Go to all that I shall send thee, and whatsoever I command thee thou shalt speak. Be not afraid of their faces: for I am with thee to deliver thee, saith the Lord" (1:7, 8).

His commission extended not only to Judah and Israel but included also the surrounding nations. He was to be God's spokesman in a period of world-wide convulsion and upheaval. It was one of those epochs in the history of mankind when in God's providence it became necessary to "pluck up and break down in order to build and plant anew." Jeremiah, as God's spokesman, was to stand before kings and priests and self-appointed prophets, most of whom were opposed to his ideals and were unsympathetic and unresponsive to his teachings. As time went on, many of his friends either died or were carried into exile. It was in the plan of God that the prophet should remain unmarried in order to be free from the cares and concerns of home and family life. He carried on his ministry in this isolation from those who might have shared his counsels and helped to bear his burdens.

His messages were delivered in the courts of the temple, in the palace of the king, and in the gates of the city, or wherever the occasion made it possible for him to get a hearing. He made large use of symbolism in his teaching. He drew lessons from the potter's wheel and from the loyalty of the Rechabites to their pledges. 35:1-10. He illustrated the utter destruction of Jerusalem and Judea by breaking the earthen pitcher at the "Potsherd Gate." 19:1, 10, 11. He demonstrated his faith in God's promises for Israel's future by redeeming, as next of kin, a field at Anathoth. 32:6-14.

His life was a life of martyrdom that finally came to its close in Egypt, whither he was taken by the remnant that fled to the land of the Nile after the fall of Jerusalem and the murder of Gedaliah, whom Nebuchadnezzar had appointed as governor of Palestine. His own family proved untrustworthy. 12:6. The people of Anathoth, his home town, laid plans to take his life. 11:19. He was put in stocks by the priests, in spite of the law of profanation against such procedures. 20:2. Even the fulfillment of his prophetic predictions did not alter the course of those who opposed him. The spirit of the age in which he lived was not the spirit of grace and mercy; it was the spirit of justice. God's people were failing Him. Mercy had been extended again and again but without avail. The time comes, in the course of human affairs, when judgment must fall and when people are compelled to reap what they have sown.

Jeremiah's Ministry During the Reign of Josiah
628-610 B.C.

It is difficult to fix definitely the date of some of Jeremiah's writings and fit them into the reign of the different kings that occupied the throne of Judah during the years of his ministry. It is, however, generally agreed that chapters 1—6 belong to the period when Josiah occupied the throne of Judah. The writer of the Book of Chronicles says that in the eighth year of his reign, 632 B.C., Josiah began to seek after the God of his father David, and in the twelfth year, 628 B.C., he began the great reformation in which he tried to eliminate idolatry and its evils from the kingdom. It was some time during this year or the year following that Jeremiah received his call from God.

It was during the eighteenth year of Josiah's reign, while the temple was being cleansed, that the book of the law was recovered. This discovery greatly accelerated the progress of the reformation. It is evident from the teachings and messages of the prophets that thus far the populace as a whole had not joined wholeheartedly in the reform movement, for Jeremiah's record indicates that the spiritual and moral conditions were still deplorably bad. During the last years of Josiah's reign, the effects of the reformation were relaxed and after his death its results were largely lost.

Jeremiah's *first recorded message* is found in chapters 2:1—
3:5, in which Israel's apostasy is graphically described. The Lord
said:

> Go and cry in the ears of Jerusalem, saying, Thus saith the
> Lord; I remember thee, the kindness of thy youth, the love
> of thine espousals, when thou wentest after me in the wilder-
> ness, in a land that was not sown. Israel was holiness unto
> the Lord, and the firstfruits of his increase: all that devour
> him shall offend; evil shall come upon them, saith the Lord
> (2:2, 3).

But after years of prosperity she had broken her sacred vows
with God and transferred her loyalty to other deities. Judah
deserted the Lord to follow after Baal. They had forsaken, the
prophet complained, "the fountain of living waters," and had accepted "cisterns that can hold no water" (2:13). The Lord said:
"I had planted thee a noble vine, wholly a right seed; how then
art thou turned into the degenerate plant of a strange vine unto
me" (2:21)? Their defilement had become so deep, he said, that
it could not be cleansed with niter or soap. 2:22. He likens them
to a "wild ass . . . that snuffeth up the wind at her pleasure"
(2:24), and yet they say, "Because I am innocent, surely his
anger shall turn from me" (2:35).

Social impurity and illicit sex relations were common practices among them. He accuses them of "[trimming their] way to
seek love" and says that "in thy skirts is found the blood of the
souls of the poor innocents: I have not found it by secret search,
but upon all these" (2:33, 34), and yet they pleaded innocence.
But the prophet said:

> Lift up thine eyes unto the high places, and see where thou
> hast not been lien with. In the ways hast thou sat for them,
> as the Arabian in the wilderness; and thou hast polluted the
> land with thy whoredoms and with thy wickedness. There-
> fore the showers have been withholden, and there hath been
> no latter rain; and thou hadst a whore's forehead, thou
> refusedst to be ashamed (3:2, 3).

A second message, chapters 2:6—6:30, was delivered in the
days of Josiah, the king, in which he intimates that Judah had
not entered wholeheartedly into the reforms that the king had

instituted. He says that "backsliding Israel" had set the pattern which Judah followed. Judah saw the corruption and pollution that followed Israel's way of life and yet Judah followed the same course. Therefore the Lord said that "The backsliding Israel hath justified herself more than treacherous Judah" (3:11). He predicted that if the nation does not repent He will redeem them "one of a city, and two of a family, and . . . will bring you to Zion" (3:14), and will give them pastors according to His heart, which shall feed them with knowledge and understanding. 3:15. He will receive them, the prophet said, even though they have nothing to offer but weeping and supplication and yet will say, "Behold, we come unto thee; for thou art the Lord our God" (3:22).

Judah's problems were not limited to those that rose within her own borders. He urges the people to assemble themselves in the fenced cities for a "lion," he says, "is come up from his thicket, and the destroyer of the Gentiles is on his way" (4:7). Some commentators think he may have reference to the appearance of the Scythian hordes that were making raids upon the cities and people of that area. He cries, "My . . . [anguish], my . . . [anguish]! . . . I cannot hold my peace, because thou hast heard, O my soul, the sound of the trumpet, the alarm of war" (4:19). But more damaging and alarming than the trumpets of war and more devastating spiritually were the activities and voices of the false prophets and the spiritual leaders of the people. "A wonderful and horrible thing is committed in the land," he says. "The prophets prophesy falsely, and the priests bear rule by their means; and my people love to have it so" (5:30, 31).

O daughter of my people, gird thee with sackcloth, and wallow thyself in ashes: make thee mourning, as for an only son, most bitter lamentations: for the spoiler shall suddenly come upon us. . . . They are all grievous revolters, walking with slanders: they are brass and iron; they are all corrupters. The bellows are burned, the lead is consumed of the fire; the founder melteth in vain: for the wicked are not plucked away. Reprobate silver shall men call them, because the Lord hath rejected them (6:26-30).

In 610 B.C. a heavy blow fell upon Judah. Josiah was killed

in the battle of Megiddo. He was spoken of as "the good king" who attempted to bring about such reforms in his kingdom as would establish its relationship with Jehovah on a sound basis. But even he was not immune to outside influences. The visit of a delegation from the rising Chaldean empire in the east was very cordial and the gifts they brought were very enticing. He could not resist the proposition of the Oriental monarch to assist him in his plan to expand his empire by blocking the invasion of the Egyptian army that was on its way to give battle to the powers of the east. Josiah met the invaders at the pass of Megiddo, where he was slain and Judah was brought under the control of the Egyptians.

Jeremiah During the Reign of Jehoahaz
609 B.C.

Following the death of Josiah, in 609, Jehoahaz, his second son, was placed on the throne of Judah. After a brief reign of three months, he was called before Necho, the commander of the Egyptian army, who relieved him of his office and sent him into exile in Egypt. One writer says that the young king was distinguished for his folly and failed to win the confidence of his "overlord," the king of Egypt, who deposed him and sent him into exile where he disappeared from the records of history.

The Reign of Jehoiakim
609-598 B.C.

Jehoiakim, Josiah's oldest son, was then placed on the throne. He was a cruel and selfish prince, given to an extravagant and luxurious life. It was during his reign that great changes took place in the relationship between Judah and the world powers of that day. Following the defeat of Egypt at the battle of Carchemish in 605 B.C., Nebuchadnezzar of Chaldea dominated the world for a period of more than a half century. The new master governed his colonial possessions with moderation and consideration, so long as his subjects paid their annual tribute and maintained order within their own boundaries. It was during the early part of his reign that Daniel and his three friends were taken to Babylon, apparently not as hostages but as young men to be trained for service in the empire.

The narrators and compilers of the material that covers the period of Jeremiah's ministry do not always place it in its chronological order. Chapters 1—6, as already noted, deal with the closing years of Josiah's reign. Chapters 7—21 cover the reign of Jehoiakim, 609-598 B.C., as do also chapters 25, 35, 36, 45, and 46. Chapters 22 and 23 belong to the brief reign of three months when Jehoiachin, second son of Josiah, occupied the throne in 598 B.C. The reign of Zedekiah, third son of Josiah, covers the period from 597 B.C. to the fall of Jerusalem in 586 B.C. Chapters 24—40 cover, with the exceptions already noted, the events of his reign. Chapters 40—52 contain some materials from his reign and also the history of the Judean colony which Nebuchadnezzar had set up at Jerusalem and its migration to Egypt where Jeremiah, so far as is known, spent the last years of his life.

Chapters 26 and 27 shed further light on the prophet's activities during the first years of Jehoiakim's reign. Jeremiah's outspoken denunciation of the nation's sin stirred up renewed animosity and resistance among the people. This was especially true of the priesthood and the ruling classes. When he had concluded his address in the court of the temple (26:1-7), the priests and prophets and all the people took him, saying, "Thou shalt surely die." They said this because he had predicted that "This house shall be like Shiloh, and this city shall be desolate without an inhabitant" (26:9).

When the princes heard of the disturbance, they convened the court in the new gate of the Lord's house, where they heard the people's complaint. There, in the presence of the princes and all the people, Jeremiah made his defense. He said:

The Lord sent me to prophesy against this house and against this city all the words that ye have heard. Therefore now amend your ways and your doings, and obey the voice of the Lord your God; and the Lord will repent him of the evil that he hath pronounced against you. As for me, behold, I am in your hand: do with me as seemeth good and meet unto you (26:12-14).

At the conclusion of his address, the princes and all the people said unto the priests and prophets: "This man is not worthy to

die: for he hath spoken to us in the name of the Lord our God"
(26:16). This verdict was supported also by the elders of the
land (26:17), and Jeremiah was released.

At the same time there was another prophet, Urijah, who
prophesied to the people in the name of the Lord. He, also, was
called to account for what they interpreted as treasonable ut-
terances which he made against the city and the nation. When
he learned of the movement for his arrest and prosecution, he
fled to Egypt. There he was arrested and, on an extradition order
of Jehoiakim, he was returned to Jerusalem where he was brought
to trial and, in spite of Jeremiah's and Ahikam's pleas for clem-
ency, he was executed.

Jeremiah knew, also, that the people of Judah were greatly
influenced by the surrounding tribes and nations and drew many
of their ideas of idolatry and licentiousness from them. Hence, his
address to the nations surrounding Palestine. During the first
year of Jehoiakim's reign he had made yokes, symbols of bondage,
which he sent to the kings of Moab, Ammon, Tyre, and Sidon,
nations that were chafing also under the rule of Nebuchadnezzar.
He admonished them that a refusal to submit to the yoke of the
Babylonian monarch would bring upon them the armies of that
nation and they would also fall under the displeasure of God,
who would punish them with famine, sword, and pestilence.
"Therefore," he urged, "hearken not ye to your prophets, nor to
your diviners, nor to your dreamers, nor to your enchanters, nor
to your sorcerers, which speak unto you, saying, Ye shall not
serve the king of Babylon." Those who submit to his rule, he said,
will be permitted to remain in their own land; they shall till it and
dwell therein. Chapter 27.

But Judah had gone beyond the point of recall. When
preaching failed to bring the people back to God, the prophet
resorted to prayer, even though the Lord had declared that He
would no longer honor prayers in their behalf.

Thus have they loved to wander, they have not refrained
their feet, therefore the Lord doth not accept them; he will
now remember their iniquity, and visit their sins. . . . [There-
fore he said] Pray not for this people for their good. When
they fast, I will not hear their cry; and when they offer burnt

offering and an oblation, I will not accept them: but I will
consume them by the sword, and by the famine, and by the
pestilence (14:10-12).

Then follows Jeremiah's pathetic plea for consideration. The
people were led astray by the prophets that prophesied lies and
led them into ways of sin that satisfied their carnal desires and
made them heedless to the call of God's spokesman. He pleads,
"Do not abhor us, for thy name's sake, do not disgrace the throne
of thy glory: remember, break not thy covenant with us" (14:21).

The prophet's life was a lonely life. He was unmarried and
had no family to whom he could turn for counsel or in whose
fellowship he could find solace and consolation. 16:1-4. The
people of his own village, Anathoth, turned traitor and conspired
against him and sought to take his life. 11:15-23. He found,
also, that his own kindred were involved in the plot. 12:5, 6. The
prophets that should have supported him contradicted him constantly and tried to undo his work. 14:13-18. The people, "every
one of them doth curse me," he said (15:10), and even God, he
thought, refused to hear and honor his prayers. In his loneliness
he cried unto the Lord, "Be not a terror unto me: thou art my
hope in the day of evil" (17:17). Jeremiah had to learn the
lesson that people of all generations have had to learn, namely,
that God cannot be persuaded to do anything that is not in
keeping with what is best for His people and His cause, even
though it may be the opposite of what seems right from man's
point of view. "Though Moses and Samuel stood before me,
yet my mind could not be toward this people: cast them out of my
sight, and let them go" (15:1), was God's conclusion.

We next hear of Jeremiah when he delivered his message
in the gate of the city, through which the royal family passed.
Here he preached his great sermon on the Sabbath. 17:19-27.
Following that we read of him in the potter's house, where he
demonstrated that a vessel may become so marred that it cannot
be repaired. It has to be broken down and remade. He intimated
that Judah was then going through such a process. 18:1-11.
Jeremiah could not conceive of a people being so unresponsive.
Even the Lord is quoted as being astounded at their attitude. The
prophet quotes:

Ask ye now among the heathen, who hath heard such things: the virgin of Israel hath done a very horrible thing. Will a man leave the snow of Lebanon which cometh from the rock of the field, or shall the cold flowing waters that come from another place be forsaken? Because my people hath forgotten me, they have burned incense to vanity, and they have caused them to stumble in their ways from the ancient paths, to walk in paths, in a way not cast up; to make their land desolate, and a perpetual hissing; every one that passeth thereby shall be astonished, and wag his head. I will scatter them as with an east wind before the enemy; I will shew them the back, and not the face, in the day of their calamity (18:13-17).

The people who had heard Jeremiah's great sermon in the potter's house said in response to his appeal:

There is no hope: but we will walk after our own devices, and we will every one do the imagination of his evil heart. For the law shall not perish from the priest, nor counsel from the wise, nor the word from the prophet. Come, and let us smite him with the tongue, and let us not give heed to any of his words (18:12, 18).

Jeremiah was arrested by Pashur, the son of Immer the priest, who was chief of the governors of the house of the Lord. He was put in stocks that were in the high gate of the house of the Lord. 20:1, 2. The following morning when he was released, he expressed himself vehemently concerning his attitude toward the whole affair. He said to Pashur that his name shall no more be Pashur, but Magor-missabib—a terror all around—for thus saith the Lord:

Behold, I will make thee a terror to thyself, and to all thy friends: and they shall fall by the sword of their enemies, and thine eyes shall behold it: and I will give all Judah into the hand of the king of Babylon, and he shall carry them captive into Babylon, and shall slay them with the sword. Moreover I will deliver all the strength of this city, and all the labours thereof, and all the precious things thereof, and all the treasures of the kings of Judah will I give into the hand of their enemies, which shall spoil them, and take them, and carry them to Babylon. And thou, Pashur, and all that dwell in thine house shall go into captivity: and thou shalt come to Babylon, and there thou shalt die, and shalt be buried there, thou, and all thy friends, to whom thou hast prophesied lies (20:4-6).

In the prayer that followed this humiliating affair the prophet declared that he decided to speak no more in the name of the Lord, but His word was in his heart, he says, "as a burning fire" so that he could not stay—refuse to speak—and in desperation he curses the day in which he was born. 20:7-18.

In chapter 36 is recorded an event that took place during the fourth year of Jehoiakim's reign. Jeremiah was divinely commanded to write in the roll of a book all the words he had spoken against Israel and Judah and the surrounding nations "from the days of Josiah, even unto this day." Acting on this command, he called Baruch and dictated all the words he had spoken. Jeremiah was apparently at the time in the custody of the law. He says, "I am shut up; I cannot go into the house of the Lord" (36:5). Hence, he instructed Baruch to go and read the roll in the hearing of all the assembly which had come from Jerusalem and all the surrounding cities. "It may be," he said, "they will present their supplication before the Lord, and will return every one from his evil way" (36:7).

The following year the roll was again read on a similar occasion. This time it struck fire! A report of this meeting was carried to the princes and to Elishama, the scribe. 36:12. The roll was read in the hearing of the group and careful inquiry was made as to how it was compiled. Baruch said, "He pronounced all these words unto me with his mouth, and I wrote them with ink in the book." The council then advised that both Jeremiah and Baruch go into hiding, "and let no man know where ye be" (36:19), for they said, "We will surely tell the king of all these words." They no doubt expected that the consequences would be serious.

The roll was sent to the king who was in his winter house, warming himself by the fire that burned on the hearth. As it was read to him, he cut off leaf after leaf and threw them into the fire. He did this in spite of the counsel of a number of his advisers and ordered the arrest of both Jeremiah and Baruch. 36:25, 26. The roll was rewritten. The prediction following this incident was that the king's dead body shall be "cast out in the day to the heat, and in the night to the frost" (36:30).

During Jehoiakim's reign, the Egyptian influence grew in Palestine. The king chafed under the rule of the Chaldeans and during the fourth year of his reign he discontinued paying tribute to Nebuchadnezzar. In addition to the invasion of the Chaldeans that was then pending, the people suffered at the hands of harassing bands of Aramaeans, Moabites, and Ammonites that overran the country and drove the peasants into the cities. Among these refugees were the Rechabites, whose loyalty to Jehovah stood in sharp contrast with the policy and practices of the king and his followers. They obeyed the commandments of Jonadab their father and kept all his precepts and did according to all that he commanded them. "Thus saith the Lord of hosts, the God of Israel; Jonadab the son of Rechab shall not want a man to stand before me for ever" (35:19).

Finally, in 598 B.C. the thing they feared came to pass. Nebuchadnezzar invaded the country and laid siege to Jerusalem. The record is not clear as to what happened to Jehoiakim. The chronicler says that he bound him with fetters to carry him to Babylon. II Chronicles 36:6. Jeremiah had said, "He shall be buried with the burial of an ass, drawn and cast forth beyond the gates of Jerusalem" (22:19).

The Reign of Jehoiachin
598 B.C.

This brought Jehoiachin (Coniah), the eighteen-year-old son of Jehoiakim, to the throne. His defiant attitude toward the Chaldeans brought again the army of Nebuchadnezzar to besiege the city. Josephus says that he surrendered on condition that the city would be left intact. This led to the first great deportation of 597 which included the royal family, all the princes and mighty men of valor, ten thousand captives, and all the craftsmen and smiths, and the prophet Ezekiel. The Chaldeans, in violation of their promise, emptied the coffers of the temple and the royal treasuries, and took also the golden vessels of Solomon and carried them to Babylon. Jehoiachin was imprisoned in Babylon for thirty-seven years until the close of Nebuchadnezzar's reign.

The Reign of Zedekiah
597-586 B.C.

Zedekiah, the third and last one of Josiah's sons to be elevated to the kingship, was then crowned king of Judah in 597 B.C. and continued to reign until the fall of Jerusalem and the final deportation of the masses to Babylon in 586 B.C.

Jeremiah continued his ministry throughout the nine years of Zedekiah's reign. The new king was inclined to treat the prophet with consideration. He was a man of some fine traits, but was not strong enough to stand against the pressures that come to one in his position. He frequently sought the counsel of Jeremiah but lacked the courage to follow the advice he gave.

Throughout the entire period of Chaldean dominion Jeremiah urged submission, because he believed firmly that the Babylonian conqueror was the servant of Jehovah, who was called to mete out justice to a disobedient nation. 27:10. The city, however, was still filled with false prophets, who predicted an early return of the exiles. "In two years they will all be back" was heard again and again on the streets and in the markets or other places where people congregated and where the problem was discussed.

During the fourth year of Zedekiah's reign, 594, Hananiah, a prophet, repeated this prediction and said that in two years Nebuchadnezzar's power would be broken. He attempted to give meaning to his words by breaking off from Jeremiah's neck a yoke or bar, a symbol of servitude which he devised and was wearing. For this act of insolence, Jeremiah predicted the early death of Hananiah because he taught the people of Jerusalem a lie. He warned this erstwhile prophet that he would die within the year and so it came to pass that "Hananiah the prophet died the same year in the seventh month" (28:17).

Jeremiah predicted that those who are now in exile will eventually rebuild the city and reclaim their homeland. He illustrated his point by the use of two baskets of figs. The figs of one basket were very good and those of the other basket were very bad, so much so that they were not usable. These latter represented the people who were left in Jerusalem at the time of the 597 deportation. They will be given, he said, to "all the kingdoms of the earth for their hurt, to be a reproach and a proverb, a taunt and a curse, in all places whither I shall drive them" (24:9). The good figs represented those of the captivity who would return and rebuild their land.

The agitation against Chaldea or Babylon did not come only from the remnant that was left in Jerusalem. Edom, Moab, Ammon, Tyre, and Sidon were among the active agitators against the rule of Nebuchadnezzar. It appears that a delegation had come to Jerusalem to influence Zedekiah against his Chaldean master and overlord. 27:3. Jeremiah warned his people, as well as those of the surrounding tribes and nations, that God will mete out punishment with the sword, and famine and pestilence to those who refuse the authority and rule of the Chaldean monarch.

But Hananiah, a son of Azur, whose home was in Gibeon, continued his propaganda of encouraging belief in the early restoration of Judah to his homeland. In the fifth month of the fourth year of Zedekiah's reign, Jeremiah was in the house of the Lord where the priests were assembled. There he heard Hananiah repeat the disturbing promises which kept the people unsettled and dissatisfied with their present state of affairs. He listened to the propagator of vain hopes and at the end of his address he said:

> *Amen:* the Lord do so: the Lord perform thy words which thou hast prophesied, to bring again the vessels of the Lord's house, and all that is carried away captive, from Babylon into this place. Nevertheless hear thou now this word that I speak in thine ears, and in the ears of all the people; the prophets that have been before me and before thee of old prophesied both against many countries, and against great kingdoms, of war, and of evil, and of pestilence. The prophet which prophesieth of peace, when the word of the prophet shall come to pass, then shall the prophet be known, that the Lord hath truly sent him (28:6-9).

A few months later Hananiah died, not knowing that his predictions had finally failed.

Jeremiah did not forget his countrymen who were taken into exile. A letter written after the deportation is recorded in chapter 29. He advised them to settle down in Babylon to build houses and plant vineyards and gardens. He urged that the young men take wives from among their own people, and raise families so that their number would not diminish but increase, and seek the peace of the city to which they were carried captive, and pray the Lord for peace thereof. In doing so, he said, they themselves shall have peace. He warned them against giving ear to the prophets that prophesy a speedy return from the captivity. He assured them that after their seventy years of servitude had been completed, the Lord would visit them and bring them back to their homeland. The tone of the entire letter bears the marks of a true pastor's heart, who is seeking the highest good of that portion of his flock which was uprooted because they failed, not only to each other as brethren, but they had failed also to live up to their highest responsibility to themselves and their God.

Zedekiah's task of governing the remnant that was left after the first deportation in 597 B.C. was not an easy one. The ablest men were gone and he, a young man of twenty-one years, was left to govern those that were not considered to be worth taking into captivity. He had to fill the positions of the government with men who were ignorant of or unschooled in the affairs of the state and the nation's relationship with other nations. Jeremiah was his ablest and most trustworthy counselor, but he was disliked by the idolatrous element, of which the population of Jerusalem and Judea was then largely composed.

Nebuchadnezzar, it appears, did not question Zedekiah's loyalty until he was informed that the king had received a delegation from the kings of Edom, Moab, Ammon, Tyre, and Sidon, whose purpose it was to form an alliance against Babylon. The false prophets of which Judah had an abundance encouraged this movement and continued their predictions of an early release of the exiles. Zedekiah became alarmed when he learned that rumors of the visit of this delegation had come to the ears of the Chaldean monarch. He then made a hurried trip to Babylon during the fourth year of his reign in order to set himself right with his sovereign overlord. Seraiah, his attendant, had taken with him some of Jeremiah's writings in which the prophet predicted the ultimate fall of Nebuchadnezzar's empire. This Seraiah was a "quiet" man and Jeremiah said:

When thou comest to Babylon, and shalt see, and shalt read all these words; then shalt thou say, O Lord, thou hast spoken against this place, to cut it off, that none shall remain in it, neither man nor beast, but that it shall be desolate forever. And it shall be, when thou hast made an end of reading this book, that thou shalt bind a stone to it, and cast it into the midst of Euphrates: and thou shalt say, Thus shall Babylon sink, and shall not rise from the evil that I will bring upon her: and they shall be weary (51:61-64).

Zedekiah's visit was evidently successful, for he was permitted to return to Jerusalem and retain his position as the head of the nation. The period of 594 to 586 was not an easy one for Jeremiah. The social and religious life of the city and also of the palace and the court was honeycombed with intrigues and excesses of all kinds. One writer says that a "man's word and his oath were strangers to each other." Sabbath observance had been largely abandoned. Idolatry and sun worship had taken over the temple in spite of Jeremiah's outspoken testimony against it.

Meanwhile, Hophra, a ruler of some importance, had risen in Egypt, and Zedekiah was persuaded to send an ambassadorial commission to him to arrange for horses and much people. Ezekiel 17:15. This was evidently in preparation for the pending attack of the Babylonians. The mission was successful. Hophra readily consented to join any movement that might bring about the downfall of the empire along the Euphrates. Zedekiah's refusal to pay the annual tribute to the Chaldeans brought Nebuchadnezzar into action and set his military machine in motion to quell this rebellion in Palestine.

The alliance, however, involved more than Judah and Egypt. Moab and Ammon, Tyre and Sidon and Edom were also involved. By this time the armies of Nebuchadnezzar were on the way toward Palestine. Somewhere along his line of march he determined by means of divination where to strike the first blow. Ezekiel 21:21. The lot fell on Jerusalem. The city was invested and the siege began in the ninth year, the tenth month, and the eleventh day of Zedekiah's elevation to the throne. It continued until the eleventh year, the fourth month, and the ninth day, when the city was broken up.

From the standpoint of hardship, disappointment, and abuse, this was perhaps the most difficult and trying period of the prophet's life. He urged submission to Nebuchadnezzar and the surrender of the city from the beginning of the invasion, but his efforts were in vain. Under the pressure of the circumstances in which Zedekiah was placed, he made a halfhearted attempt to set himself right with the God of his fathers. He ordered all the Hebrews to release their servants and set free their slaves, most of whom had, no doubt, become indentured by debt. According to the law of Moses such persons were to be set free every seventh (sabbatical) year. This law had evidently not operated for some time, but now that danger was threatening the very existence of the nation, the people complied.

Reports in the meantime had arrived that the Egyptian army, under the leadership of Hophra, was on the march to support Zedekiah. Nebuchadnezzar withdrew his army from Jerusalem in order to repulse this invasion. The Egyptians then withdrew without risking a battle and the Babylonian general returned to Jerusalem to resume the siege. During the absence of the Babylonian army, the Jews who had freed their slaves at once forced them back into bondage. During this period Jeremiah made plans to withdraw from Jerusalem and retire to his home at Anathoth. He was arrested at the gate of Benjamin and was charged with falling away to the Chaldeans. After being flogged, he was imprisoned in the dungeon of Jonathan, the scribe. 37:12, 13.

Zedekiah sent for Jeremiah when the Chaldeans returned from their Egyptian campaign to continue the siege and inquired, "Is there any word from the Lord?" Jeremiah replied: "There is: for, said he, thou shalt be delivered into the hand of the king of Babylon. Moreover Jeremiah said unto king Zedekiah, What have I offended against thee, or against thy servants, or against this people, that ye have put me in prison? Where are now your prophets which prophesied unto you, saying, The king of Babylon shall not come against you, nor against this land" (37:17-19)? Then he made a touching plea that he might not be returned to prison. He said:

> Therefore hear now, I pray thee, O my lord the king: let my supplication, I pray thee, be accepted before thee; that thou cause me not to return to the house of Jonathan the scribe, lest I die there (37:20).

On orders of the king, he was then committed to the guard court with the promise that so long as there was any bread in the city, he would be given a loaf each day. From thence he again took up his predictions of the fall of the city. In spite of his abuse and mistreatment, his message was always the same. He steadfastly maintained that the security of a nation cannot be determined by temple sacrifices and rituals. These had their place in his time but were in themselves not a guarantee of relief from the consequences of sin. Only sincere confession, repentance, and obedience to God can restore a people to their standing as His children. There was in Israel at that time a way of worship that included altars, sacrifices, and services which represented truths that would enable them to maintain a proper relationship with God. But they chose, instead, ways of worship that enabled them to satisfy their basest desires at their shrines and altars. Their disregard of Jeremiah's reproofs of their apostasy finally led to their downfall.

As a result of his persistent predictions of the fall of the city and his denunciations of the idolatry among the people, the prophet was moved, from the guard court where he had been confined, to a dungeon where he sank into the mire to his waist, until he was released on the plea of an Ethiopian slave. 38:1-13. He was again summoned before the king and asked the oft-repeated question regarding the fate of Jerusalem. He hesitated to answer and expressed his fear of being put to death. He questioned whether the king would hearken to the counsel which he would by force of his conviction be compelled to give. Zedekiah responded under oath that he would neither be put to death nor handed over to those who sought to slay him. 38:14-16. The prophet then replied without hesitation and assured him if he would surrender, his life would be spared and the city would not be destroyed, but if not, that he, the king, would be compelled to suffer and he and his family would be taken by the Chaldeans. 38:17-23. The king then warned Jeremiah on the pains of death to make no mention of this conference. 38:24.

The fate of the city hung on the decision of a wavering king who knew what was right but was afraid of the sentiment of the people and feared to trust himself to the care of God. He therefore refused the counsel of the best adviser he had because his predictions were not acceptable to the population at large.

The day of reckoning had finally come! On the ninth day of the fourth month in the eleventh year of Zedekiah's reign, the city was broken up and all the princes and the king of Babylon came in and sat in the middle gate. *The city had fallen* as Jeremiah said it would. Its glory was gone! The thing which the false prophets had said all along could not happen had finally come to pass.

When Zedekiah and his army saw what had taken place, they fled. The king and his family and retinue left by way of the king's garden and headed for the Jordan Valley. They were captured in the hills toward Jericho and were brought before Nebuchadnezzar's headquarters at Riblah in the land of Hamath, where their fate was decided. The king saw all his sons slain before his eyes, and all the nobles. Then his own eyes were put out and the world became dark forever. 39:6, 7. Jerusalem was sacked. The palace and buildings were burned; the walls of the city were demolished and the temple treasures were carried away to a strange land, to Chaldea or Neo-Babylonia, where they were stored in treasure houses. Nebuzaradan, the commander of the guard, slew all the nobles of Judah and carried into captivity all its people, except the poor who were considered to be too impotent to cause trouble. To them the conqueror gave the vineyards and fields. 39:9, 10.

When disposition had been made of the royal family and the nobility and their families, Nebuchadnezzar gave orders that

Jeremiah should be given good treatment. He was allowed to choose his own future, either accompany the captives into exile or remain in Judea with the remnant. Jeremiah chose the latter. He was then released and was given food and a reward and returned to the ruins of his country and its impoverished people. 40:4-6.

A new government was set up in Palestine under control of the conqueror. Gedaliah, who dwelt among the remnant that stayed in the land, was appointed governor. The Jews who had fled the country during the siege began to return. Among them was Ishmael, "a son of royal seed." A report was circulated that a movement was on foot among the Ammonites to have Gedaliah murdered and install Ishmael as governor. Gedaliah refused to believe this report. The insurrection, however, took place. Gedaliah was killed. Not only did they slay the remnant of the Jews that were loyal to the governor but also the Chaldean garrison that was stationed in Judea to see that the orders of their monarch would be obeyed. This tragic incident led to the migration of a large number of the Jews to Egypt. They took Jeremiah with them against his protests.

This movement to Egypt was, however, not the answer to their problem. They continued their idolatrous worship and practices in spite of the opposition of the prophet. He said:

Ye have seen all the evil that I have brought upon Jerusalem, and upon all the cities of Judah; and, behold, this day they are a desolation, and no man dwelleth therein, because of their wickedness which they have committed to provoke me to anger, in that they went to burn incense, and to serve other gods, whom they knew not, neither they, ye, nor your fathers (44:2, 3).

The prophet's words went unheeded. "Then all the men which knew that their wives had burned incense unto other gods, and all the women that stood by, a great multitude, even all the people," replied, saying:

As for the word that thou hast spoken unto us in the name of the Lord, we will not hearken unto thee. But we will certainly do whatsoever thing goeth forth out of our own mouth, to burn incense unto the queen of heaven, and to pour out drink offerings unto her, as we have done, we, and our fathers, our kings, and our princes, in the cities of Judah, and in the streets of Jerusalem: for then had we plenty of victuals, and were well, and saw no evil (44:16, 17).

The ministry of Jeremiah was a long and faithful one. He loved peace but was in conflict with the majority of the people all of his active years. He spent his life battling against idolatry, while upholding the righteousness of God. To the casual observer all his efforts would appear to have been in vain. But time has vindicated his claims for the cause of Jehovah and the principles he upheld. He insisted that Nebuchadnezzar's success was not due to the superiority of the gods he worshiped, but rather that he was an instrument in the hands of Jehovah to punish the people through whom God had chosen to make Himself known. The idea of the efficacy of idol worship seems to have been a widely spread fallacy among the pious sinners in Israel. It was not only held by the refugees in Egypt, but also by many of the exiles in Babylon that the children suffer automatically because their parents have sinned. In this case, it was certainly true. They suffered because their fathers had sinned, but they were not held responsible. Jeremiah said that "in those days they shall say no more, The fathers have eaten a sour grape, and the children's teeth are set on edge. But every one shall die for his own iniquity" (31:29, 30). This doctrine has Messianic implications that found their fullest expression in the mission of Him who was born at Bethlehem centuries later and of whom it was said:

But he was wounded for our transgressions, he was bruised for our iniquities: the chastisement of our peace was upon him; and with his stripes we are healed (Isaiah 53:5).

No one knows what finally happened to Jeremiah. Tradition has it that he was slain in Egypt. Out of the loneliness and sorrows of his exile, among a strange people in a foreign land, have come a series of five dirges known as the *Lamentations of Jeremiah*. These compositions contain descriptions of the siege of Jerusalem, the hunger and starvation and suffering of the people. They reveal the same sensitive temper that is so prominent throughout all of his writings.

Some critics question the Jeremian authorship of the Book of Lamentations. It appears to have been written by someone who was in the city and witnessed the suffering that prevailed at that time. He speaks of having been the laughingstock of the people, of having been cast into a dungeon, of children swooning in the streets, and of those who had "sodden their own children" in order to satisfy their hunger. In both books, Jeremiah and the Book of Lamentations, the troubles of Israel are traced to the same source, i.e., the personal and national sins of the rulers, the priests, the false prophets, and misplaced confidence in political allies. The writer's philosophy is phrased in the sayings of Israel's great poet-king: "He that goeth forth and weepeth, bearing precious seed, shall doubtless come again with rejoicing, bringing his sheaves with him" (Psalm 126:6).

In Jeremiah's time these promises appeared to be long in coming to maturity. But one wintry night a star stood over Bethlehem and proclaimed to the inhabitants of Babylon, perhaps descendants of those exiles who one time sat by its rivers and wept as they remembered Zion, that a KING is born and the day of the redeemer had come. Remembering this promise of hope, this lonely prophet, looking out of the gloom of his Egyptian exile, could well say of the Lord's mercies:

They are new every morning: great is thy faithfulness.

The Lord is my portion, saith my soul; therefore will I hope in him.

The Lord is good unto them that wait for him, to the soul that seeketh him.

It is good that a man should both hope and quietly wait for the salvation of the Lord.

—Lamentations 3:23-26.

18 | Ezekiel, the Prophet of the Exile

Late in the seventh century B.C. Judah's Indian summer came to an abrupt end. A major shift of military might and power had taken place. A people spoken of as the "river people," or "swamp people," rose in the lower Tigris-Euphrates Valley under the leadership of Nabopolassar, 675-605 B.C. This capable leader together with Cyaxares of Media, dealt the final blow that broke the power of the Assyrians who had dominated the political situations of the east for more than two centuries. This noted monarch led the armies of this coalition to victory in 612 B.C. when Nineveh fell and Assyria's glory came to its end. Nabopolassar's son, Nebuchadnezzar, succeeded his father as king of Babylon and defeated the remnant of the Assyrians and the armies of Egypt at Carchemish in 605 B.C. and captured Jerusalem in 598 B.C. He maintained his position as the ruling monarch of the empire until his death in 561 B.C. He was succeeded by his son, Evil-merodach, who released Jehoiachin, captive king of the Jews, from his thirty-seven years of imprisonment and gave him a place at his table above that of all the other captive princes. The reign of Evil-merodach lasted but three years. He was murdered by his brother-in-law, Neriglissar, who, it appears from the Biblical records, was a staff officer at the siege of Jerusalem. Jeremiah 39:3, 13. His successful reign was brief and came to its end in 556 B.C. His infant son Labashi-Marduk became king, but at the end of nine months he was deposed by the priestly party and Nabonidus, a man of priestly descent, was placed on the throne, which position he held for eighteen years, 556-538. He had been a successful officer in the Babylonian army and was for that reason entrusted with the affairs of the nation.

The new sovereign was, however, not primarily interested in political matters. He was a religious enthusiast, a devoted disciple of some special gods, and an antiquarian of note. He therefore turned over to his son, Belshazzar, the affairs of state while he and his daughter, the princess Belshalta-nana, devoted themselves to the building of temples, one at Ur and another at Haran. His brilliant daughter had served for a time as ambassadress to Ur, where she became a high priestess of the temple of the moon-god and a patroness of the famous boys' school of that city. She shared her father's antiquarian interests and is credited with having founded the first museum of which there is any record. She and her father brought their collection of antiques and archaeological specimens to Ur where they were carefully classified, cataloged, and mounted for display.

During his reign Nabonidus did not lose altogether his interest in the affairs of the government. He was, as he should have been, concerned about the conduct of his son Belshazzar. Among the records of his concern is the following statement:

As for me, Nabonidus, king of Babylon, save me from sinning against thy great divinity. A life of many days grant as thy gift. As for Belshazzar, the first-born son, proceeding from my loins, place in his heart fear of thy great divinity; let him not turn to sinning, let him be satisfied with the fulness of life.

While Belshazzar was frittering away the strength of the empire, and his father was puttering over his temples and antiques, a new figure loomed up on the eastern horizon. Cyrus the Persian, of whom Isaiah had spoken as the anointed of God (45:1), rose up in the east and Media and Lydia fell in rapid succession before his armies. In 539 B.C. Babylon fell also while

Belshazzar, its erstwhile king, and a thousand of his lords were indulging in a feast of debauchery.

This is a brief review of the political situation within which the exiles of Judah and Jerusalem lived after the conquest of their homeland.

Israel and Judah in Exile

The thing that the people of Israel thought could not happen had finally, in accordance with the predictions and warnings of their loyal prophets, come to pass. Jerusalem, their last hope, had fallen into the hands of pagan powers and a large and prominent part of its population was on its way into exile. For centuries the reigning monarchs of the North and East, as also those of the south country along the Nile, had looked covetously upon this prosperous little buffer state that lay between their holdings.

The process of removing the Israelites from their land began in 734 B.C. when the Assyrians carried away the first group from the Northern Kingdom. By 721 B.C. this project was practically completed and the land was repopulated with people taken from other countries. The exiles of Israel were settled in territory of the Medes, whose empire at that time extended from the borders of India to the Black Sea. Historians speak of this deported group as the "lost tribes of Israel."

But even before that the two and one-half tribes, Reuben, Gad, and one half of the tribe of Manasseh, that had settled on the east side of the Jordan at the time of the conquest of Canaan by Joshua, had been carried away by the Assyrian conquerors. Daniel and his three companions together with others were taken from Jerusalem to Babylon in 606 B.C. Jehoiachin and his mother, Nehushta, the queen, his entourage, and ten thousand of the best and most capable of its citizens and their families, were taken to the Tigris-Euphrates Valley in 596 B.C. and settled on lands along these rivers. Among them was a prophet, Ezekiel, who was to figure largely in their affairs during the years of their exile.

The destruction of Jerusalem and the deportation of a prominent part of its population were a severe blow to the people whose claim to Palestine dates back to the days of Abraham.

They had, with the exception of periodic sojourns in Egypt, occupied it with varying security and success during all those
years up to the time of the Chaldean invasion. They believed
throughout all this time that nothing like this calamity could befall them. But they had not reckoned with all the factors that
entered into the situation. Their continued complacency and
waywardness in the presence of the evils of their time finally
led to their defeat.

Fortunately the kings of the east, Nebuchadnezzar of Babylonia, Darius of Media, and Cyrus of Persia, were considered
benevolent rulers in their day when compared with those of
Assyria and other nations with which the Israelites had come in
contact earlier, or even with those of the modern states of the
Soviets, the Nazis, and Fascists of the recent past. The exiles were
given lands on which they could settle. The soil was composed
of rich alluvial deposits and crops grew and produced abundant
yields where water for irrigation was available. Many of the exiles
became successful in business and still others like Daniel and
his three friends were educated for service in the government,
where they occupied positions of honor and renown. The temple
treasures and vessels of the Lord's house were held intact
throughout the reign of Nebuchadnezzar, and also throughout the
reigns of the Medes and Persians. Ezra 1:7-11.

But the displaced settlers were homesick. They were a people in a strange land, among a race whose culture and interests
differed widely from those of these uprooted pilgrims whose
shattered hopes cut deeply into their lives, as is always the case
when memories come thronging out of the past. They needed
more than homes and food. They needed the steadying influence
and power of the divine spirit to tide them through the maze and
bewilderments of their defeats and losses as well as the strange-
ness and temptations of their new surroundings. Their mission
had not reached its fulfillment. They were still a people through
whom God was to reveal Himself and His workings in the hearts
of men. Therefore He, in His providence, provided them with
a spokesman, a prophet whose duty it was to keep alive among
them the faith of Abraham, which they had aforetime been on
the verge of losing when during their sojourn in Egypt they

were intimately exposed to the religious practices of a people whose ceremonies and idols were made attractive and impressive. Here in this strange land, between the Tigris and Euphrates rivers, they were to be exposed again to the same situations and problems. The attitude of the native population of Babylonia toward these alien people was that of hate, tolerance, and respect. The attitude of the government, it appears, was considerate.

Among the exiles there was a prophet named Ezekiel, who was destined to become their counselor, their spiritual leader and adviser. We know almost nothing of his childhood and background, except that being a priest he must have come from the line of Levi. He was a person of unusual personal qualities and was, no doubt, considered by some a queer and peculiar character. He was the prophet of hope at a time when conditions seemed hopeless. He was to keep the embers of faith alive and fan them into a flame that would keep the exiles together until the day when they could return to their homeland.

His call came out of a dust storm. His charge was given in the form of a roll. One would judge that the book that bears his name was written by himself. With few exceptions it was written in the first person. The events of history, concerning which he writes, come as nearly as one can determine in consecutive and chronological order. The book begins with his call and closes with the vision of the ever-widening stream that flows from under the *eastern gate* of the temple to an unbounded destination.

His home appears to have been kept open to the people of his parish, which extended to the borders of the land occupied by the exiles and beyond. We read of delegations calling at his home for consultation and counsel. Among them were commissions and delegations from Jerusalem. 33:21. His manner of imparting knowledge and of delivering his messages was unusual, so much so that he was spoken of, perhaps reproachfully, as a speaker of parables. 20:49. His discourses are loaded with visions, parables, allegories, symbolical action, and picturesque illustrations.

Scholars and commentators usually divide the book into three sections as follows:

1. Chapters 1—24. This section covers the period of four

and one-half years, from the date of the prophet's call in the fifth
year of the exile to the siege of Jerusalem in 588 B.C.

2. Chapters 25–32 deal with prophecies which were delivered against the nations that had contributed to Israel's delinquency or that had joined in the wars against her or had rejoiced over her misfortunes and sorrows.

3. Chapters 33–48 are largely futuristic in their content and
contain visions of the restoration of Israel and beyond.

Ezekiel's Call

The prophet, in speaking of his call, says that it came in the
thirtieth year, in the fourth month and the fifth day of the
month, when he was by the River Chebar, "that the heavens
were opened, and . . . [he] saw visions of God" (1:1). The date
here given evidently has reference to his age. He gives also
definitely the date of his call to the prophetic ministry. It was
on the "fifth day of the month, which was the fifth year of king
Jehoiachin's captivity" and imprisonment when Ezekiel was in the
land of the Chaldeans by the River Chebar and the hand of the
Lord was there upon him. 1:2.

What happened that day was an event that was not to be
forgotten. A whirlwind in the desert is in itself frequently an
occurrence that will be remembered. In this case he describes
the infolding fire and the four living creatures with their
mysterious faces and hands that appeared like burning coals.
And above the firmament that was over their heads was a throne
upon which was the likeness of the appearance of a man and
over it "the appearance of the bow that is in the cloud in the day
of rain." This, says the prophet, was "the appearance of the likeness of the glory of the Lord." (See 1:4-28.)

The commission or charge Ezekiel received that day was not
inspiring, but it was challenging. The voice said:

Son of man, I send thee to the children of Israel, to a rebellious nation that hath rebelled against me: they and their
fathers have transgressed against me, even unto this very
day. For they are impudent children and stiffhearted. . . .
And thou shalt say unto them, Thus saith the Lord God. And
they, whether they will hear, or whether they will forbear,

. . . yet shall know that there hath been a prophet among them (2:3-5).

Then a hand gave the prophet a roll of a book, the words of which he was to absorb and deliver to his people. His mission was a bitter one, for the faces of his audience were hard. 3:8.

This complex symbol of the majesty and power of the omnipotent God reappeared again and again during the prophet's ministry. He was destined to become a lonely man far removed from his homeland among a people who were embittered with their losses and misfortunes. Here, in these pagan surroundings, he was delegated to indoctrinate, instruct, and reprove an erring race and restore a faith that was badly infected with the seeds of idolatry and godlessness. Many of them in spite of their misfortunes still held, it appeared, to idolatrous modes of worship and maintained that such practices were not inconsistent with the worship of Jehovah, which also consisted of altars and rites and ceremonies. Some of them evidently complained that they were made to suffer for sins which others had committed (28:2, 25; 33:10, 17, 20) and accused the Lord of dealing inequitably and unjustly with them. They were encouraged in their critical attitude by prophets who predicted that they would, within a short time, be permitted to return to their former homes.

Ezekiel went, in bitterness and in the heat of his spirit, to assume his tasks. When, however, he came to the exile camp by the River Chebar, "sat where they sat," and saw their destitution, loneliness, homesickness, and despair, he remained there astonished—stupefied—for seven days. There he saw again the "glory of the Lord" and the spirit entered into him and he was set upon his feet and warned to speak only when the Lord moved him to do so, "for they are a rebellious house," he said.

The destruction of Jerusalem, which appeared to be inevitable, lay heavily upon the soul of the prophet. The 390 years of Israel's vacillating loyalty to Jehovah and Judah's forty years of rebellion are graphically set forth by Ezekiel in a dramatic act in chapter 4. For 390 days he personally was to lay siege to a miniature city which God had designed to pay for Israel's iniquity and forty more days for the iniquity of Judah. During this period he was to eat only limited siege rations, "bread by weight,

and with care" and "water by measure, and with astonishment"—
stupefaction. The fate of the nation was illustrated later when
one day he shaved his head with a barber's razor and divided the
hair carefully by weight into three parts. He burned one third
by fire in the midst of the city. Another third was cut to pieces,
violently, with a knife, and the remaining third was scattered
to the wind. Of this latter portion he was instructed to take "a
few in number" and tie them in his skirts. Thus was told in a
sad, picturesque way the story of the fate of the people who
once possessed Jerusalem, but who were then in the process of
destruction by warfare, famine, and exile. Of the latter portion,
but few, in the providence of God, would be saved. One can
imagine that the peculiar acts and conduct of this man would
draw large crowds to witness his performances. Some, no doubt,
turned away in disgust; others mocked; and a few, pitifully few,
took the lesson to heart.

judgement

Ezekiel is exact in giving dates, although the base from
which his reckonings are made is not always clear. He says, in
chapter 8, that in the sixth year, the sixth month, and the fifth
day of the month, a delegation of the elders of Judah sat before
him and that the hand of the Lord was upon him. From a
mysterious image a hand reached out, took him by a lock of his
hair, and transported him to Jerusalem, to the temple where he
saw again the image he had seen in the storm on the plains of
Babylon. He was led from room to room within the temple and
was shown the abominations that were being practiced there.
Through a secret door he gained admittance to the inner chamber
whose walls were covered with images of creeping things, abominable beasts, and all the idols of the house of Israel. There, too,
he saw seventy men of the ancients of Israel, among whom was
Jaazaniah, the son of Shaphan, a Rechabite, a sect that had
been pledged to a life of primitive simplicity and purity. Now
one of their number was with the apostates of Israel who, with
smoking censors in their hands, were worshiping the imagery
portrayed on the walls. He saw women sitting at the north door
of the temple, weeping and worshiping Tammuz, the god of
agriculture, whom they, no doubt, implored to come back and
restore the harvests that had failed. Between the altar and the

*likely famine encouraged this
in their attitude of unbelief, and failure
to recognize judgement*

porch he saw twenty-five men facing the east and worshiping the sun. Chapter 8. Then he saw again the image he had seen on the plains, this time lifting itself and departing from the temple. It settled on a mountain toward the east. 10 and 11:1-23. God had departed from His temple. His house was emptied of His glory and the city was doomed.

The rumors of an early return of the exiles, however, persisted in spite of the unfavorable news from Jerusalem, whose existence was thought to be secure because the temple of God was there. This agitation prevented the exiles from settling down in their foreign homes and taking advantage of the opportunities that their new master made available to them. Nor did they want to accept the penalty that God had laid upon them for their unfaithfulness. Hence, the "word of the Lord" came again to Ezekiel, saying, "Son of man, thou dwellest in the midst of a rebellious house, which have eyes to see, and see not; they have ears to hear, and hear not" (12:2). Therefore, he was instructed to prepare his belongings as one who readies himself for flight from an enemy. He packed his goods in the presence of those who looked on, dug a hole in the wall of his house, covered his face as one who does not wish to be recognized, and at twilight he bore his belongings upon his shoulders as one who is fleeing from a beleaguered place. When those who were standing by asked, "What doest thou?" then he explained the meaning of his acts. 12:3-9. This burden, the prophet said, concerns the princes of Jerusalem and all the house of Israel. "Like as I have done, so shall it be done unto them" (12:11).

Ezekiel was constantly opposed by prophets whom he accuses of prophesying "out of their own hearts" (13:2). He likens them to foxes of the desert and to builders that build with untempered mortar that cannot withstand the elements of the weather. He compares them to lewd women who adorn themselves with strange garments to attract men and hunt for their souls. 13:17-23.

He refers to a conference with the elders of Israel who had come to his house (chapter 14), whom he accuses of having put "the stumblingblock of their iniquity" before the people. He has no word of consolation for them and reaffirms his prediction of

Judah's downfall and famine and pestilence which he assures them cannot be avoided even though Noah, Daniel, and Job were involved in the sufferings.

Ezekiel is fond of allegory and makes extensive use of illustrations and figurative language. He likens Jerusalem to an unwanted child who at birth was left in an open field with its "navel" untreated, unwashed, and unsalted, and unswaddled. This waif was found by a stranger who adopted her and bestowed upon her his love and his wealth and gave her a home. She grew into a beautiful woman and then played the harlot and bestowed her love and substance upon lewd lovers. Chapter 16. He compares Jehoiachin and Zedekiah to vines that grew between two great eagles, Egypt and Babylon, by whom they were uprooted and carried away. Chapter 17.

The source of Judah's trouble lay in the past, and the people placed the blame for their distress on their own ancestors. "The fathers have eaten sour grapes, and the children's teeth are set on edge," they said. 18:2. Ezekiel admits that Judah's trouble had its source in the past but insists that the people of his day are not suffering because of what their ancestors did, but for what they themselves are doing. He blames Josiah's wife, Judah's queen, for having contributed largely to the evils of her time, and the waywardness of her sons who succeeded their father to the throne. He says their mother was a lioness, "she lay down among lions, she nourished her whelps [Jehoahaz, Jehoiakim, Jehoiachin, a grandson, and Zedekiah] among young lions. And . . . [they] learned to catch the prey" (19:2, 3). Beginning with Jehoahaz they followed each other to the exalted position of the throne of Judah. Historians tell us of their misrule and of their tragic fate. Jehoahaz was taken to Egypt where he disappeared; Jehoiakim came to a tragic death in Jerusalem; Jehoiachin, a grandson, spent thirty-seven years in a Babylonian prison; and Zedekiah, blinded after he saw his own children killed, died in exile. The mother, though she had "strong rods for the sceptres . . . was plucked up in fury," Ezekiel said, "cast down to the ground, and the east wind dried up her fruit." She was "planted in the wilderness, in a dry and thirsty ground" (19:11-13).

On the tenth day of the fifth month of the seventh year, the

prophet had another meeting with the elders of Israel who came
to inquire of the Lord. 20:1. But information from that source
was not available. "As I live, saith the Lord God, I will not be
enquired of by you" (20:3). But Ezekiel had something to say
and what he said was not a message that inspired hope. 20:5-49.
One cannot be certain whether chapters 21 and 23 are part of
the record of this meeting, but the message is full of predictions
of destruction. The armies of Chaldea were on the march to
Jerusalem, the prophet said. He speaks of the field marshal,
halting at the crossroads to determine, by divination, where to
strike the first blow. The lot fell upon Jerusalem. 21:2-26. The
tenth day of the tenth month of the ninth year was a never-to-be-
forgotten day in Ezekiel's life. It was the day when the siege began. He was instructed to mark the date on the calendar. 24:1, 2.
He says sadly, "So I spake unto the people in the morning: and
at even my wife died" (24:18).

Prophecies Against the Nations That
Contributed to Israel's Fall

Ezekiel's prophecies, against the nations that surrounded
Judah, continued with bitterness. The people and tribal bands
that surrounded Israel and Judah were never reconciled, it appears, to have this people who had grown strong and powerful
during their sojourn in Egypt reclaim the lands which were
promised to Abraham their father centuries earlier. Ammon and
Moab, whose father (Lot) had benefited by Abraham's generosity, looked grudgingly upon the success of the returning Hebrews. Edom shared their animosity, as did Tyre and Sidon,
whose streets resounded with the noises of the markets and the
exploits of sailors who brought home with them the wares and
vices of the lands beyond the sea.

Dark and gloomy as the future appeared, the prophet's messages are, nevertheless, sprinkled with words of hope. The day
will come, the Lord said, "When I shall have gathered the house
of Israel from the people among whom they are scattered, and
shall be sanctified in them in the sight of the heathen, then shall
they dwell in their land that I have given to my servant Jacob"
(28:25).

In the twelfth year of the captivity, the tenth month and the fifth day of the month, a messenger who had escaped from Jerusalem came to Ezekiel's house and informed him that the city had fallen. 33:21. The prophet says that the hand of the Lord was upon him. The evening before the tragic news came he was speechless. People, he says, were still talking against him by the walls and in the doors of the houses, saying, "Come, I pray you, and hear what is the word that cometh forth from the Lord. . . . With their mouth they shew much love, but their heart goeth after their covetousness" (33:30, 31). To them he was just "a very lovely song of one that hath a pleasant voice, and can play well on an instrument: for they hear thy words, but they do them not" (33:32).

Now that Jerusalem had fallen, and their armies were defeated and destroyed, another great deportation took place. Israel's hope, at that time, may well have struck a new low. Surely the prospect was not an inspiring one. Only the poor were left in the land. Then the Lord took Ezekiel out to a valley filled with dry bones, bleached in the sun and weatherworn by the winds and storms of the desert. One who looked for life could hardly have found a more unpromising prospect. The prophet was commanded to preach to these "dry bones." As he spoke, there was a stir and out from among them arose an army exceedingly great. 37:1-10. "These bones are the whole house of Israel," the Lord said. Now that Jerusalem is lost, the people say, "Our bones are dried, and our hope is lost" (37:11). "Therefore . . . say unto them, . . . I will open your graves, and . . . bring you into the land of Israel. And ye shall know that I am the Lord" (37:12, 13).

In the five and twentieth year of the captivity, on the tenth day of the month of the fourteenth year after the city was smitten, the prophet was taken in visions of God to Jerusalem. There he was shown the plan of the new city and of the temple. He looked out from the eastern gate and saw again the image of the glory of God that he first saw by the River Chebar, and which he had last seen as it departed from the desecrated temple some years before. Now the glory of the Lord returned again to His temple and to His people, this time by way of the *eastern gate*. He was with

His people once again. Through them, in the course of time, would come the Messiah, the world's greatest gift at Bethlehem. He saw also the flow of a new stream which issued out from under the threshold eastward. At first it was a mere trickle which increased in volume as it flowed. A man with a measuring rod followed its course. At the distance of a thousand cubits it was ankle deep; at two thousand cubits the waters reached to a man's knees; at three thousand the waters came to his loins. Beyond that it became a stream to swim in and farther on it became a flood that could not be passed over. Chapter 47. Such was the life-giving stream that had a small beginning but increased in its flow and brought life and hope to all the lands through which it flowed and will continue in its course unto the end of time.

Hebrews in the School of Adversity

The people of the Northern Kingdom who were deported in 722 B.C. were absorbed by the population of the nations among whom they lived. They appear no more in history as a people. After the fall of Jerusalem in 586 B.C., some fifty thousand, all told, were deported to Babylon, or Chaldea, as it was then known. Among them were what was considered the ablest and best of the group. The greater number of those that were left in Palestine finally migrated to Egypt where they probably identified themselves with those who had previously settled in that country. They were located at first in the Lower Nile country in and around Tahpanhes and Migdol. When, however, their trading privileges were withdrawn, some of them returned to Palestine and others settled in Upper Egypt near Memphis and Pathros and on an island in the River Nile near Assuan. This group, however, does not figure in the affairs of Palestine after the Babylonian conquest, except as individuals or small groups may have returned to their former homeland.

Great changes took place in their way of living and their outlook on life during the years of their sojourn in Babylonia. They had been taken from a small country made up largely of hills and valleys from which the husbandman succeeded in coaxing from the soil, with considerable effort, the means of his livelihood. The government was constantly confronted with the task of warding off marauding bands of invaders that threatened to encroach upon their territory. In Babylonia or Chaldea conditions were different. During the greater part of their sojourn in that country the government was strong and stable. The soil was good and the land was easily tilled. A network of irrigating ditches covered the country and crops yielded abundantly. One would say that on the whole the government was benevolent and their property, such as they were able to accumulate, was secure. Many of them prospered. Some of them acquired wealth. Others became engaged in business affairs and some of them held positions of eminence and honor in the government.

They enjoyed also a large measure of religious freedom. But they were without their temple, their altars, and their paraphernalia of worship. Consequently, they had to devise other ways and means of perpetuating their faith. They had with them their book of the law, to which they no doubt turned for consolation. After the first years of uncertainty and homesickness were over, they settled down and made use of such means as were available in order to maintain themselves physically and spiritually. The synagogue, which was destined to occupy such a large place in their lives, was probably brought into existence during the captivity. Here their children were taught and it appears that a form of worship was developed that greatly influenced all the later years of their existence. A new class of leaders known as the scribes grew out of this situation, and in the years that followed they largely molded the thought and life of the group. Their influence continued through the following centuries until the fall of Jerusalem in A.D. 70, the final dispersion, and beyond.

These disasters and defeats, filled with sorrows and hardship, were purifying measures within a maturing race that gave to the world a knowledge of Jehovah, the living God, and gave to mankind the Scriptures which bear a revelation of God and a record of their experience that, together with the New Testament which is also a book of Jewish origin, has become the source of knowledge out of which the Christian Church grew. Since that time Israel has been a nation within the nations, and continues so, except for the small portion that again occupies a part of the soil that was one time their homeland.

The prospect that looked so hopeless as the exiles sat by the rivers of Babylon and wept was in the long run turned into victory. The "dry bones" of the valley were brought to life, not by the incantations of the priests, nor by the fires that burned on their altars, nor by the means of tithes and offerings, but by the spirit of God, who said, "[I] shall put my spirit in you, and ye shall live!"

Thus the seed of Abraham still survives. Their exilic experience broadened their understanding of their mission and gave them more lofty ideals to live by. It enabled them, also, to give to the world a legacy of spiritual truth, that has enriched the cultures of all the races and places, whomsoever and wheresoever it touched, and shed upon them a Light Divine!

19 | Daniel, Statesman and Counselor of Kings

After the fall of Jerusalem in 605 B.C., Nebuchadnezzar instructed Ashpenaz, the master of his eunuchs, to select certain specially qualified men of the children of Israel, "of the king's seed, and of the princes . . . such as had ability in them to stand in the king's palace." From this statement it would appear that they were to be in some way connected with the royal family. They were to be selected on the basis of their personality, physical soundness, and intellectual ability, men whom "they might teach the learning and the tongue of the Chaldeans." They were not hostages nor prisoners of war, but civilians that were to be educated and trained for service in the government. Among those of the children of Israel or Judah who became prominent were Daniel, Hananiah, Mishael, and Azariah. Their Hebrew names were dropped at once when they arrived in Babylon and they were given new names as follows: Daniel was called Belteshazzar, Hananiah was named Shadrach, Mishael's name was changed to Meshach, and Azariah was given the name Abednego. Of this group, Daniel became eminent above all the others. His leadership ability became evident from the beginning and he rose rapidly to positions of highest trust, dignity, and honor in the empire. He early won the confidence of Nebuchadnezzar and when the kingdom fell to the Medes and Persians, he was retained in the service of the succeeding monarchs during the seventy years of his public life. He was distinguished not only for his sagacity and shrewdness but also for his piety and his devotion to the God of his fathers to whom he was steadfastly loyal. His contemporaries classified him already, in his own time, with such of their great heroes as Noah and Job. Ezekiel 14:14, 20; 28:3.

Daniel is listed in the Bible among the prophets. His ministry, however, differed widely in many respects from that of other prophets. He was a seer, and an interpreter of dreams and visions that had futuristic content. He was, in that respect, able to foresee events and movements that lay beyond his day and time. There is almost no record of sermons that dealt with the moral, social, or spiritual problems of his time, although it is evident from his life and attitude that he was deeply concerned about such affairs. He was a statesman who occupied high and responsible positions of trust in a succession of Gentile governments. He performed the function of his office with honesty and in accordance with such principles as were in harmony with the will of the God he knew. To Him he bore faithful witness in all his dealings with the kings and potentates of his day.

The book that bears his name does not give the reader a biographical sketch of his life. It consists rather of a series of episodes or incidents that are taken from the reigns of four kings under whom he served. Chapters 1–4 deal with three different incidents that took place during the reign of King Nebuchadnezzar. Chapters 5, 7, 8 deal with happenings that took place during the reign of Belshazzar. Chapters 6 and 9 deal with events that occurred during his service at the court of Darius, the Mede. Chapters 10, 11, 12 give the record of his vision of the glory of the Lord while he served at the court of Cyrus.

Nebuchadnezzar, the king of Babylon under whom Daniel first served, was a true son of Babylon, says Goodspeed in his history of the Babylonians and Assyrians. He was not an Assyrian. He was a man of peace, not of war. He was a devotee of religion and culture and not of organization and administration. His strength as a world ruler lay in his inheritance. His father set up the organization and introduced the forms of government and methods of operation and control which were bequeathed as it were by the Assyrians. His father had also sponsored an alliance with the Medes by which Nebuchadnezzar benefited. He shared the ruthless energy, enjoyed the luxury, and when necessary exercised the means of cruelty that characterized the reign of the great Semitic monarchs of his time. He was inclined toward religion and some of his inscriptions express a loftiness of sentiment that stands unequaled in the annals of the royal literature of the pagan world.

> O eternal prince, Lord of all being!
> As for the king whom Thou lovest, and
> Whose name Thou hast proclaimed,
> As was pleasing to Thee,
> Do Thou lead aright his life,
> Guide him in a straight path.
> I am the prince obedient to Thee,
> The creature of Thy hand.
> Thou hast created me and
> With dominion over all people,
> Thou hast instructed me.
> According to Thy grace, O Lord,
> Which Thou dost bestow on all people,
> Cause me to love Thy supreme dominion,
> And create in my heart
> The worship of Thy god-head.
> And grant whatsoever is pleasing to Thee,
> Because Thou hast fashioned my life.

see p 206

Nebuchadnezzar's reign was vigorous and successful, but his dynasty was painfully unstable and unsuited for the high office and responsibilities to which his descendants fell heir. His son, son-in-law, and grandson who succeeded him occupied the throne a little more than six years when the nobles, tired of their rule, placed Nabonidus on the throne which he left, with its problems, cares, and responsibilities, largely to his irresponsible son, Belshazzar, who brought the onetime glorious kingdom of the Chaldeans to its end. Historians tell us little of the misrule of this playboy, and practically all we know is what, according to Daniel, took place on the fateful night when the kingdom fell into the hands of the Medes and Persians, and what can be gathered, meagerly, from the archives of the past.

The first problem that was to test the faith and loyalty of these three young Hebrews came when they were issued their food. It may be assumed with confidence that rations from the king's table would be wholesome and acceptable. But to the Hebrews there were other problems involved. It consisted, in all probability, of food that had been offered to idols and as such it would not be acceptable to the Jews. To have outrightly refused it on such grounds would almost certainly have created unfavorable reactions from the palace. Daniel then wisely suggested to those who served them that during a trial plan for ten days they should be served very simple, but wholesome food. This appeared to have been acceptable to the servants, who likely enjoyed the portions from the king's table during this period. The plan worked so satisfactorily that it was continued. The tact and shrewdness with which this problem was handled were manifested frequently during Daniel's long years of service in the state, which he served with prominence and honor until 486 B.C., while his disheartened countrymen languished in exile by the rivers of Babylon, waiting longingly for the day when their deliverance should come.

Nebuchadnezzar, it appears from such records as are available, was during the years of his reign troubled with dreams. One of them was so impressive that it virtually haunted him, even though he could not recall what it was. The wise men, soothsayers, and astrologers that occupied a prominent place in the Oriental courts were supposedly able to take care of such matters, but in this case they failed. This drew from the baffled monarch a rash order that all of them, including Daniel and his three friends, should be slain. The test of whether their interpretation was true was to be determined by their ability to tell what the dream was. Through Arioch, the captain of the king's guard, Daniel secured an audience with the king. Again, his calmness and cool judgment prevailed. He saw no reason, he said, for hasty action and assured the king that if given time he would show him its meaning. During a period of prayer, Daniel and his three friends called upon their God that His "mercies" might be made known. Then the answer came to Daniel in a night vision. The beautiful little prayer of chapter 2:20-23 expresses his gratitude to Him who holds all the secrets of the ages in His mind.

Blessed be the name of God for ever and ever: for wisdom and might are his: and he changeth the times and the seasons: he removeth kings, and setteth up kings: he giveth wisdom unto the wise, and knowledge to them that know understanding: he revealeth the deep and secret things: he knoweth what is in the darkness, and the light dwelleth with him. I thank thee, and praise thee, O thou God of my fathers, who hast given me wisdom and might, and hast made known unto me what we desired of thee: for thou hast now made known unto us the king's matter.

Daniel then called for an audience with the king and assured him that the secret was not revealed to him so that his reputation might be established or enhanced but that the king might know the thoughts of his heart. 2:30. The meaning of the mystical image which the king saw in his dreams was described. Nebuchadnezzar was to have a large part in the world system of kingdoms which was symbolized by the image. It was to be a kingdom of power and strength and glory whose borders would extend to every place where the children of men dwell and where the beasts of the field and fowls of the heavens are. 2:37, 38. After him there should rise another kingdom, he said, and a third kingdom which shall rule over the earth. This shall be succeeded by a fourth kingdom strong as iron with feet of iron mingled with clay. This is to be followed by a kingdom set up by God Himself and the kingdom of iron shall be destroyed by a "stone [that] was cut out of the mountain without hands."

Daniel's integrity was established. The king was satisfied with the answer, and recognized the God of the Hebrews as a "God of gods, and a Lord of kings." Daniel was then promoted to a position that included the administrative affairs of the whole province of Babylon. At the request of Daniel, his three friends were set over the affairs of the province of Babylon and Daniel sat in the gate of the king. 2:48, 49.

The Hebrews who had been so signally honored and promoted were soon to learn that their position did not exempt them
from further temptation and danger. A convocation of all government officials, great and small, was called to attend the dedication of an image, perhaps a shaft, topped with an image, ninety
feet tall and nine feet square at its base. In order to assure himself of a good audience, the king made attendance at this cere-
mony compulsory on the pains of death. After the services
certain ones of the children of the Hebrews were accused of not
having participated in the exercises. This involved three of the
four Hebrew children, Shadrach, Meshach, and Abednego, upon
whom the king had bestowed great honors. Again, their loyalty
to Jehovah and their faith in Him were manifested when to the
amazement of the king they survived the flames of the fiery
furnace. Again they were promoted and their God was exalted.

Once more the king had a dream that troubled him (4:4, 5),
and again his wise men and astrologers and magicians failed him
and Daniel was called upon to give the interpretation. This time
the fate of the king himself was involved. Daniel, when he heard
the dream and realized what it all meant, was astonished—stunned
—for an hour. But with the king's encouragement he gave the
interpretation. "The dream," Daniel said, is "to them that hate
thee, and the interpretation thereof to thine enemies!" You are
the tree. Your greatness has increased and reached unto heaven
and your dominion to the end of the earth. The "watcher" which
came down from heaven cried mightily, "Hew the tree down,"
and scatter the leaves and branches, but bind the stump with an
iron band. This symbolized the king's fall. His heart was to be
changed from a man's heart to a beast's heart. Therefore Daniel
urged, "O king, let my counsel be acceptable unto thee, and
break off thy sins by righteousness, and thine iniquities by shew-
ing mercy to the poor; if it may be a lengthening of thy tran-
quillity" (4:27).

Twelve months went by. Time may have mellowed the shock
which followed the interpretation of the strange dream. Then,
as this mighty monarch walked in the palace of the kingdom of
Babylon one day and pondered upon his great accomplishments,
he said, "Is not this great Babylon, that I have built for the house

of the kingdom by the might of my power, and for the honour
of my majesty?" While the words were yet in his mouth, the
writer says, a voice from heaven pronounced his doom, saying,
"O king Nebuchadnezzar, to thee it is spoken; Thy kingdom is
departed from thee" (4:30, 31). That same hour he was driven
from men and lived like the animals of the field. The writer says
that he "did eat grass as oxen, and his body was wet with the dew
of heaven, till his hairs were grown like eagles' feathers, and his
nails like birds' claws" (4:33).

Time passed by, but the kingdom was in good hands. Before this calamity struck, he had placed Daniel and his friends
in positions of power and trust. When the time of his deliverance
had come, the king says:

At the end of the days I Nebuchadnezzar lifted up mine
eyes unto heaven, and mine understanding returned unto me,
and I blessed the most High, and I praised and honoured
him that liveth for ever, whose dominion is an everlasting
dominion, and his kingdom is from generation to generation.
. . . At the same time my reason returned unto me; and for
the glory of my kingdom, mine honour and brightness returned unto me; and my counsellors and my lords sought unto me; and I was established in my kingdom, and excellent
majesty was added unto me. Now I Nebuchadnezzar praise
and extol and honour the King of heaven, all whose works
are truth, and his ways judgment: and those that walk in
pride he is able to abase (4:34, 36, 37).

Daniel and Belshazzar
Prince Regent During Reign of Nabonidus

Belshazzar was apparently coregent with his father Nabonidus, who turned over to his son the affairs of state while he was
absorbed with his archaeological pursuits and his temples and
books—a field in which, as already noted, he made noteworthy
discoveries and achievements. The problems of the nation, however, did not entirely rise out of the political situation of his time.
Secular records of that period indicate that great changes had
taken place in the social and commercial life of the country.
Ezekiel speaks of his people having been carried into a "land

of traffick" and set in a "city of merchants" (Ezekiel 17:4). The pre-eminence of commercial pursuits and industrial life and activity had brought about great changes in the social and economic life of Babylon. The distinctions between the noble and the common man were tempered by the spirit of commercial and business relationships. Even the names of kings and princes appear in documents which describe ordinary business transactions. Neriglissar's documents show that he borrowed money to build a house, and Belshazzar, the reigning monarch, sold wool and took security for its payment as any ordinary merchant would. Merchant princes and ecclesiastical lords, it appears, had taken the place of the old aristocracy.

Daniel also was a man given to dreams. He says in chapter 7 of his book that in the first year of Belshazzar he "had a dream and visions of his head upon his bed," and that he then "wrote the dream, and told the sum [or gist] of the matters" (7:1). Four great beasts, he says, rose up out of the earth. The first one was like a lion with wings like an eagle. Its wings were plucked and it was made to stand upon its feet like a man and was given a man's heart. The second one, like a bear, raised itself on its side and had three ribs in its mouth. It was told to arise and devour much flesh. The third had the form of a leopard with four wings of a fowl upon its back. Dominion was given to it. The fourth beast was dreadful and terrible and strong with teeth of iron. It was diverse from all the others and had ten horns. It was destructive and devoured and broke in pieces its antagonists, and the residue it stamped with its feet. While he was considering this beast a little horn with eyes arose upon its head and its mouth spoke great things. He looked, he says, until the thrones were cast down and the "Ancient of days" did sit. A fiery stream issued and came forth from him. Thousands and ten thousand times ten thousand stood before him, and the judgment was set, and the books were opened. He saw the beast with the horn slain and the rest of the beasts had their dominion taken away but their lives were prolonged for a season. Then he saw one like the Son of Man come with the clouds of heaven to the Ancient of days and He was given dominion and a kingdom in which all people, regardless of race or nationality or language,

should serve Him. His kingdom is an everlasting kingdom that
shall not be destroyed. It has its beginning in the realm of time
and continues on to where time shall be no more. 7:1-14.

The interpretation of the vision was given to Daniel by one
who stood by. The beasts which he saw are four kings, the messenger said, that shall rise, but the saints of the Most High shall
prevail. The fourth beast shall be different from the other kingdoms. It shall speak words against the Most High, and shall wear
out the saints and think to change times and laws, but in the
judgment his dominion shall be taken away and the kingdom
shall be given to the saints who shall serve and obey him. Daniel
says in conclusion that his thoughts greatly upset him or troubled
him, but he kept the matter in his heart. 7:15-28.

In the third year of Belshazzar another vision appeared to
him while he was at Shushan in the palace, in the province of
Elam by the River Ulai. He saw a ram which had two horns.
The two horns were high, but one was higher than the other and
the higher one came up last. The ram pushed westward and
northward and southward and swept everything before it. While
he was considering this, he says, he saw an he-goat come out of
the west and destroy the ram. Out of this last power was to come
a little horn that would wax strong and take away the daily
sacrifice. The place of the sanctuary would be cast down, and
be trodden underfoot for two thousand three hundred days when
it shall be cleansed. 8:1-14.

When the vision was explained, the messenger Gabriel said
that the ram with two horns represents the kings of Media and
Persia. The rough goat is the king of Greece and the great horn
is the first king. Daniel says he was faint and sick for a number
of days. Then he rose up and attended to the king's business.
8:15-27.

Belshazzar's reign was drawing to its close. Cyrus of Persia
had risen and become a new power to be reckoned with in the
east. His success caused alarm among the older states of the
Orient and they prepared themselves to resist his progress. In
545 an alliance of Lydia, Egypt, Sparta, and the war party of
Babylon was defeated by Cyrus. Babylon's time had now come.
Historians say that in October 539 B.C. the Medes and Persians

broke through the defenses of Opis and Belshazzar's army was driven back. With the fall of Sippar, the king took refuge within the defenses of Babylon, within whose lofty walls he doubtless felt secure. The Persian general, Gobryas, it is thought, found friends within the fortifications of the city who opened the gates and the city fell. Belshazzar and a thousand of his lords were at that time banqueting and engaged in a drunken revelry when suddenly a mysterious hand wrote a startling message on the wall. In the panic that followed, the queen, who was perhaps Belshazzar's mother, remembered Daniel, whom Nebuchadnezzar had made master of the wise men and astrologers, and suggested that he should be sent for and consulted. When he arrived on the sordid scene, the king met him and promised to reward him and clothe him in scarlet with a golden chain around his neck if he would interpret the mysterious writing. Daniel waved all these aside with the remark, "Let thy gifts be to thyself, and give thy rewards to another; yet I will read the writing unto the king, and make known to him the interpretation" (5:17). Following a short address in which he reminded Belshazzar of the great things God had done for Nebuchadnezzar in giving him a large kingdom before which all kings and nations trembled, and yet in spite of that he exalted himself and lifted up his heart and hardened his mind in pride; then God deposed him and took his glory from him and sent him to live with the beasts of the field, to teach him that "God ruled in the kingdom of men, and that he appointeth over it whomsoever he will," Daniel said:

And thou his son, O Belshazzar, hast not humbled thine heart, though thou knewest all this; but hast lifted up thyself against the Lord of heaven; and they have brought the vessels of his house before thee, and thou, and thy lords, thy wives, and thy concubines, have drunk wine in them; and thou hast praised the gods of silver, and gold, of brass, iron, wood, and stone, which see not, nor hear, nor know: and the God in whose hand thy breath is, and whose are all thy ways, hast thou not glorified: then was the part of the hand sent from him; and this writing was written. . . . MENE, MENE, TEKEL, UPHARSIN. . . . God hath numbered thy kingdom, and finished it. . . . Thou art weighed in

the balances, and art found wanting. . . . Thy kingdom is
divided, and given to the Medes and Persians (5:22-28).

The writer of the Book of Daniel says, "In that night was
Belshazzar the king of the Chaldeans slain. And Darius the
Median took the kingdom, being about threescore and two years
old" (5:30, 31).

The city, the great Babylon, had fallen. Nabonidus was
captured and exiled in the east. Belshazzar was killed. Cyrus,
who was to become the new master of the east, worshiped at the
ancient shrines and honored the gods who he believed had given
the mastery over the lands and people whom he had conquered.
This, says one writer, was the turning point in the history of the
world. A master of another race had come on the scene and begun to build on the ruins of the mighty Semitic communities that
had for centuries dominated the affairs of the eastern world. The
culture and ideals of the newly enthroned people, the Aryan, were
formed "under other skies" and were thenceforth to be woven
into the cultures of the people of the east.

Daniel and Darius
(Chapters 6, 11, 12)

Daniel says that Darius was sixty-two years old when he was
appointed governor of Babylon and he ruled two years, after
which Cyrus became the sole ruler. He placed the affairs of the
government in the hands of a council, which consisted of one
hundred and twenty princes. Over this body was a council of
three presidents, of which Daniel was first. 6:2. It was to this
body of three that the princes were to give an account of their
work in order to make sure that the business of the king was
handled properly. Daniel, the records say, was esteemed above
all the princes because of the excellent spirit that was in him.
The chronicler says that the king had considered setting him
over the whole realm. This stirred up a spirit of animosity among
the princes that were on the governing staff with Daniel. They
said, correctly, that no fault could be found with the way he con-
ducted the affairs of his office, or with his character and religion.
If any occasion was to be found against him at all, it would have
to be found concerning his religious practices. It was then that

an attempt was made on his life by persuading the king to issue a decree forbidding for a period of thirty days any petition to any God or man save to the king, on the penalty of being cast alive into the lions' den. The writer then tells of Daniel's faithfulness to his religion and mode of worship and of the king's effort to save him from the evil designs of the princes. He tells also of the king's anxiety during the time that Daniel spent with the lions and of his joy when he was rescued unharmed. The record says that Daniel prospered during the time of his connection with the court of Darius. (See chapter 6:4-24.)

Daniel and Cyrus

The first year of Darius, the Mede, which was the third year of Cyrus, the king of the Persian Empire, was a year of visions for Daniel. Great changes were in the process of taking place, some of which were to reshape the destiny of the Jews in Babylon. It was revealed to Daniel, by means of a vision, that there were to be yet three kings of Persia and a fourth one who should be far richer than they all. The latter would, by his wealth, stir up all the nations against the realm of Greece, who after having conquered Persia was to rule "with great dominion," but in the end his kingdom would be broken into four pieces. This prophecy brings history to the days of Alexander the Great, who pressed his conquests to the borders of India and died while reveling in the pleasures of his conquered subjects in this remote corner of his far-flung domain. Daniel's message includes an outline, as it were, of the struggle for world power among the rival kings which finally resulted in a shift in the seat of authority from the east to the west, where it has remained until the present day.

During the days while these visions were in progress, Daniel says that he was in mourning for "three full weeks. I ate no pleasant bread, neither came flesh nor wine in my mouth, neither did I anoint myself." On the twenty-fourth day of the month, when he was by the great river Hiddekel, the Tigris, he saw a person that looked like a being from another realm, who spoke to him and informed him of the struggle he had with Cyrus in behalf of the exiles. Chapter 10. It appears that this struggle may have had to do with the great decision that finally led to the edict that gave the Hebrew exiles the liberty to return to their Palestinian homes.

It was during the third year of Cyrus that the prophet was shown the meaning of this message. 11, 12. On the screen of time he was given a glimpse of the world's history and he saw that behind the conflict of the nations and the struggle for world dominion, there is the hand of an Unseen Power, that ultimately decides their destiny. It is with this Invisible Force that the saints of God, as also all the nations of the world, have to reckon. Great movements were at that time in the making and were about to take place by which the people of Israel were to be shifted again to the place, designed for them in the divine plan, where their predestinated mission could be accomplished.

The period of their chastisement was drawing to its close. Israel was about to be delivered and sent home, where its people could resume the place God intended for them and where they would, under the blows of Gentile powers, be trampled underfoot for a long time. He was shown, too, that above the tangled skein of world politics, violence, selfishness, and intrigues, there is One who yet overrules the designs of men and finally directs the course of history. Historians tell us of the rise of Alexander the Great, whose armies seemed unconquerable, but whose power finally degenerated under the heat of licentiousness and pleasures of his newly acquired possessions in the East. Egypt, Syria, and Rome, Antiochus Epiphanes, Pompey, the Herods, and the Caesars all fell under the strokes that were designed by the Unseen with which people finally have to reckon. In the fullness of time when Michael, the prince, who was predestinated to stand for his people, arose, the force of earthly powers was doomed to crumble. Under this same power those who were foreordained to be the people of God lost their standing because they rejected His Son who came to save them from their sins.

Daniel asked how long it would be until "the end of these wonders." In reply, the messenger who was clothed in white linen raised his hand unto heaven and said, "It shall be for a time, times, and an half; and when he shall have accomplished to scatter the power of the holy people, all these things shall be finished" (12:7). And he, "the man clothed in linen," said:

Go thy way, Daniel: for the words are closed up and sealed till the time of the end. Many shall be purified, and made white, and tried; but the wicked shall do wickedly: and none of the wicked shall understand; but the wise shall understand. And from the time that the daily sacrifice shall be taken away, and the abomination that maketh desolate set up, there shall be a thousand two hundred and ninety days. Blessed is he that waiteth, and cometh to the thousand three hundred and five and thirty days. But go thou thy way till the end be: for thou shalt rest, and stand in thy lot at the end of the days (12:9-13).

The Message of Daniel

The Book of Daniel is full of mysteries. It is, in a sense, a message to the people of all times. He exalts the mystery and sovereignty of God who is the final authority and power with which people of all ages will have to reckon. He overruled the prince of Persia and sent the exiles home. He supplemented the wisdom of Daniel with thoughts and knowledge beyond his own wisdom and his own thoughts that enabled him to perform his mission with justice and honor in the highest courts the world of his time had to offer. One wonders, too, whether his messages may have been designed to warn the exiles whose mission was still unfinished that their troubles were not ended when they again reached the homeland. Their removal from Babylon did not eliminate "the prince of the power of the air," with whom people must reckon until the end of time—a change of location on earth does not eliminate that problem. There was still Greece, the Seleucidae, the Ptolemys—successors of Alexander when his empire was divided in 323 B.C.—that had to be reckoned with. There was also the Maccabean struggle against these rivals who contended for possession of Palestine and its people. And finally they had to deal with and endure the might of the Caesars and Rome's power until the fall of Jerusalem in A.D. 70 and thereafter. The Book of Daniel has a message of consolation for the believing people of all generations. The prophet, it appears, foresaw the coming of the new covenant, a new order of worship that was not limited to a set time or attached to a specified place, but was suitable and adaptable to all conditions and places until the end of time. His message and his predictions are not free from difficulties, but are filled with hopeful notes for the people of the ages until the Messiah comes again.

20 | Zechariah, Prophet And Priest

Capable scholars, both Jewish and Christian, have from early times conceded that they failed "to find their hands" in the exposition of the visions and sayings of the prophet Zechariah and that "they passed from one cloud to another until they were lost." This prophet's writings are difficult because there is so much of historical, apocalyptic, and eschatological material intermingled. Time also has dimmed the lines between the historical and predictive elements of the book and thus laid the groundwork for a wide range of interpretation of its content.

There are, however, some things that are clear. The authorship of this collection of sayings and sermons is not seriously questioned nor is the date of its composition. The author is identified in the opening chapter as the son of Iddo. Verses 1, 7. He was contemporary with Haggai and lived at Jerusalem with the exiles that had returned from the captivity in 536 B.C. to reclaim, repopulate, and rehabilitate their land and, above all, to rebuild their temple and re-establish their worship. He was called to his ministry rather early in life, for he is spoken of as a "young man" (2:4). He entered upon the duties of his office in 520 B.C., the same year in which his contemporary, Haggai,

began his ministry, and continued his labors until the temple
was completed. The tasks of these men, Zechariah and Haggai,
were beset with discouragements and difficulties. Opposition
rose from the people who had occupied the land during the years
of Judah's exile. Out of this situation grew problems that required judgment, wisdom, patience, and courage on the part of
those who were called upon to guide the repatriates through the
maze of difficulties with which they were confronted.

The Book of Zechariah falls naturally into two parts. Chapters 1–8 contain introductory material, together with a series of
visions concerning the future of Israel and of the time in which
they lived. Chapters 9–14 contain two addresses in which there
exists a large element of Messianic and other predictions concerning Israel and Judah's future.

The returning exiles were poorly prepared for the situation
they found in Palestine. Most of them were born, no doubt, on
foreign soil or had only faint memories of the land they left in
their childhood when they were taken to Babylon as children.
The prophets who accompanied the returning group saw that the
major problem of the new arrivals was not that of regaining possession of the land, critical as that may have been. Their major
problem was spiritual. If reclaiming their land and establishing
homes was to be the chief object of their migration, then they
might as well have stayed in Babylonia. If, however, the re-
establishment of their worship and the rebuilding of their faith
was to be their main purpose, then, as is always the case, they
must be satisfied with such things as they could have and exalt
and make glorious the things in which they believed.

The statement of the prophet in chapter 1:11 indicates that
the nations were at peace with each other. Historians, however,
tell us of discontent, insurrections, and unrest within the Persian
Empire. The statement, "the earth sitteth still, and is at rest"
(1:11), may have had reference to their attitude toward Judah.
Then, too, the great nations of the west that figured so prominently in the affairs of the world in later years do not appear
to have been active at this time. During this period of "ease" the
Lord said, "I am returned to Jerusalem with mercies: my house
shall be built in it . . . and a line shall be stretched forth upon

Jerusalem. . . . My cities through prosperity shall yet be spread abroad" (1:16, 17).

Work on the construction of the temple was begun soon after their return from Babylon, but the opposition of the surrounding tribes brought all the building operations to a halt. The foundation of their house of worship had been laid amid great rejoicing, but there the work stopped and the superstructure was not erected until years later. The altar of burnt offering had been set in its place, but it appears that there were no priests worthy to offer up the sacrifices (3:3), and the people as a whole had grown indifferent. Haggai had aroused interest in the rebuilding of the temple, but it remained for Zechariah to see the project through to its completion in 516 B.C.

Zechariah's first sermon was a call to repentance. He says that in the eighth month of the second year of Darius, the word of the Lord came to him saying:

The Lord hath been sore displeased with your fathers. Therefore say thou unto them, Thus saith the Lord of hosts; Turn ye unto me, . . . and I will turn unto you. . . . Be ye not as your fathers, unto whom the former prophets have cried, saying, Thus saith the Lord of hosts; Turn ye now from your evil ways, and from your evil doings: but they did not hear, nor hearken unto me, saith the Lord. Your fathers, where are they? and the prophets, do they live for ever (1:2-5)?

The prophets of their fathers' time were gone. Historians tell the story of what happened to them. When the people turned from their evil ways and obeyed the Lord, they prospered. But the prophets tell also what happened when they did not obey. Their bodies were buried in foreign soil and their children were left in foreign lands among a strange people.

On the twenty-fourth day of the eleventh month of the second year of Darius, Zechariah saw among the myrtle trees that were "in the bottom" a rider on a red horse. "Behind him were there red horses, speckled, and white." While the prophet was pondering upon this vision, he was informed that these are the messengers of the Lord whom He had sent out to explore the world. This was the message they brought back: "We have walked to and fro through the earth, and, behold, all the earth sitteth still, and is at rest" (1:11). There was at that time but little evidence of the momentous movements that were in the making in the west which were to shake the earth and uproot the kingdoms of the east as the prophets had prophesied. (See Daniel 7 and 11.) God, it appears, was getting things ready to usher in an age in which He would reveal Himself, not through visions nor through the testimony of prophets and seers, but by the greatest of all the prophets of all the ages, *His own Son*.

Then the scene changed and in its place came the vision of the four horns of iron. The prophet says that he inquired about the meaning of these symbols and was told that these horns represent the powers that scattered Israel, Judah, and Jerusalem. 1:18, 19. Following that, he saw the vision of four carpenters or, as translated by some, the four smiths.

> Then said I, What come these to do? And he spake, saying, These are the horns which have scattered Judah, so that no man did lift up his head: but these [the carpenters] are come to fray [to make afraid, discomfit] them, to cast out the horns of the Gentiles, which lifted up their horn over the land of Judah to scatter it (1:21).

The returning exiles had hardly expected to find the opposition which they encountered when they came back to their former homeland. But the enemy they met was subtle and frequently operated under the guise of friendship to draw them into situations that defeated them in their effort to establish themselves in their homes and restore their worship. They learned through the years how devastatingly destructive such contacts and associations can be.

When Zechariah lifted up his eyes again, he saw a man with a measuring line in his hand. He asked, "Whither goest thou?" and the man replied: "To measure Jerusalem, to see what is the breadth thereof, and what is the length thereof" (2:1, 2). Then the prophet said:

> And, behold, the angel that talked with me went forth, and another angel went out to meet him, and said unto him, Run, speak to this young man, saying, Jerusalem shall be inhabited as towns without walls for the multitude of men

and cattle therein: for I, saith the Lord, will be unto her a wall of fire round about, and will be the glory in the midst of her. Ho, ho, come forth, and flee from the land of the north, saith the Lord: for I have spread you abroad as the four winds of the heaven, saith the Lord. Deliver thyself, O Zion, that dwellest with the daughter of Babylon. For thus saith the Lord of hosts; After the glory hath he sent me unto the nations which spoiled you: for he that toucheth you toucheth the apple of his eye (2:3-8). Sing and rejoice, O daughter of Zion: for, lo, I come, and I will dwell in the midst of thee, saith the Lord. And many nations shall be joined to the Lord in that day, and shall be my people: and I will dwell in the midst of thee, and thou shalt know that the Lord of hosts hath sent me unto thee (2:10, 11).

The Arraignment of Joshua the High Priest

The righteous have always had their accusers. Joshua, the high priest, was brought before the bar of justice. The desecration, it appears, had reached the inner part of the sanctuary and involved the one who was ordained to minister at the altar of the Most High. He was charged by Satan, as ministers often are, of being unworthy of the high office to which he had been called. His vestments were stained with the grime of unholy contacts. But Joshua was a "brand plucked out of the fire" and Israel's God was a "pardoning God." The priest's filthy garments were removed from him. His iniquity was taken away and he was clothed with a change of raiment. His office was restored to him and those that stood before him were instructed to set a fair mitre on his head and clothe him with a change of raiment. 3:4, 5. The angel that stood by him proclaimed his restoration:

If thou wilt walk in my ways, and if thou wilt keep my charge, then thou shalt also judge my house, and shalt also keep my courts, and I will give thee places to walk among these that stand by (3:7).

The ministers of the Lord have an impressive mission to perform. This was true in the days of Zechariah. It is always true, even in modern times. Thus the Lord spoke and said:

Hear now, O Joshua the high priest, thou, and thy fellows that sit before thee: for they are men wondered at: for, behold, I will bring forth my servant the BRANCH. For behold the stone that I have laid before Joshua; upon one stone shall be seven eyes: behold, I will engrave the graving thereof, saith the Lord of hosts, and I will remove the iniquity of that land in one day. In that day, saith the Lord of hosts, shall ye call every man his neighbour under the vine and under the fig tree (3:8-10).

People of all times have had to be reminded of the unfailing source of strength (and) power that is available to them. The prophet next saw another wonder. He says that the angel that had talked with him "waked . . . [him], as a man . . . is wakened out of his sleep" (4:1). He looked and saw a "candlestick all of gold, with a bowl upon the top of it." There were seven lamps thereon, and seven pipes were connected to the seven lamps, "which are upon the top thereof: and two olive trees by it, one upon the right side of the bowl, and the other upon the left side thereof" (4:2, 3). The angel said, "This is the word of the Lord unto Zerubbabel, saying, Not by might, nor by power, but by my spirit, saith the Lord of hosts" (4:6). The task of rebuilding the house of the Lord must have looked like an impossible task to the builders because of the opposition they were meeting from the local people. But now that power from an unfailing source was available, Zerubbabel could proceed with assurance that the task which he had begun would be completed. 4:8, 9.

But there was also a vision of warning. The flying roll which the prophet saw was a reminder of the curse that is upon everyone that is dishonest or swears falsely and deals unjustly.

I will bring it forth, saith the Lord of hosts, and it shall enter into the house of the thief, and into the house of him that sweareth falsely by my name: and it shall remain in the midst of his house, and shall consume it with the timber thereof and the stones thereof (5:4).

Zechariah then beheld another vision. He saw an ephah, a measuring box or bushel, which the angel said goeth forth.

He said moreover, This is their resemblance through all the earth. And, behold, there was lifted up a talent of lead: and this is a woman that sitteth in the midst of the ephah. . . . This [the prophet was told] is wickedness. And he cast it into the midst of the ephah; and he cast the weight of lead upon the mouth thereof. Then lifted I up mine eyes, and looked, and, behold, there came out two women, and the wind was in their wings; for they had wings like the wings of a stork: and they lifted up the ephah between the earth and the heaven. Then said I to the angel that talked with me, Whither do these bear the ephah? And he said unto me, To build it an house in the land of Shinar: and it shall be established, and set there upon her own base (5:6-11).

The prophet says that he "turned and lifted up . . . [his] eyes, and looked" and he saw four chariots come out "from between two mountains; and the mountains were mountains of brass." The first chariot was drawn by red horses; the second one by black horses; the third one by white horses; and the fourth one by "grisled and bay [spotted] horses." These chariots, he was informed, were the agencies of heaven sent out to administer justice throughout the world, and quiet or satisfy the spirit of God. 6:1-8.

Two years after Zechariah had begun his ministry, a deputation came to him to inquire about the propriety of observing certain feasts that were being kept annually in commemoration of the tragic events connected with the siege and fall of Jerusalem and the captivity. 7:1-3. The siege of Jerusalem began in the tenth month (II Kings 25:1); the fall of Jerusalem occurred in the fourth month (Jeremiah 52:6); the destruction of the temple in the fifth month (Jeremiah 52:12); and the murder of Gedaliah in the seventh month (II Kings 25:25). The question involved here was the day of mourning and fasting which was observed for the destruction of the temple. Zechariah's reply was: First, that God does not recognize self-appointed fasts or feasts. When questions arise concerning such matters, the people, he said, should follow the word of God rather than the established rules of men. 7:4-7. Second, since disobedience and failure or neglect in the administration of justice and in the application of mercy in their dealings with each other was the cause of the destruction of the city and their deportation to a foreign country, such dates should not be made the occasion of memorial observances, but they should rather be observed with the performance of good deeds toward each other.

These are the things that ye shall do; Speak ye every man the truth to his neighbour; execute the judgment of truth and peace in your gates: and let none of you imagine evil in your hearts against his neighbour; and love no false oath: for all these are things that I hate, saith the Lord (8:16, 17).

The last six chapters of the Book of Zechariah present problems to interpreters. In the first part, chapters 1–8, one has no difficulty in identifying the speaker whose name is frequently given. His sayings are dated. The visions are clearly stated and their meaning is interpreted. Much of this is missing in the last section (9–14). The content and structure of the material in this part of the book are different from the first part. For that reason, some commentators question the authorship of Zechariah and attribute it to some unnamed person. The problems involved here are real, yet they are not of such a nature that they necessarily invalidate the authenticity of its content nor the authorship of the person to whom the book is ascribed. One commentator says that chapters 9–11 constitute an oracle of promise to the New Theocracy. He says:

In general, this section contains promises of a land in which to dwell, a return from the exile, victory over a hostile world power, also temporal blessings and national strength and closes with a parable of judgment brought on by Israel's rejection of Jehovah and their shepherd. More specifically, in chapter 9, Judah and Ephraim, restored, united, and made victorious over their enemies, are promised a land and a king; in chapter 10, Israel is to be saved and strengthened; in chapter 11, Israel is to be punished for rejecting the shepherding care of Jehovah.[1]

Verses 1-8 of chapter 9 contain an oracle of doom upon the nations surrounding Palestine, the home of the rehabilitated Jews. The message is directed to the cities of Syria, Hamath, Tyre, Sidon, Ashkelon, Gaza, and Ashdod. Bastards, or mongrels born of a Jewish father and pagan mothers shall dwell in Ashdod,

1. Robinson, *The Twelve Minor Prophets*, p. 152.

the prophet says, and the pride of the Philistines shall be cut off. 9:6.

Judah's struggle for survival included its contact with the Greeks whose conquest was being pressed to the borders of the then known eastern world powers. During that time, Zechariah predicts, God will protect His people. Verse 8 of chapter 9 is by some commentators interpreted as having reference to their experience with Alexander the Great when he was on his way to the east during his triumphal campaign by which he brought the political supremacy of the Orient to its end. The Lord said:

And I will encamp about mine house because of the army, because of him that passeth by, and because of him that returneth: and no oppressor shall pass through them any more: for now have I seen with mine eyes (9:8).

But he admonishes them to look to the right source for strength in their struggle and says:

Turn you to the strong hold, ye prisoners of hope: even today do I declare that I will render double unto thee; when I have bent Judah for me, filled the bow with Ephraim, and raised up thy sons, O Zion, against thy sons, O Greece, and made thee as the sword of a mighty man (9:12, 13). And the Lord their God shall save them in that day as the flock of his people: for they shall be as the stones of a crown, lifted up as an ensign upon his land. For how great is his goodness, and how great is his beauty! corn shall make the young men cheerful, and new wine the maids (9:16, 17).

Chapter 10 deals with the triumphant return and restoration of Judah and Israel. In the past they were plagued with idolatry and led by dreamers that "spoke unrealities," but now, the Lord says, He will "strengthen the house of Judah" and "save the house of Joseph, and . . . bring them again to place them; for I have mercy upon them: and they shall be as though I had not cast them off" (10:6).

Chapters 12–14 are definitely futuristic. The Lord says that Jerusalem shall be a "cup of trembling" and intoxicating bowl, an attracting place. But it shall also be "burdensome stone," a heavy stone, so much so that all who burden themselves to remove or destroy it shall be destroyed, for in that day, saith the Lord, "all that burden themselves with it shall be cut in pieces" (12:2, 3). In that day when the enemy shall move against Jerusalem, saith the Lord:

> I will smite every horse with astonishment [consternation], and his rider with madness [fury]: and I will open mine eyes upon the house of Judah, and will smite every horse of the people with blindness. And the governors of Judah shall say in their heart, The inhabitants of Jerusalem shall be my strength in the Lord of hosts their God. In that day will I make the governors of Judah like an hearth of fire among the wood, and like a torch of fire in a sheaf; and they shall devour all the people round about, on the right hand and on the left: and Jerusalem shall be inhabited again in her own place, even in Jerusalem (12:4-6).

This is a time not only of physical and political deliverance but also of spiritual redemption and rehabilitation. The prophet says:

> Then shall the Lord go forth, and fight against those nations, as when he fought in the day of battle. And his feet shall stand in that day upon the mount of Olives, which is before Jerusalem on the east, and the mount of Olives shall cleave in the midst thereof toward the east and toward the west, and there shall be a very great valley; and half of the mountain shall remove toward the north, and half of it toward the south (14:3, 4).

Then the people, he says, shall flee to the valley of the mountains which shall reach unto Azal. They "shall flee, like as . . . [they] fled from before the earthquake in the days of Uzziah king of Judah." Then the Lord shall come and all the saints with Him. "And it shall come to pass in that day, that the light shall not be clear, nor dark," but:

> It shall be one day which shall be known to the Lord, not day, nor night: but it shall come to pass, that at evening time it shall be light. And it shall be in that day, that living waters shall go out from Jerusalem; half of them toward the former sea, and half of them toward the hinder sea: in summer and in winter shall it be. And the Lord shall be king

over all the earth: in that day shall there be one Lord, and his name one (14:7-9).

The Book of Zechariah is a fitting close to a turbulent period in the history of a nation through whom God chose to make Himself known to the people of that time and of all time. Though Israel was a race with limitations, it had also traits of character and an element of strength that grew out of the faith of its founder and its patriarchs and was kept alive through the centuries by its prophets and teachers. Through them the Redeemer was brought forth who was to establish a kingdom that knows no race nor clan but which consists of those who are redeemed by the blood of the Lamb that was slain on Calvary. It will reach its fullness when He comes in the clouds to receive His own to Himself.

"And so at last, it may be you and I
In some far realm of blue Infinity
Shall find together some enchanted shore
Where Life and Death shall be no more,
Leaving Love only and Eternity."

21 | Haggai, the Prophet of the Restoration

The history of the restoration of Palestine to the Jews is told in the books of Ezra and Nehemiah. With the fall of Babylon in 538 B.C. the onetime great empire came to its end and its dominion in world affairs ceased. It became a part of the great Persian state that was to dominate the political situation of the east for the greater part of the following two centuries. Cyrus became the new monarch. His attitude toward the displaced people that were scattered throughout the domain of the Chaldean kings was one of consideration and friendliness. He was tolerant of every religious belief and, it appears, treated their adherents with consideration and respect.

Babylonia had become wealthy through the exploitation of its conquered provinces and their people. Many of them, with what they may have salvaged of their wealth, were settled in and around Babylon. Nebuchadnezzar's reign was marked with a benevolent spirit toward the exiles who occupied prescribed lands and positions in his domain. But many thousands of them were never entirely reconciled to their situation. This was especially true of those that had been deported from Palestine. When Cyrus came to the throne, he sensed this ferment of restlessness and understood the cause of it. He therefore entered upon a policy that was rare in that day and issued an edict which enabled any or all of those who had been forcibly deported to return to their native lands. He gave them liberty to worship their gods in whatever manner had been their custom. He ordered also that their paraphernalia and materials of worship, which their former conquerors had confiscated, should be restored. This concession evidently occasioned great joy as the word was passed from village to village among the Hebrews. One of their poets writing about it says:

When the Lord turned again the captivity of Zion,
we were like them that dream.
Then was our mouth filled with laughter,
and our tongue with singing:
Then said they among the heathen,
The Lord hath done great things for them.

Turn again our captivity, O Lord,
as the streams in the south.
They that sow in tears shall reap in joy.
He that goeth forth and weepeth,
bearing precious seed,
Shall doubtless come again with rejoicing,
bringing his sheaves with him.
—Psalm 126.

The Return of the Exiles Under Zerubbabel
538 B.C.

It is evident, though, that but few if any of the actual exiles returned. Those that were babes in their mothers' arms at the time of the final deportation in 586 were now past fifty years old and their fathers, most of them, were no doubt dead and were buried in foreign soil. Many, too, had prospered and had no desire to return. Others were engaged in business and some of them in the affairs of the government. Many of them had inter-married with the Babylonians and were held by family ties. Besides that, life in Babylonia was attractive and numbers of them had by that time adopted the customs and religion of the country. It is doubtful, too, whether all who had retained their faith in Jehovah desired to go back to the former home of their fathers. There seem to have been a considerable number who remained but had enough interest in this venture to contribute liberal sums of gold, vessels of silver, with goods, beasts of burden, and precious things to strengthen the hands of their brethren.

The total number "of the congregation" that finally undertook the long journey was forty-nine thousand, eight hundred and ninety-seven persons. This number included the freeholders, family heads, wives, children, servants, and maids. Ezra 2:64, 65. The chattels, which the caravan brought along, consisted of seven hundred and thirty-six horses, two hundred and forty-five mules, four hundred and thirty-five camels, six thousand, seven hundred and twenty asses. Ezra 2:66, 67. Besides this, they brought with them the vessels of the Lord's house and all the gold which Nebuchadnezzar had taken from the temple. These treasures were delivered to Sheshbazzar, who is by some scholars identified with Zerubbabel, a prince of Judah, who brought them with "them of the captivity" to Jerusalem.

"So the priests, and the Levites, and some of the people, and the singers, and the porters, and the Nethinims, dwelt in their cities, and all Israel in their cities" (Ezra 2:70). On the first day of the seventh month they gathered as one man in Jerusalem to observe the Feast of the Tabernacles. It appears to have been a rather uneasy gathering, "for fear was upon them because of the people of those countries" (Ezra 3:3). After that they offered their daily sacrifices and those of the "new moon," and all of the set feasts of the Lord were consecrated. Ezra 3:5. In the second month of the second year the foundation of their temple was laid amid great rejoicing. Ezra 3:8.

The conditions to which these exiles returned were not like those which their ancestors had left fifty years earlier. They no longer constituted an independent nation. They were under the rule of the king of Persia. Palestine was more or less occupied by wandering tribes and some of the descendants of the Jews who were not deported at the time of the conquest. The Samaritans, a mixed race that was imported from other lands at the time the Northern Kingdom went into exile in 722 B.C., were prominent, as were also bands of the descendants of Moab and Ammon and others who had always looked with envy upon the fields and cities of Judah before its people went into exile. No sooner had they settled in the cities and villages of their ancestors and established their altars than some of the inhabitants of the land asked to join in their worship. These situations created problems that the returned exiles had to contend with for many years.

The opposition, which had been brewing since the arrival of the Jewish repatriates in Palestine, came to a head when the Jews refused to allow the local people to have any part in the building of their temple or in their worship. The Samaritans wrote a letter to the king of Persia, accusing them of having been a rebellious nation in the past and informing him that they were now building the walls of the city and if permitted to do so they would again, they reported, rebel against the king. A copy of the letter is found in Ezra 4:12-16. This brought from the king an order, a copy of which is found also in Ezra 4 (verses 17-22), in which the Jews were directed to bring their building program to a halt. This brought the work to a close for a period of sixteen years.

In 520 the prophets Haggai and Zephaniah became active and urged the builders to proceed with their work. Haggai's first message is recorded in the book that bears his name. It was delivered the first day of the sixth month of the second year of Darius I. "This people say," he said, "The time is not come, the time that the Lord's house should be built. . . . Is it time for you," he said, "to dwell in your cieled houses, and this house lie waste" (Haggai 1:2-4)? His sermon brought results and work on the building was again started on the twenty-fourth day of the sixth month of Darius the king. On the twentieth day of the seventh month Haggai spoke again to the people and assured them that though this temple may seem as nothing in comparison with the one they knew before its destruction, yet the glory of this latter house that grew out of people's penury and sacrifice, he said, will be greater than of the one that came out of Solomon's wealth and extravagance. 2:9.

His next sermon was delivered on the twenty-fourth day of the ninth month of the second year of Darius, in which he re-

proved them for their perverted sense of values. He assured them
that from the first day that the foundation stone was laid God
would bless them; even though the seed for the next harvest was
still in the bin and the trees of their groves and orchards had not
yet brought forth fruit, they might, nevertheless, rest assured of
the Lord's blessing upon them. This was a challenge to their faith.

When the enemies, who had obstructed the building plans
of the returned exiles, saw what was going on, they again wrote
to Darius and said that their intruders claimed that Cyrus had
given them permission to re-establish their worship and to build
a house for their God. Darius authorized a search of the records
and found in the archives of the palace at Achmetha, in the
province of the Medes, a copy of the decree. He then ordered
the opposition to cease and "let the work of this house of God
alone; let the governor of the Jews and the elders of the Jews
build this house of God in his place" (Ezra 6:7). And, further-
more, he ordered that an appropriation of money be made from
the king's tribute "beyond the river" to complete the building and
to provide animals for sacrifices. Ezra 6:8, 9. Ezra reports in
his writings (6:15) that the house was finished on the third day
of the month of Adar in the sixth year of the reign of Darius.

The last word from Haggai, of which we have record, came
on the twenty-fourth day of the month. It was a special message
for Zerubbabel, the governor, delivered on the same day as the
last address. It was a message of hope. He predicted that the
kingdoms of the world would be overthrown by their struggle
for power, and the heavens and the earth would be shaken, he
says. "In that day, saith the Lord of hosts, will I take thee . . . and
will make thee as a signet: for I have chosen thee, saith the Lord
of hosts" (2:23).

The little book that bears Haggai's name was the first recorded message of prophecy to the Jews who had returned from
a seventy-year period of exile to reclaim the land which God
centuries earlier promised to Abraham, their ancestor. They resettled their land in the face of overwhelming odds. They were
a small group when compared with those who chose to stay in
the land to which they were taken years earlier. It was through
them that the race kept its identity and God's redemptive pur-

pose was being carried out. Their temple looked unimportant when compared with the glory of the one they lost during the siege when Jerusalem fell. Their achievements probably were insignificant in comparison with the accomplishment of those who chose to stay by the rivers of Babylon, but they preserved a faith that was in danger of being lost and gave to the world a message of hope that did not reach its highest fulfillment until centuries later.

22 | Malachi, the Last of the Canonical Prophets

Events took an unexpected turn in the East where the Jewish people lived during the period of the Exile. In spite of the stigma, humiliation, and suffering they had to bear as a conquered and alien people, they rose above their situation and won many favors at the hands of the officials of the country to which they were taken. No one could have anticipated the influence that members of the forlorn group, removed from their native land after the fall of their Holy City, would exercise among the people who were their conquerors. Nor could anyone have foreseen the rise of some of their members to positions of influence and honor which they came to occupy in the affairs of the country to which they were taken. Daniel, as already noted, early won the confidence of the monarch under whom he served for many years. He rose from one position of trust to another during the reign of Nebuchadnezzar and his successors. He reached the pinnacle of his career under Cyrus, when he was appointed prime minister, the most influential position in the empire. Nehemiah, another Jew of exilic origin, became the trusted cupbearer of the king Artaxerxes. Mordecai sat in the gate of the king, which, according to the usage of the term, would indicate that he was a judge of the king's court, the highest judicial honor the nation could bestow, and was retained as the king's counselor. Esther, an orphan girl, became the queen of Ahasuerus, who is identified as the great Xerxes, whose kingdom extended from India to Ethiopia.

Momentous events were taking place, also, among nations that previous to that time were little known, which changed the course of history for all time. The Ionians, a people of the Mediterranean area, challenged the kings and military might of the East where the political power had resided from the dawn of known history. They threw off the yoke of Persia at Marathon in 490 B.C. This battle is known in history as one of the "decisive battles" of the world. The seat of power was then shifted from the Orient to the West. New names now began to appear in the records. Thermopylae, Salamis, Plataea, and others mark spots on the globe where gory events took place in order to prevent the Asiatic armies from overrunning Europe and other lands of the western world.

There is no record of the rehabilitated Jews of Palestine having been drawn into that struggle prior to the Maccabean revolt in 166 B.C. As colonials, however, they could hardly have escaped all the demands for taxes and supplies, such as were customarily imposed upon people of their status. It is probable, too, that some of their men served as recruits in the armies of the contending nations under whose jurisdiction they lived.

The attitude of the rulers of Persia was favorable toward the Jews who returned to Palestine in spite of the opposition of those who had occupied the land during the time of the Exile. The repatriated settlers had authority from the ruling monarchs of the East to carry forward their rehabilitation and building program, and establish their worship in accordance with what their custom had been. The natives, who had occupied Palestine during the absence of the Jews, looked with suspicion and concern upon the people who came to reclaim their country and rebuild their cities and their temple. Letters, containing complaints and accusations, continued to pass between the tribal leaders and the king of Persia, which finally brought the building and reconstruction program of the Jews to a halt for a period of sixteen years. Ezra, ch. 4. The matter, as already noted, was finally brought before Darius, the king, who, upon making search of the records, found that the Jews were within their rights according to the Decree of

Emancipation issued by Cyrus, and he permitted them to continue their work. Ezra 5, 6. As a result of the decree and the ministry of Haggai and Zechariah, Zerubbabel resumed his work on the house of God, which was completed on the third day of the month of Adar, in the sixth year of the reign of Darius. The dedication was observed with rejoicing and gladness. The priests were set in their divisions, and the Levites in their courses, for the service of God, as it is written in the book of Moses. Ezra 6:16-18.

The Jews to whom the land had been restored, however, soon discovered that there were problems which they perhaps had not anticipated. The lands which they came to reclaim were now in possession of those who were left in the country at the time of the great deportation or were occupied by others who had encroached upon the territory at the time when it was vacated. Ezra says that the adversaries of Judah and Benjamin came to Zerubbabel and offered to assist in the construction of the temple, for, said they, "We seek your God, as ye do; and we do sacrifice unto him since the days of Esar-haddon king of Assur, which brought us up hither" (Ezra 4:2). This offer was promptly rejected by Zerubbabel and his elders. This abrupt refusal stirred up opposition and Ezra records that "the people of the land weakened the hands of the people of Judah" and hindered them in their building. They hired counselors against them and continued to annoy and frustrate their purposes throughout the reigns of Cyrus, Darius, Ahasuerus, and Artaxerxes. As noted in a previous chapter, a copy of a letter written to the king is found in the fourth chapter of Ezra, as is also a copy of the decree of Artaxerxes ordering the building and construction activities at Jerusalem to cease.

The intermingling of the races on the social level, however, continued and resulted in marriages between the Jews and the Samaritans and other groups among whom they lived. Later, when Nehemiah came on the scene, he complained that the races and clans had become so intermixed through marriages that their children spoke half in the language of Ashdod and could not speak in the language of the Jews at all. Nehemiah 13:24. This situation greatly troubled some of the Jewish colonists. Hanani, a brother of Nehemiah who was the cupbearer of the king Artaxerxes, met Nehemiah at Shushan, the winter home of the king. He, in company with others, had lately returned from Jerusalem and had dire reports to give concerning the situation at that place. The walls of the city, they said, had not been rebuilt, and the gates that were burned with fire had not been restored. The remnant that had been left there of the captivity were in great affliction and reproach. Nehemiah 1:2, 3. This report deeply grieved Nehemiah and he went into a season of humiliation and prayer. The fate of his people affected him so much that his condition became noticeable to the king when he was served his wine, and he was led to inquire as to the cause of his grief.

As a result of the conversation that followed, Nehemiah was granted a leave of absence to go to Jerusalem, under a military escort, for a period of time to remedy the situation. He carried with him letters from the king, addressed to the governors beyond the River Euphrates, requesting security for Nehemiah and his convoy as they traveled through their territory, and also a letter to Asaph, the keeper of the king's forest, by which he was authorized to allow Nehemiah to draw timbers and materials from the forest for the gates of the palace and for the walls of the city and for his own house. Nehemiah 2:7-9.

Nehemiah and his caravan arrived in Jerusalem ca. 444 B.C. His arrival was, however, not looked upon with favor by the local tribesmen. He makes special mention in his writing of "Sanballat the Horonite, and Tobiah the servant, the Ammonite, and Geshem the Arabian. These men, he says, were exceedingly grieved when they learned that he had come to seek the welfare of the Hebrews. Nehemiah 2:10. He found conditions in as deplorable a state as they had been described by the party he had met at the gates of Shushan.

After having spent three days in the city, he went out alone by night to explore the place. He started from the gate of the valley and followed the remnant of the wall to the dragon well, from there on to the dung port, and from thence to the gate of the fountain and the king's pool. All along the route there was no place for the beast he rode to pass. He returned by the gate of the valley and found nothing but remnants of destruction.

His call for helpers to rebuild the wall met with a ready response from the Jews, but it brought only scorn and ridicule from the local tribal leaders. Sanballat became enraged, but Tobiah in a mood of humor said, "If a fox go up, he shall even break down their stone wall" (Nehemiah 4:3). But undaunted by ridicule and opposition, the writer says that the employees worked with a will and in fifty-two days the wall was completed and the gates were restored.

But Nehemiah discovered that there were problems more serious than those that pertained to walls and buildings. The economic and spiritual conditions were bad. The country had gone through a period of drought and many of the new settlers had mortgaged their lands to buy food and even to pay the king's tribute. The nobles took advantage of the situation and charged the people high rates of usury which added to their already heavy burdens. Some of them even sold their brethren into servitude in order to get money to live by or to collect what was due them. Nehemiah handled this situation with vigor. He ordered the lands restored to their owners, "shook . . . [his] lap" against the moneylenders and the collectors of interest, and invoked the judgment of God upon those who had taken advantage of their brethren in order to make secure their loans or to enrich themselves by the failure of the more unfortunate ones. Nehemiah 5:1-13.

During all this time Nehemiah himself bore the expense of the reconstruction of the walls and buildings. He had at times, he says, as many as one hundred and fifty men at his table, together with those that came among them from the heathen. He gives an itemized list of the variety of food that was served and says that "for all this required not I the bread of the governor, because the bondage was heavy upon this people" Nehemiah 5:17, 18).

The social problems that existed among them were even more serious than the economic conditions. Intermarriage with the pagan tribes that occupied the land was widely practiced. He says he contended with them and "plucked off their hair" and took oaths of them to discontinue the practice. Nehemiah 13:23-26. Nehemiah called a convocation of the Jewish popula-

tion at which the law of Moses was read in the hearing of all the
people. The Feast of the Tabernacles was restored and the temple
worship was again set in order. The marriage regulations prescribed by the law were put into effect under the supervision of
Nehemiah. Bargaining, buying, and selling were carried on on
the Sabbath day between the Jews and the hucksters on the
outside of the city as had been done before the walls were rebuilt. He ordered the gates closed and served notice on the
traffickers that he would "lay hands on . . . [them]" if they would
persist in luring the people to purchase their wares on the
Sabbath.

The enclosure of the city within its walls was, however, not
the answer to their whole problem. Letters passed between
the nobles of the city and the tribal leaders on the outside, many
of whom were drawn together by marriage ties within their families. Rumors of disloyal motives on the part of Nehemiah were
spread among the people and threats designed to intimidate him
were current. He however, permitted none of this to interfere
with the work he had undertaken in order to salvage the colony
for the Lord's cause.

When the walls were finished and the affairs of their worship
set in order, with the appointment of the porters, singers, and
Levites, he appointed his own brother, Hanani, ruler over the
city and Hananiah ruler over the palace and gave such instructions as he deemed necessary to protect the people from their
opposers on the outside.

About this time a new name appears in the history of the
Judean colony. Ezra, who is described as a loyal Jew and "a ready
scribe in the law of Moses," arrived in Jerusalem.[1] There is
some uncertainty as to the date of his arrival on the Jerusalem
scene, but it is evident from Nehemiah's writings that he was
in the city in time to participate in the marriage reforms which
the governor had instituted. It appears also that the Persian
rulers were interested in having the Jewish colony in Palestine
succeed. Artaxerxes made liberal provision for the expedition led
by Ezra. He was given financial aid from the king and his

1. See Bright, *A History of Israel*, pp. 376-86. Also Schultz, *The Old Testament Speaks*, p. 230.

counselors, such as each one "freely offered," and from the people, such as they contributed "willingly" (Ezra 7:15, 16). He carried with him, also, letters from the king, addressed to those through whose provinces he was to pass, requesting that they contribute silver in the amount of one hundred talents and stipulated quantities of wheat, oil, wine, and salt. The decree also exempted from taxation the priests, Levites, singers, and all others employed in the worship services of the temple. Ezra 7:24.

In addition to the Jews the expedition included also some of the children of Israel, Nethinims, temple servants and slaves. They left Persia in the seventh year, on the first day of the first month of the reign of King Artaxerxes, and arrived in Jerusalem on the first day of the fifth month. The record says that "Ezra had prepared his heart to seek the law of the Lord, and to do it, and to teach in Israel statutes and judgments" (Ezra 7:10).

The conditions which Ezra found in Jerusalem were not inspiring. They were in fact lamentable. The princes came to him with complaints that the people, including the priests, had intermarried with the people of the land and were participating in all the abominations of the neighboring tribes and the Egyptians. Ezra says, "When I heard this thing, I rent my garment and my mantle, and plucked off the hair of my head and of my beard, and sat down astonied [appalled]" (Ezra 9:3).

At the time of the evening sacrifice he arose, fell on his knees, and offered a remarkable and impressive prayer and confession of sin. Ezra 9:5-15. Then there gathered unto him out of Israel a large congregation of men and women, among whom was Shechaniah who spoke for the people and urged that Ezra take steps to correct the evils that prevailed among them. "This matter," he said, "belongeth unto thee: we also will be with thee: be of good courage, and do it" (Ezra 10:4). Acting upon this counsel, he called for a general assembly of all the "children of the captivity" to meet in Jerusalem within three days. The date was set for the twentieth day of the ninth month. Failure to attend was to be punishable by the forfeiture of the absentee's substance and excommunication from the congregation. When the day came, there was a "great rain." The crowd was large and many of the people were without shelter. Hence, they petitioned

for an extension of time to the first day of the tenth month, which
was granted. Ezra was uncompromising and exacting in his
judgments. It was true then as it is now that a nation or a church
can be only as pure as its homes and people are pure. Among
those who had violated the marriage laws of the Jews and had
taken "strange wives" were the sons of the priests, who "gave their
hands" and promised that they would put them away and
offered appropriate sacrifices to atone for their sin. Ezra 10:18, 19.

Nehemiah speaks of a meeting where "all the people
gathered themselves together as one man into the street that was
before the water gate; and they spake unto Ezra . . . to bring the
book of the law of Moses, which the Lord had commanded to
Israel. . . . And Ezra the scribe stood upon a pulpit of wood . . .
[and] read in the book in the law of God distinctly, and gave the
sense, and caused . . . [the people] to understand the reading"
(Nehemiah 8:1-8). This brought about a great revival among
the Jews of Jerusalem and Palestine. The Feast of the Tabernacles was restored, and the seed of Israel separated themselves
from all strangers and confessed their sins and the sins of their
fathers. Nehemiah gives a list of those who signed the covenant
and entered into a curse and into an oath to walk in the law of
God, which was given by Moses, the servant of God. They
pledged themselves to observe and do all the commandments of
the Lord and His judgments and His statutes, and not give their
daughters to the people of the land nor take their daughters for
their sons. Nehemiah 10:28-30.

Nehemiah says that in all this time he was not in Jerusalem
but had returned to Shushan in the thirty-second year of
Artaxerxes. After certain days, he says, he obtained leave from
the king to return to Jerusalem. On his arrival in Judea, he found
that the great revival had spent its force and irregularities had
again found a place in the conduct and practices of the people.
Eliashib, the high priest, had prepared a chamber in the courts
of the house of God for Tobiah, the Ammonite. Nehemiah ex-
pelled him and ordered all his "household stuff" thrown out of the
chamber, and after a thorough cleansing he restored the vessels
of the Lord's house to their proper place. Nehemiah 13:7-14.
He discovered, also, that one of the sons of Eliashib, the high

priest, had married the daughter of Sanballat, the Horonite. He says they "chased him" away. Nehemiah 13:28. He found, too, that there was a general neglect in the collection of the tithes and that the Levites were working in the fields to earn their livelihood. The bartering between the fishmongers of Tyre and other merchants was being carried on on the Sabbath day as it had been before the walls were restored. He says, also, that he saw some "treading wine presses" and "lading asses" and "bringing in sheaves" in violation of the pledges they had made during the revivals of Ezra. Nehemiah 13:15, 16.

The problem of maintaining the spiritual life of a people is a perennial task. But God was not without a spokesman during those days. Haggai and Zechariah spoke in His behalf during the earlier years after the return of the Jews from the captivity. They urged repentance and reforms and saw the temple completed and worship restored. Malachi, the last of the canonical prophets, came on the scene during Nehemiah's time, *ca.* 444 B.C. We know nothing about this prophet except what we can glean from his writings. Scholars debate whether the title of this little book, Malachi—My Messenger, was actually his name or whether it was a term which described his official relationship to God. Since, however, many Jewish names are significant, this should not pose a serious problem. His ministry was a call to faith at a time when the life of his people was ebbing into worldliness and ungodliness which were stimulated by the influence of an alien people who refused to be separated from the children of Abraham who had come to reclaim their land.

Malachi's style is peculiar. He follows the scribal question and answer method of instruction. His little book contains only fifty-five verses and is usually considered as consisting of two sermons or polemics (1:6 to 2:9 and 2:10 to 4:3). The first discourse is addressed to the priests who had become lax and willfully disobedient in their ministrations in the sanctuary and at the altar. The prophet deals specifically with important questions which have to do with people's relationship to God and also with their relationship with each other. The first question is fundamental. It is a statement of God's relationship with His people which governs His attitude toward them.

I have loved you, saith the Lord. Yet ye say, Wherein hast
thou loved us (1:2)?

The people pleaded ignorance throughout the entire dis-
cussion, as though ignorance or lack of knowledge constituted
sufficient cause for their conduct. They overlooked the facts of
their history. Throughout all the years of their existence as a
people they were conserved because the hand of God inter-
vened in their behalf. He disciplined the nation by sending His
judgments upon them. He delivered them when they themselves
were unable to do so. It appears that at the very beginning He
recognized a violation of the law of progeniture in order that
Jacob might become his father's heir and the founder of a nation
through which He would reveal Himself and His purposes for
mankind. He disciplined the Israelites by sending them into
bondage and bringing them again to their promised land. The
roads which they traveled throughout their existence were lined
with evidence of God's guidance which they could not but recognize, but now that His will stood in the way of their desires
they raised questions that involved His integrity.

The second proposition is directed to the priests who sacri-
ficed the sanctity and honor of their position to satisfy their
personal desires. It appears that they showed less respect for
God than they required for themselves from their children or their
servants.

A son honoureth his father, and a servant his master: if
then I be a father, where is mine honour? and if I be a master,
where is my fear? . . . O priests, that despise my name. And
ye say, Wherein have we despised thy name (1:6)? Ye offer
polluted bread upon mine altar; and ye say, Wherein have
we polluted thee? In that ye say, The table of the Lord is
contemptible. And if ye offer the blind for sacrifice, is it not
evil? and if ye offer the lame and sick, is it not evil (1:7, 8)?

He challenges them to attempt to pay their obligations to the
government with sick and diseased animals and see what the
consequences would be. He says, "I have no pleasure in you,
. . . neither will I accept an offering at your hand." He admonishes
the priests of the sanctity of their position. His covenant with
Levi was one of life and peace and the law of truth was in his

mouth and iniquity was not found in his lips. He was the messenger of the Lord of hosts, but now the priests, the sons of Levi,
have departed from his way and have caused many to stumble at
the law and have corrupted the covenant.

> Therefore have I also made you contemptible and base
> before all the people, according as ye have not kept my ways,
> but have been partial in the law (2:9).

It seems that the problem of intermarriage with their pagan
neighbors was constantly recurring. This matter comes up again
and again throughout their history. The prophet charges Judah
with having dealt treacherously and with having committed an
abomination in Israel and Jerusalem and profaned the holiness of
God by marrying women who worshiped strange gods. They
knew that this was not to be; hence, the Lord promised through
the prophet that He would deal impartially with them regardless
of their station in life. Even those who offer offerings at the altar
will not be spared. 2:12. Again they pleaded ignorance and
asked, "Wherefore?" He replied:

> Because the Lord hath been witness between thee and the
> wife of thy youth, against whom thou hast dealt treacherous-
> ly: yet is she thy companion, and the wife of thy covenant.
> And did not he make one? Yet had he the residue of the
> spirit. And wherefore one? That he might seek a godly
> seed. Therefore take heed to your spirit, and let none deal
> treacherously against the wife of his youth (2:14, 15).

Again, the prophet charges the people with having wearied
the Lord with their insincerity in dealing with each other and
by their attitude toward the commandments of God. Yet they
said: "Wherein have we wearied him?"

> When ye say, Every one that doeth evil is good in the sight
> of the Lord, and he delighteth in them; or, Where is the God
> of judgment (2:17)?

Israel's loyalty to God was very spotted. There were times
when they earnestly sought to walk in His ways. Then again
their ardor cooled and their interest in divine things declined.
The group that returned from Babylon came, no doubt, with
noble motives and good intentions, but in their struggle to establish themselves in the midst of pagan surroundings they lapsed

again and became involved with the people among whom they lived. The prophet charges them with having forsaken the ordinances of God and with having failed in bringing the tithes and offerings. He interprets this as robbery and says they are cursed with a curse, for they have robbed God, even the whole nation. Again they plead ignorance and ask: "Wherein have we robbed thee?" He replies, "In tithes and offerings."

Bring ye all the tithes into the storehouse, that there may be meat in mine house, and prove me now herewith, . . . if I will not open you the windows of heaven, and pour you out a blessing, that there shall not be room enough to receive it (3:10).

And lastly they are reproved for having misrepresented God. He says: "Your words have been stout against me. . . . Yet ye say, What have we spoken so much against thee" (3:13)? He replies:

Ye have said, It is vain to serve God: and what profit is it that we have kept his ordinance, and that we have walked mournfully before the Lord of hosts? And now we call the proud happy; yea, they that work wickedness are set up; yea, they that tempt God are even delivered (3:14, 15).

Malachi, the last of the Old Testament prophets, in spite of the gloomy outlook of his own time, closes his ministry with promises that have colored the hopes of the faithful with a glow that will warm their hearts and shed a light upon their pathway until the end of time. He says:

Then they that feared the Lord spake often one to another: and the Lord hearkened, and heard it, and a book of remembrance was written before him for them that feared the Lord, and that thought upon his name. And they shall be mine, saith the Lord of hosts, in that day when I make up my jewels; and I will spare them, as a man spareth his own son that serveth him (3:16, 17).

* * *

But unto you . . . shall the Sun of righteousness arise with healing in his wings; and ye shall go forth, and grow up as calves of the stall. And ye shall tread down the wicked; for they shall be ashes under the soles of your feet in the day that I shall do this (4:2, 3).

Behold, I will send you Elijah the prophet before the coming
of the great and dreadful day of the Lord: and he shall turn
the heart of the fathers to the children, and the heart of the
children to their fathers, lest I come and smite the earth
with a curse (4:5, 6).

The Old Testament closes with Israel broken into two great
divisions—the remnant in Palestine and the large body scattered
throughout the east, no longer as bondsmen and captives among
the nations but as colonists. Whatever voices spoke in their
behalf were not included in the canonical writings, but we get
echoes of them, now and then, in the historical records of the
"silent years."

From the time of Malachi to John the Baptist the world was
filled with nations that were struggling for supremacy. The
eastern powers tried to maintain the dominant position they had
held for centuries, but they were challenged by great new forces
that were rising out of the west. The he-goat with the great horn
between his eyes, which Daniel saw in a vision years earlier,
settled the question of political dominance when Alexander the
Great led his victorious army eastward and conquered the ancient
strongholds where political power and military might had resided from known history. The Persian Empire fell before his
army in 330. His rule over Palestine covered a brief period of
nine years, 330 to 321 B.C. After his death in 321 his empire
fell apart. In the contest that followed, the house of the
Ptolemys of Egypt prevailed in Palestine, which remained under
its control for a period of 120 years. During this time more than
a million Jews were settled in Egypt. In 198 B.C. Antiochus of
Syria secured control of Palestine and proceeded at once to force
upon the Jewish people the culture and religion of the Greeks.
This brought on the Maccabean revolt and under the leadership
of Judas Maccabaeus and his sons, the Jews won their independence in 166 B.C., which they maintained until 40 B.C., when
Palestine became a Roman province and a part of the great Roman Empire.

The Jewish people had waited long and hopefully for the
voice of the messenger of whom the prophet Malachi had spoken.
Then one day the silence of the centuries was broken when a

recluse who had come up out of the wilderness appeared along
the River Jordan and cried, saying: "Repent ye: for the kingdom
of heaven is at hand. . . . Prepare ye the way of the Lord, make
his paths straight" (Matthew 3:2, 3). The day of which the
prophets had spoken had come! The Messiah was at hand and a
new era was about to begin.

23 | Conclusion

There is a considerable volume of predictive prophecy in the writings of the Old Testament prophets that foretells conditions and events that lie in the future, far beyond the time in which the prophets lived and labored. Some of these writings and sayings are Messianic in their content and have reference to the advent, life, and ministry of our Saviour. Among them is the great fifty-third chapter of Isaiah. There are other references, also, such as the one found in Isaiah 61:1, which Jesus used as the basis of His discourse in the synagogue at Nazareth on the Sabbath following His return from the River Jordan where He had been baptized and was pointed out to the multitude as the Messiah by John the Baptist. Luke says that He went into the synagogue as His custom was and when the scroll was handed to Him, He read from the Book of Isaiah:

> The Spirit of the Lord is upon me, because he hath anointed me to preach the gospel to the poor; he hath sent me to heal the brokenhearted, to preach deliverance to the captives, and recovering of sight to the blind, to set at liberty them that are bruised, to preach the acceptable year of the Lord (Luke 4:18, 19).

After having read this Scripture, He closed the book and gave it to the minister and sat down. He then began to teach and confirmed the validity of the Messianic implications of what He had read by saying: "This day is this scripture fulfilled in your ears" (Luke 4:21). He quoted from the prophets, also, on other occasions and said that they have reference to Himself. During His ministry He refers to other prophetic sayings which He says were then in the process of fulfillment. He spoke frequently of a kingdom which, He declared, is "not of this world" and uses a series of parables to illustrate the nature of it. Matthew 13:2-35 and 25:1-30. Jeremiah spoke also of a "righteous Branch" and a king who, he says, "shall reign and prosper, and shall execute judgment and justice in the earth" and under whose benign rule Israel shall dwell safely. Jeremiah 23:5. Micah spoke of a kingdom in which weapons of war shall be beaten into plowshares and spears into pruninghooks and nations shall learn war no more. Micah 4:1-5. Isaiah's prediction is almost identical with that of Micah. He says:

It shall come to pass in the last days, that the mountain of the Lord's house shall be established in the top of the mountains, and shall be exalted above the hills; and all nations shall flow unto it. And many people shall go and say, Come ye, and let us go up to the mountain of the Lord, to the house of the God of Jacob; and he will teach us of his ways, and we will walk in his paths: for out of Zion shall go forth the law, and the word of the Lord from Jerusalem. And he shall judge among the nations, and shall rebuke many people: and they shall beat their swords into plowshares, and their spears into pruninghooks: nation shall not lift up sword against nation, neither shall they learn war any more (Isaiah 2:2-4).

These few passages of Scripture taken from the writings of the prophets, together with the teachings of Jesus and the apostles, furnish the material out of which has grown a wide range of opinion regarding the nature, character, and place of the kingdom of which the prophets wrote and spoke. The question is, Do they mean that there will be a literal kingdom on the earth over which Christ will rule in person, and does it exist within the limits of a thousand years? Or is the kingdom of which they speak a spiritual one and is it in existence now and does it consist of the redeemed who live and follow the way of life prescribed by the Saviour, rather than the way of the unregenerate and ungodly? Will the kingdom enter upon its fullest attainment at the time of the resurrection when the saints shall be separated from the unregenerate and ungodly at the judgment and will then reign with Christ in glory throughout the ages to come?

Scholars and Bible students recognize the existence of this material which is found in both the Old and New Testaments, but they differ widely in their interpretation of it. This accounts for the several schools of thought that have risen through the centuries, whose modes of interpretation are, for the sake of convenience and identification, indicated by the prefixes which are added to the word "millennium." They are, therefore, classified as postmillennial, premillennial, and amillennial. This, however, does not mean that the advocates of each view necessarily agree on all the details of the main proposition. There is, in fact, a wide range of opinion within each group. For example, the fundamentalists and the Russellites are for the most part premillennial in their views, but they differ greatly in their interpretation of the details of the kingdom prophecies. This is true, also, of the other schools of thought.

It must be said, too, that they do not always plead their cause with charity or respect for those with whom they disagree. Some even venture to make a person's interpretation of this doctrine the test of his orthodoxy and the basis or foundation of his salvation. Dr. G. L. Murray in his book entitled *Millennial Studies* has this to say:

> Any discussion of the millennial theories inevitably leads to a theological battleground, on which one has to risk the sacrifice of his reputation and popularity. This is a subject on which many Christians have no opinon, but on which others have such definite conclusions that they can hardly be induced to read or consider anything at variance with their present theories. . . . We believe that every phase of the truth is important, but we just as steadfastly deny that

any theory of the millennium is to be regarded as proof of either orthodoxy or salvation.[1]

The word "millennium" derives from two Latin words: *mille* meaning thousand, and *annus* meaning a year. The postmillennialists believe that the millennium will be past when the Lord returns the second time to judge the world. They think of this era as "The Golden Age" which will precede the end of the world. This condition, they believe, will be brought about through the preaching of the Gospel and the widespread missionary movements which, together with the resultant educational, social, legislative, and reform movements, will eventually result in bringing in the new age. The premillennialists believe that the present world order will continue to degenerate and the millennium will be ushered in with the second coming of Christ, who will then reign with His saints for a thousand years. This view is especially dominant in what is known as the "Fundamentalist" and Bible School groups, and some of the sects like the followers of Charles Russell, the founder of the Russellites, the Seventh Day Adventists, and others. The amillennialists do not believe that there will be a literal "thousand-year" reign of Christ on earth. They rather believe that the kingdom teachings of the prophets and of Jesus and the apostles have reference to a spiritual kingdom which is in existence now and consists of the redeemed saints of God. This kingdom, they believe, will attain its consummation at the second coming of Christ when those that "sleep in . . . [him]" will arise and together with them that are alive at that time will go to "meet the Lord in the air." I Thessalonians 4:14-17 (cf. Matthew 13:1-52; Mark 4:1-29, and Luke 8:4-18).

It is altogether possible, and probable, that neither, nor any, of the differing schools of interpreters has the full answer to all the problems that are involved in this doctrine. The Scriptures, however, state clearly what the essentials of salvation are upon which citizenship in the kingdom is based. It is, therefore, wise that one should be primarily concerned with faith and the nature of his responsibility as a child of the kingdom and await with patience the glory which the AGES will reveal. Whatever that is, we may rest assured, will transcend any concept that we, with

1. Murray, G. L., *Millennial Studies*, p. 83. Baker Book House, 1948.

our present knowledge, limitations, and understanding, can formulate. Awaiting, then, His second coming, when the glories of His kingdom will be revealed, may we labor on until He comes in the clouds to receive His own.

"At length there dawns the glorious day
By prophets long foretold;
At length the chorus clearer grows
That shepherds heard of old.
The day of dawning Brotherhood
Breaks on our eager eyes,
And human hatreds flee before
The radiant eastern skies."